# BIBLE
*for Young Catholics*

# BIBLE
## *for Young Catholics*

Paraphrase and commentary by
Anne Eileen Heffernan, FSP

Illustrations by
Deborah J. White

Pauline
BOOKS & MEDIA
BOSTON

Nihil Obstat:
    Rev. Thomas W. Buckley, STD, SSL

*Imprimatur:*
    †Bernard Cardinal Law
    Archbishop of Boston
    December 9,1997


Library of Congress Cataloging-in-Publication Data

Heffernan, Anne Eileen.
    Bible for young Catholics / paraphrase and commentary by Anne
Eileen Heffernan ; illustrations by Deborah J . White.
        p.   cm.
    Includes bibliographical references.
    Summary: Paraphrases the Old and New Testaments and provides
introductions to each book of the Bible along with illustrations, maps, and
information about the history, geography, and theological teachings.
    ISBN 0-8198-1158-0 (paperback)
    1. Bible—Paraphrases, English.   2. Bible—Juvenile literature.
    3. Catholic Church—Doctrines—Juvenile literature.   [1. Bible—
Paraphrases.]   I. White, Deborah J., 1953–      ill.   II. Title.
    BS551.2. H4365   1998
    220.9'505—dc21                                                98–13644
                                                                            CIP
                                                                            AC

The Daughters of St. Paul wish to thank Celia M. Sirois for her diligent reading of
this paraphrase and commentary and her very helpful suggestions.

*Cover design:* Sergia Ballini, FSP

Printed and published in the U.S.A. by Pauline Books & Media, 50 Saint Pauls Avenue, Boston, MA 02130-3491

www.pauline.org

Pauline Books & Media is the publishing house of the Daughters of St. Paul, an international congregation of
women religious serving the Church with the communications media.

3 4 5 6 7 8                                                                07 06 05 04 03 02

# BIBLE

## *for Young Catholics*

*Presented to* _____

*By* _____

*On* _____

*With best wishes for* _____

_____

_____

# SACRAMENTS
## *I Have Received*

*I received Baptism on* _____

*at* _____ *Church.*

*I was baptized by* _____

*My sponsors were* _____

*and* _____

*I received Confirmation on* _____

*at* _____ *Church.*

*I was confirmed by* _____

*My sponsor was* _____

*I first received Reconciliation on* _____

*at* _____ *Church.*

*I received my First Communion on* _____

*at* _____ *Church.*

# CONTENTS

# INTRODUCTION

The Bible is a collection of writings ("books") that are holy to Jews and Christians. It is also called Scripture or the Scriptures. "Bible" means "the Books" or "the Book." "Scripture" means "the Writings."

The Bible is God's message to us, in which he tells us about himself and his plan for us. His plan is to bring us to live with him forever—thanks to the saving life, death and resurrection of Jesus and the help of the Holy Spirit. He invites us to believe in him, to hope for eternal life, and to love him and one another.

More than three thousand years ago, God began to make this plan known to the Israelites in Egypt. God wanted them to learn about him and eventually to tell the world about him. With the help of Moses, he led them out of Egypt. He brought them safely through the sea and into the wastelands of Sinai, where he made an agreement with them: they would be his people and he would be their God.

After God brought his people into the Promised Land, the Israelites passed on their wonderful story from one generation to another. They found it always new. Much later, after they had been taken away to Babylon, more stories were told, even about the beginnings of the human race. Gradually all the stories were written down and made more and more complete.

Then, after a long time, changes stopped being made, and the Hebrew Scriptures were finished. These Scriptures make up a large part of our Old Testament.

Our New Testament, too, started with stories—stories about Jesus that were told by the apostles and disciples to other early Christians. After several years, they began to be written down, and sometime later changes stopped being made. Our whole Bible was complete.

But even though the Bible will not change anymore, it is alive—the living Word of God. God inspired the people who wrote the Scriptures. Through what they wrote, he speaks to us today.

Those authors lived in particular times and places. To know what God was saying through them, it's helpful to learn something about who they were and when and where they lived. By identifying the author and original audience of a Bible passage and the kind of writing that was used (history, poetry, etc.), we hope to understand what God was saying then and there. That can help us understand what God is telling us here and now.

Bible-reading is a way of conversing with God. When we read, God speaks to us. Then we can respond, talking with God about the reading and/or about our own lives. We can praise and thank God, ask his forgiveness, and ask his help. In other words, Bible-reading can help us to pray.

This paraphrase of the Bible gives priority to the historical books and other stories. It also presents each of the other books (laws, poetry, words of encouragement, wisdom literature, instructional letters and prophecies), providing an introduction and at least a sample of the text. Explanations throughout the text appear in italic type or in footnotes. In the back of this book you will find: definitions and spellings; a time chart; information about history, geography and archaeology; theological and other information for parents and ideas about how to use the Bible more in the home.

# INTRODUCTION TO THE OLD TESTAMENT

The Old Testament is the first part of the Catholic Bible. It is made up of the Hebrew Scriptures and some other writings dating from before Jesus' time. For Christians, the Hebrew Scriptures find their completion in Christ. But they are also important in themselves.

The Old Testament is a story of people physically on the move—whether journeying toward the Promised Land, returning from exile or fighting to regain their religious freedom. It is also a history of people on the move toward the God who made them his people. As we read the Old Testament, we can see that the Hebrew people grew in their understanding of who God is, what he offers his children, and what he expects of them.

We Christians are spiritual descendants of Abraham, father of the Hebrews and "friend of God." Like the Jewish people in every generation, we are called to read Scripture to deepen our understanding of who God is, how much he loves us and how we should love him in return.

# THE BOOK OF GENESIS

The first book of the Bible is called *Genesis,* which means "the Beginnings." It contains stories that people told for centuries before anyone wrote them down. The stories in the first eleven chapters are about prehistoric times. (See glossary, p. 318, ff.) They don't contain science or history. Instead, they tell us basic truths about God and people.

*Genesis* belongs to the *Pentateuch.* "Pentateuch" means "five books." The books of the Pentateuch are the first five books of the Hebrew and Christian Bibles or Scriptures. Jewish people call the Pentateuch "the *Torah,*" the Law.

*Genesis* begins with a story of the creation of the world and everything in it, including human beings. Through this story of creation, God through the human writer tells us that God loves and cares for us members of the human race in a special way.

**Genesis 1**

In the beginning God created heaven and earth. The earth was wasteland, and the deep waters were covered by darkness. But the spirit of God was soaring above the waters. God said, "Let there be light." And there was light. God saw that the light was good. Then God separated the light from the darkness. He called the light "day," and he called the darkness "night." Evening came and then morning. It was the first day.

God said, "Let there be a dome in the middle of the waters, and let it divide the waters from each other." So God made the dome to divide the waters under the dome from the waters above it. And God called the dome "sky." Evening came and then morning. It was the second day.

God said, "Let the waters under the sky come together in one place and let dry land show." And that was what happened. God called the dry land "earth," and he called the gathered waters "the sea." God saw that it was good. Then God said, "Let the earth produce grass and plants that make seeds—trees that produce their own kinds of fruit with seeds inside." And that was what happened. God saw that it was good. Evening came and then morning. It was the third day.

God said, "Let there be lights in the dome of the sky to separate day from night, to mark the times for celebrations, to separate the days and years, and to shed light on the earth." And that was what happened, God made the two great lights—the stronger light to rule over the day, and the weaker light to rule over the night—and the stars. God saw that it was good. Evening came and then morning. It was the fourth day.

God said, "Let the waters be filled with groups of living things, and let birds fly above the earth against the dome of the sky." So God created huge sea-monsters

and different kinds of living things with which the waters are filled, as well as different kinds of flying birds. God saw that it was good. Then God blessed them, saying, "Be fruitful and multiply, so as to fill the waters of the seas, and let the birds multiply." Evening came and then morning. It was the fifth day.

God said, "Let the earth produce different kinds of living things—cattle, reptiles and wild animals." And that was what happened. God saw that it was good. Then God said, "Let us make human beings in our image, resembling us, and let them rule over the fish of the sea, the birds in the sky, the cattle, and all the earth."

So God created human beings in the image of himself. He created them as male and female. Then God blessed them. He said to them, "Be fruitful and multiply, so as to fill the earth and take care of it; and rule over the fish of the sea, the birds in the sky and everything alive that crawls on the ground." God also said, "Look, I am giving you every seed-producing plant on the whole earth, and every tree on which there is seed-producing fruit. You will have these for food." And that was what happened.

Then God looked at everything he had made, and it was very good. Evening came and then morning. It was the sixth day.

And so, the sky and earth, with everything in them, were finished. And on the seventh day God rested from all the work he had done.

## The Second Story of Creation

**Genesis 2**

*The second creation story tells some of the same truths that the first story does, but in different order.*

When the Lord God made earth and heaven, there weren't any bushes or plants on the earth, because the Lord God hadn't sent rain. Instead, water flowed out of the ground.

The Lord God molded a man out of dust from the ground. Then he blew the breath of life into his nostrils. Adam ["man"] became alive.

Then the Lord God planted a garden in Eden, toward the east, and there he put Adam, whom he had made. And from the ground the Lord God made all sorts of beautiful trees grow. They produced delicious fruit. In the middle of the garden stood the tree of life, and also the tree of the knowledge of good and evil.

The Lord God told Adam, "You may eat fruit from any tree in the garden. But you must not eat fruit from the tree of the knowledge of good and evil. On the day you eat that, you will certainly die."

Then the Lord God said, "It is not good for Adam to be alone; I will make the right partner for him." He made Adam very drowsy, so that he fell asleep. Then he took out one of Adam's ribs and built the rib into a woman. He brought her to Adam. And Adam said, "At last, this person comes from my own bones and flesh. She will have the name Woman."

Adam and his wife were without clothes but they did not feel ashamed in front of each other.

## Our Parents Turn from God

**Genesis 3**

The serpent, who was the most clever animal that the Lord God had made, said to the woman, "Maybe God told you, 'You must not eat fruit from the trees in the garden.'"

The woman said to the serpent, "We do eat fruit from every tree in the garden, except the tree in the middle of the garden. God has given this order: 'You shall not eat that tree's fruit—you shall not even touch it—or you will die.'"

The serpent answered the woman, "You will not die at all! Instead, God knows that the day you eat it your eyes will be opened and you will know good and evil."

Then the woman noticed that the tree's fruit looked delicious and beautiful. It would also help her to know more. So she took some of the fruit and ate it. She also gave some to her husband. He ate it too. Then they realized that they had no clothes on. So they sewed fig leaves together and made clothes for themselves.

*This is the Bible's way of saying that something changed inside Adam and Eve after their sin. They lost much of their self-control.*

As the day cooled, they heard the Lord God's voice ringing out in the garden. Adam and his wife hid among the trees,

avoiding the Lord. But the Lord God called out and asked, "Where are you?"

Adam answered, "I heard your voice and was afraid because I didn't have any clothes on, so I hid."

God replied, "Who told you that you needed clothes? Have you eaten fruit from the tree that I warned you about?"

Adam answered, "It was the woman you gave me to be my partner. She gave me fruit from the tree, and I ate it."

Then the Lord God said to the woman, "Why did you do this?" The woman answered, "The serpent tricked me, so I ate it."

The Lord God said to the serpent, "Since you have done this, as long as you live you shall crawl on your belly and swallow dust. Besides that, I will make you and the woman enemies of each other, and also your descendants and her descendant. He will strike you on the head and you will strike him on the heel."

To the woman he said, "You will give birth to children in pain. Your husband will make life hard for you."

And he said to Adam, "Since you have listened to your wife and have eaten fruit from the tree that I told you not to eat from, the ground will give you thorns and thistles. With sweat on your face you will eat your bread, until you return to the ground, since you were taken from it. You are dust, and you will become dust again."

Adam gave his wife the name "Eve," since she would become the mother of everyone alive.

The Lord God made clothes out of animal skins for Adam and his wife and dressed them. Then he sent them out of the garden of Eden.

## Cain and Abel

**Genesis 4–5**

Adam came together with Eve, his wife, who became pregnant and gave birth to Cain. Later she gave birth to his brother, Abel.

Abel tended sheep, and Cain farmed the land. After a while, Cain brought an offering to the Lord from his crops, and Abel brought some of his lambs. The Lord showed that he was pleased with Abel and his offering, but he did not show that he was pleased with Cain and his offering. Cain burned with anger and went around with his head down.

The Lord asked Cain, "Why are you so angry and downcast? If you act right, can't you hold your head up? But if you don't act right, sin will crouch at the door, ready to pounce on you. Yet you can defeat sin."

But Cain said to his brother Abel, "Let's go out into the field." When they were in the open field, Cain attacked Abel and killed him.

Then the Lord asked Cain, "Where is Abel, your brother?"

He answered, "I don't know. Am I in charge of my brother?"

But God insisted, "What have you done? I can hear your brother's blood crying out to me from the ground. You must leave the land that opened its mouth to

receive your brother's blood from your hand! Even if you farm the land, it won't give you its harvest any longer. You will wander over the earth."

Cain said to the Lord, "My punishment is too hard to take! If you send me away and I have to hide from your presence, anybody who meets me will kill me."

But the Lord said to him, "Revenge will be taken on anybody who kills Cain."

*This section of Genesis shows us that killing of human beings is displeasing to God. But it also shows that God does not give up on someone who has committed a serious sin.*

Cain left the Lord's presence and settled in the land of Nod, east of Eden.

Adam came together with his wife again. She gave birth to a son, whom she named Seth.

*Genesis tells us that from the sons—and daughters—of Adam and Eve, the human race began to grow. One of Seth's descendants was Noah.*

The Lord saw that people's wickedness had increased throughout the world and that every thought in their minds was evil. He was sorry that he had made human beings. So the Lord said, "I will erase from the face of the earth the humanity that I have created. I am sorry that I made them." But Noah was pleasing to the Lord.

# Noah and the Flood

**Genesis 6–9**

Noah was a good and honest man. He tried to stay close to God. He became the father of three sons: Shem, Ham and Japheth.

The earth was filled with violence. So God said to Noah, "I have decided to put an end to human beings, because the earth is full of violence. I am going to destroy them together with the earth. Make yourself an ark of resin wood, with storerooms inside it. Coat it with pitch inside and out. You must make a roof for the ark. You must also put the door of the ark in its side. Make the ark with lower, second and third floors.

"I am going to bring down a flood of water on the earth to destroy everything living under the sky. But I will make a covenant with you. You are to go into the ark—you and your sons, as well as your wife and your sons' wives. And from all living things you are to bring a pair of each—they must be male and female—into the ark, so that they may stay alive with you. You must get every kind of food that there is and bring it in with you for yourselves and for them." Noah did everything just as God had told him.

Then the Lord said to Noah, "Go into the ark, you and all your family. In this generation you are the only person I have seen doing what is right. In seven more days I will begin to pour down rain on the earth. It will rain for forty days and forty nights, wiping off the face of the earth everything I have made."

So Noah and his sons, as well as his wife and his sons' wives, went into the ark.

And after seven days, it happened: the waters of the flood came over the earth. All the springs of the great deep burst, and the floodgates in the sky broke open. For forty days and forty nights water poured down on the earth.

The water became so deep that the ark began to float. As the water kept rising, the ark drifted on its surface. Then the water rose to such a height that the highest mountains were drowned. Therefore, all animals died that moved on the earth, and every human being. Only Noah was left and those with him in the ark. The water rose above the ground for a hundred and fifty days.

But God kept Noah in mind, as well as all the wild and tame animals that were with him in the ark. So God sent a wind over the earth, and the water level began to drop, since both the springs of the deep and the floodgates in the sky had closed again. The waters kept shrinking from the earth.

After forty days Noah opened the window he had made in the ark, and let out a raven. It came back again and again, while the waters were drying up from the earth. Then, in order to see whether the waters had lessened, he let out a dove. But, since there was water all over the earth, the dove found no place to put its feet and returned to him in the ark. Stretching out his hand, Noah brought it in. After seven more days he sent the dove out again. At evening the dove came back to him, carrying an olive leaf in its beak. Noah realized that the waters had lessened. He waited again, and after seven more days he let the dove go again. It did not come back.

By the first day of the first month, the water had dried up from the earth.

God then said to Noah, "Come out of the ark, you yourself and your wife, your sons and your sons' wives. Bring out all the animals that are with you, whether birds, or beasts, or any sort of reptiles that crawl on the ground, so that they may fill the earth, be fruitful and multiply."

So Noah came out and, with him, his sons, his wife and his sons' wives. All the animals and all sorts of reptiles and birds—everything that moved on the earth—came out of the ark, family by family.

Then Noah built an altar to the Lord and offered animal sacrifices on the altar.

And the Lord said in his heart, "I will never again punish the earth because of human beings. It is true that the human mind plans to do evil from its youth, but I will never again kill all living things, as I have done. From now on, planting and harvesting, cold and heat, summer and winter, day and night will never fail through all the ages of the earth."

God blessed Noah and his sons. He said to them, "Be fruitful and multiply on the earth and increase on it." Then God said to Noah and his sons, "I am going to set up my covenant with you and with your descendants, and also with every living thing that is with you. Never again shall all living things be wiped out by the waters of a flood; never again shall there be a flood to make the earth a wasteland."

God went on to say, "The sign of the covenant that I am making forever between myself, yourselves and every living thing in your care is my rainbow, which I have set in the clouds. It is the sign of the covenant between myself and the earth. Whenever I bring clouds over the earth, the rainbow will appear in the clouds, and I will remember my covenant, the covenant between myself, yourselves and every living thing. Never again shall the waters of a flood destroy all living things."

## The Tower of Babel

**Genesis 11**

*The first eleven chapters of Genesis tell us about times that are called "pre-historic." We don't have any written records dating from those times. We only have stories that were written much later. These stories are not important for their details but for the message they give us.*

*The story of Babel tells about a group of people who wanted to do something good (build a tower) for the wrong reason (pride).*

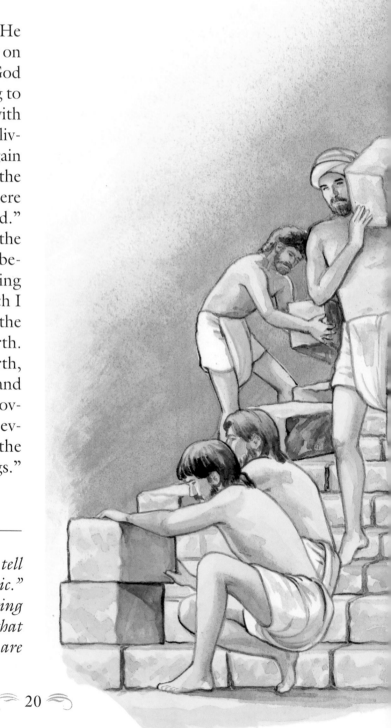

us build ourselves a city with a tower that reaches the skies. That will make us famous. Otherwise, we might scatter over the whole surface of the earth."

But the Lord came down to take a look at the city—especially the tower. Then the Lord said, "Here is one people, all of whom have the same language! If they have started by doing this, they will be able to do anything they want. Let's go down and confuse their language so they can't understand each other."

So since the Lord scattered them from that place over the whole earth, they stopped building the city. This is why it was given the name Babel, for there the Lord confused the language of the whole world, and then scattered the people from that place over the whole earth.

## God Calls Abram

**Genesis 12**

Abram was a descendant of Noah's son Shem. His family moved from Ur, near where the rivers Tigris and Euphrates meet, to Haran (modern Syria). Abram lived with his wife, Sarai, his father and his nephew, Lot. Abram and Sarai didn't have any children. After a while, Abram's father died.

The Lord said to Abram, "Leave your land, your relatives and your father's home to go to a land that I will show you. I will make a great nation come from you. I will bless you and make your name great. You will be a blessing. In you all the communities on earth will be blessed."

Abram took Sarai his wife and his brother's son, Lot, as well as all their things

When the whole world had the same language and the same words, as people moved eastward, they found a plain in the land of Shinar, where they settled. So they said to one another, "Come on! Let us make bricks and bake them in an oven." They had bricks for stones, and tar for mortar. Then they said, "Come on! Let

and their servants, and started out for the land of Canaan. When they arrived in Canaan Abram went into the land as far as the holyplace of Shechem. Even though the Canaanites were in the land at that time, the Lord appeared to Abram and said, "I will give this land to your descendants." Abram built an altar to the Lord, who had appeared to him.

With his family and servants, Abram traveled through Canaan and the Negeb, the dry region south of Canaan, then continued on into Egypt. Afterwards they returned to the hilly region in the center of Canaan.

## Abram and Lot Separate

**Genesis 13**

Abram was very rich in livestock, silver and gold. But Lot, too, who was traveling with Abram, had sheep, cattle and tents. The land could not support them if they stayed together. There was quarreling between Abram's herdsmen and Lot's.

So Abram said to Lot, "Since we are close relatives, let there not be any argument between me and you, or between my shepherds and yours. The whole land is available. Please, let us separate. If you turn to the left, I will turn to the right; and if you turn to the right, I will turn to the left."

When Lot looked around, the Jordan plain caught his eye, because the whole of it was well watered. So, Lot chose the whole Jordan plain for himself and traveled east. Abram settled in the land of Canaan, while Lot settled among the towns of the plain; he pitched his tents near Sodom.

After Lot had left, the Lord said to Abram, "Lift up your eyes, and from where you are look north and south, east and west, for I will give you and your descendants forever all the land that you can see. Travel up and down the land and across it, for I will give it to you."

## Rescue

**Genesis 14**

Four foreign kings and their fighting men invaded the territory around the cities of Sodom and Gomorrah, and five local kings called up their men and went out to fight. Since the raiders were stronger, the local kings lost the battle. They and many of their people escaped. But some people, including Lot, were captured and taken away.

Someone hurried to tell Abram about this. Abram rode out to catch up with the the raiders. With him went his servants, who were trained fighting men, and his Amorite friends, Eshcol, Aner and Mamre, with their servants. They caught up with the raiders at night, surrounded them, attacked them and chased them out of the territory.

Abram brought back all the booty, as well as Lot, his brother's son, Lot's possessions, the women and the other people who had been captured.

The king of Sodom went out to meet Abram when he returned. And Melchizedek, king of Salem, brought out bread and wine (he was a priest of God most high) and blessed Abram in these words, "May God most high, Creator of heaven and earth, bless Abram. And blessed be God most high, who turned your enemies over to you." Abram gave Melchizedek a tenth of the booty.

The king of Sodom said to Abram, "Give me the people, and keep the booty for yourself." But Abram replied to the king of Sodom, "I will not take as much as a thread or a sandal-strap or anything that is yours. Just let my servants have what they have used, and let Aner, Eshcol and Mamre have their share."

## God Renews the Promise

**Genesis 15–17**

After these events, the word of the Lord came to Abram in a vision with this message: "Don't be afraid, Abram. I am your reward." But Abram replied, "What can you give me when I am going to die without children?"

"Your own son shall be your heir." The Lord took him outside and said, "Look at the sky and count the stars if you can." And he promised him, "That is how your descendants will be." Abram believed the Lord, and the Lord was pleased with him for this.

Time passed. At Sarai's suggestion, Abram fathered a son by Sarai's slave-girl,

Hagar. This was a custom that people accepted in those days. Abram named the boy Ishmael. By now, Abram was very old.

The Lord appeared to him and said, "I am God, the Almighty. Live in my presence and be whole-hearted. I will make a covenant between myself and you and will multiply your descendants." Abram bowed down, and God continued, "You will become the father of many nations. Therefore, your name will not be Abram any longer. Your name will be Abraham, because I make you the father of many nations. To you and to your descendants I will give the land where you are living—the whole land of Canaan. I will be your God."

Again, God said to Abraham, "As for Sarai, your wife, you shall not call her Sarai, but her name is Sarah. I will bless her and give you a son through her too. Yes, I will bless her. Kings of peoples will be descended from her."

As he bowed down, Abraham laughed, saying to himself, "Can a man a hundred years old be the father of a child, or can Sarah give birth at the age of ninety?" So Abraham replied to God, "May Ishmael live on in your presence!"

But God insisted, "Not at all! Sarah, your wife, is going to give you a son, whom you will name Isaac and with whom I will make a covenant. But I have also listened to what you have said about Ishmael. I will bless him and give him many descendants."

## The Three Visitors

**Genesis 18**

The Lord appeared to Abraham again, when he was sitting at the entrance of his tent around noon. Abraham lifted his eyes to look around and saw three men standing near him. He ran to meet them, and bowing to the ground said, "Sir, please be so kind as not to pass by me. Let the servants bring some water and wash your feet. Then rest under a tree while I bring a little food so you can refresh yourselves. Then you may go on." They replied, "All right, do what you have said."

While they were eating, one of the men asked, "Where is Sarah, your wife?"

He replied, "She is there in the tent."

The man said, "When I return to you a year from now, Sarah, your wife, will have a son."

Sarah was listening at the entrance of the tent, which was behind him. Abraham and Sarah were old. So Sarah laughed to herself. But the Lord said to Abraham, "What is Sarah laughing at? Is anything beyond the Lord's wonderful power? By the time that I return to you—one year from now—Sarah will have a son."

Then, because she was afraid, Sarah lied, saying, "I didn't laugh."

But he replied, "You didn't? Yes, you did!"

## Abraham's Prayer for Sodom

**Genesis 19**

The men stood up and started out toward Sodom, while Abraham walked with them to say good-bye. The Lord was thinking, "Shall I hide from Abraham what I am going to do? I have chosen him, so that he may tell his sons and his servants to follow the ways of the Lord, do-

ing what is right." So the Lord said, "The complaints against Sodom and Gomorrah are very great, for their sin is very serious. I will go down and see whether their actions match the complaints that have reached me. I want to know."

The two men continued on toward Sodom, but Abraham stayed in the Lord's presence. Abraham asked, "Are you going to wipe out even the upright people along with the wicked? There may be fifty upright persons inside the city. Will you wipe out the place without paying attention to the fifty upright persons who are in it? It certainly isn't like you to do something like that."

The Lord replied, "If in Sodom I find fifty upright persons, I will forgive the whole place for their sake."

Abraham realized that there might not be fifty upright persons in Sodom, so he continued to bargain. What if there were forty-five upright persons? Forty? Thirty? Twenty?

Each time, the Lord said he would not destroy the city if that many upright people could be found there.

Again Abraham said, "Let not my Lord grow angry if I speak just this last time. Maybe ten can be found there."

And he said, "I won't destroy it for the sake of the ten."

The two men (angels) arrived at Sodom in the evening and discovered that the people of the city really were living very bad lives. There were not even ten upright persons in the city.

At sunrise, the angels urged Lot to take his wife and daughters and escape from the city without looking back. They left the city, but it is said that Lot's wife did look back and was turned into a pillar of salt.

As soon as Lot and his daughters had reached a safe spot, there was a great disaster. It may have been a combination of earthquake and lightning, setting fire to the tar pits near the cities. The cities of the plain were destroyed.

That morning Abraham looked out toward Sodom and Gomorrah. He saw smoke rising from the ground like the smoke of a furnace.

## Isaac—and Abraham's Test

**Genesis 21–22**

As the Lord had promised, Sarah gave a son to Abraham when he was very old. They named him Isaac, which is related to the Hebrew word for laughter. Sarah said, "God has given me a chance to laugh."

Sometime later, God tested Abraham. God called to him: "Abraham!" He replied, "Here I am."

He continued, "Take Isaac your son, whom you love so much, and go to the land of Moriah. Offer him up as a burnt offering on one of the mountains that I will show you."

So the next morning Abraham got up early, saddled his donkey, took along two of his servants, as well as his son Isaac, chopped wood for the burnt offering, and started out toward the place that God had told him about. On the third day Abraham raised his eyes and saw the place far away. So he said to his servants, "Stay here with the donkey, while I and the boy go there and worship; then we will return to you."

Abraham took the wood for the burnt offering and laid it on the shoulders of Isaac his son, while in his own hands he took the fire and the knife. They were both walking side by side, when Isaac said to his father Abraham, "Father!"

He replied, "Yes, son."

He went on to say, "Here are the fire and the wood. But where is the lamb for the burnt offering?" Abraham replied, "My son, God himself will give us the lamb for the burnt offering."

They came to the place that God had shown him. There Abraham built an altar and set the wood in order. Then he tied up Isaac, his son, and laid him on the wood. Abraham reached out and gripped the knife to kill his own son. But the angel of the Lord called to him from heaven: "Abraham, Abraham!"

He replied, "Here I am."

The Lord said, "Don't lay a hand on the boy. Don't harm him. Now I know that you fear God, since you have not held back your own son from me." When Abraham raised his eyes, he saw a ram caught by the horns in a clump of bushes. He went and took the ram, which he offered as a burnt offering in place of his son.

The angel of the Lord called to Abraham a second time and said, "Since you have done such a thing— that is, since you have not held back your own son from me—I will bless you very much and will make your descendants as many as the stars in heaven and as the grains of sand on the seashore. And because you have listened to my voice, all the nations of the earth will be blessed in your descendants."

## Jacob and Esau

**Genesis 23–28**

In those times, people were free to pasture their flocks and herds on any land that was not being farmed. So Abraham, who was a sheep-owner, did not actually have any land in Canaan until his wife, Sarah, died. Then he bought a cave at Hebron and buried Sarah there.

After that, Abraham sent one of his servants to find a wife for his son Isaac from among their relatives in Haran. The servant came back with Rebekah, a beautiful young woman. She and Isaac were married, and after some time they had twin sons, Esau and Jacob, who turned out to be very different from one another.

Meanwhile, Abraham died. Isaac and Ishmael buried him next to Sarah.

When the twins grew up, Esau became an expert hunter, but Jacob was a home-loving sort of man. Isaac preferred Esau. He liked to eat the wild game that Esau brought home. Rebekah preferred Jacob.

Jacob was clever and one day he tricked Esau into selling him his rights as the first-born son. This pleased his mother, Rebekah, because Jacob was her favorite son.

When Isaac was old and his eyesight had grown dim, he called Esau and said to him, "My son, as you see, I am old and do not know when I will die. Since this is how things are, take your quiver and bow, go out into the countryside and kill some

game for me. Then prepare tasty meats for me the way I like, and bring them for me to eat so I may give you my special blessing before I die."

Rebekah overheard this conversation and thought of a way for Jacob to receive Isaac's special blessing. She asked Jacob to kill two kid goats from the flock, so she could cook them before Esau returned. Jacob would bring the meat to his father and receive the blessing meant for Esau. Jacob objected, because it was a risk, but his mother talked him into it. She covered his smooth hands and neck with pieces of hairy goatskin, so the almost blind Isaac would think the young man really was Esau. Rebekah also gave Jacob Esau's best clothes to put on. Then she handed Jacob the tasty dishes of meat and the bread she had prepared.

Jacob went in to his father and said, "Father!"

He answered, "Who are you? My son?"

Jacob said to his father, "I am your elder son, Esau. I have done as you told me. Please get up, take a seat and eat some of my game, so you may give me your special blessing."

Isaac asked, "How did you find it so soon, my son?"

He answered, "The Lord your God sent it in my direction."

Isaac continued, "Bring me the meat, so I may eat of my son's game and give you my special blessing." Jacob brought him the meat, and he ate. Jacob also brought him wine, and he drank. Then his father Isaac said to him, "Please come closer, my son, and kiss me." As Jacob came closer and kissed him, Isaac could smell the fragrance of his clothes. So he blessed him in these words:

"Here is the fragrance of my son! Like the fragrance of a field that the Lord has blessed. May God, then, give you dew from heaven and fruitful lands on earth, along with plenty of grain and wine. May peoples serve you and nations bow down to you. Be ruler over your brothers, and may your mother's sons bow down to you."

Right after Isaac had finished blessing Jacob, and Jacob had left, Esau came in from hunting. He, too, prepared tasty dishes that he brought to his father, saying, "Let my father get up and eat some of his son's game, that you may give me your special blessing."

But his father Isaac replied to him, "Who are you?"

He said, "I am Esau, your elder son."

Isaac was agitated with violent convulsions as he said, "Then, who was it that caught some game and brought it to me? I ate everything and then blessed him. And he will stay blessed!"

When Esau heard this, he uttered a loud, bitter cry and said to his father, "Bless me, father—me too!" But Isaac said, "Your brother came in underhandedly and got away with your blessing."

But Esau said to his father, "Do you have only one blessing, father? Bless me, father—me too!" And Esau cried aloud and wept.

So Isaac his father replied, "You shall make a living with your sword, but shall serve your brother. Yet, you shall tear to pieces the yoke he will place on your neck."

Esau was very angry with Jacob, who had taken advantage of him twice. He knew that their father would not live much longer and planned to kill Jacob after the period of mourning.

Rebekah, his mother, learned about this. So she hinted to Isaac that Jacob needed to take a wife from their own people. Isaac thought it was a good idea and decided to send Jacob to his uncle Laban in Haran. In this way Jacob escaped his brother's anger.

Jacob started for Haran. At sunset he stopped to spend the night in the spot where he found himself. Taking one of the stones of that place, he used it as a pillow. In a dream he saw a ladder set up on the ground, with its top reaching into the sky. Angels of God were climbing up and down. He also saw the Lord standing beside him. The Lord said, "I am the God of Abraham your father, and the God of Isaac. I will give you and your descendants the land on which you are lying. Also, I will be with you and guard you wherever you go and bring you back to this land."

Jacob woke up and said, "The Lord is really in this place; but I did not know." And in his heart, he continued, "How awesome is this place! This is God's house. In fact, this is the gate of heaven." So the next morning he got up early, and taking the stone that he had made his pillow, he stood it up and poured oil on it. He named that place Beth-el [house of God].

Then Jacob made this promise: "If the Lord God is with me and guards me on this journey that I have begun, if he gives me food to eat and clothes to put on, if he brings me safely back to my father's house, the Lord will be my God. This stone that I have set up shall be God's home. Lord, I will give back to you one tenth of everything you give me."

## The Deceiver Is Tricked

**Genesis 29–31**

Jacob continued on toward Haran, where he found the home of his mother's brother, Laban. His uncle gave him a great welcome, and Jacob began to help take care of the sheep. After about a month, Laban asked what Jacob would like as pay. "I will serve you seven years for Rachel, your younger daughter," said Jacob. Laban had two daughters, but Jacob liked the younger, Rachel, who was pretty. Laban agreed.

But when the seven years were up, Laban tricked Jacob into marrying the elder daughter, Leah, who was still single.

"Why have you tricked me?" Jacob asked in anger.

Laban answered, "It isn't our custom to give the younger daughter in marriage before the elder one." Then he invited Jacob to marry both of them and work another seven years for Rachel. Because Jacob loved Rachel, he agreed. (In those times some men had two or more wives.)

After the second seven-year period, Jacob wanted to return to Canaan, but he was poor. So he stayed on with Laban a while longer, and because he was clever, he slowly built up his own flocks of sheep andgoats.

At last, Jacob left with his wives, children and flocks. By this time his family was large—two wives and their maid-servants, eleven sons and a daughter. His sons' names were Reuben, Simeon, Levi, Judah, Dan, Naphtali, Gad, Asher, Issachar, Zebulun and Joseph, the son of Rachel. Jacob's daughter was named Dinah.

## Return to Canaan

**Genesis 32–35**

Jacob sent messengers ahead of him to his brother Esau, who lived in the land of Edom. He told them: "This is what you will say: 'Jacob, your servant, says this: I have been staying with Laban until now. I have oxen, donkeys, flocks, and servants. I am sending word that I would like to be on friendly terms with you.'"

The messengers returned to Jacob with this news: "We went to see your brother Esau. But he is coming to meet you, and there are four hundred men with him."

Jacob was very much afraid, so he divided the people with him, as well as the flocks and cattle, into two camps, for he thought, "If Esau attacks one of the camps and destroys it, the other camp will escape."

Then Jacob prayed, "O Lord, God of my father Abraham and God of my father Isaac, who have said to me, 'Return to your country and to your relatives, and I will be with you,' I don't deserve all your kindness and the faithfulness you have shown to your servant. Your goodness can be seen by the fact that I crossed the Jor-

dan with only my staff, but now I own enough things for two camps. Please rescue me from the hand of Esau. I am afraid that he may strike me down, together with the mothers and children. Yet you have said, 'I will surely be good to you and make your descendants like the sands by the sea.'"

Then Jacob chose some of his best goats, sheep, cattle and donkeys and sent them ahead of him in flocks and herds. To the servant in charge of each group he said, "When my brother Esau meets you and asks, 'Whose servant are you, where are you going and for whom are these animals you are herding?' you will say, 'Your servant Jacob's. This is a gift sent to you. He himself is just behind us.'" Jacob was thinking, "Let me make up to him with the gifts, and let me meet him afterwards. Maybe he will welcome me kindly."

That night a mysterious man attacked Jacob in the dark and wrestled with him until dawn. Neither would give in.

At last the man said, "Let me go, for day is coming." But Jacob answered, "I will not let you go unless you bless me."

He asked him, "What is your name?"

He said, "Jacob."

The man said, "They will not call you 'Jacob' any longer, but 'Israel,' for you have struggled with God and men, and have won."

Jacob asked, "Please, tell me your name."

But he answered, "Why are you asking about my name?" Yet, he did bless him.

*Was it an angel? Was it God himself? Jacob didn't know. But he had a new name,*

*Israel, which meant he had fought with "God and men."*

Jacob looked up and saw Esau coming, and with him were four hundred men. So he placed the maid-servants with their children in the front, then Leah with her children, and then Rachel with Joseph. He walked ahead of them. He bowed to the ground seven times before he reached his brother. But Esau ran to meet him and hugged and kissed him.

Then, as he looked around, seeing the women and children, Esau asked, "Whose are these? Are they yours?"

Jacob answered, "The children are the favor that God has given to your servant."

Then Esau asked, "What was your purpose with all those flocks and herds that I met?"

Jacob answered, "I wanted to find favor with you."

But Esau said, "Brother, I have plenty. Keep what you have."

But Jacob replied, "Oh no! Please accept my gift from my own goods, both because God has been gracious to me and because I have all I need." Because he insisted, Esau accepted.

After they had spoken for a while, Esau returned to his home at Seir, to the south, while Jacob, his family and his servants continued west and entered Canaan.

On the way, Rachel gave birth to her second son, Benjamin, and died. Jacob was sad, for he loved Rachel very much. As Rachel's sons, Joseph and Benjamin, grew, Jacob showed that these two were his favorites.

## Joseph and His Brothers

**Genesis 37**

When Joseph was seventeen, he used to tend the sheep with his brothers, and he would tell his father whenever they did something wrong. Israel (Jacob) gave him a multicolored robe. Seeing that their father had a special love for him, his brothers hated Joseph and would not speak to him kindly.

They hated Joseph all the more when he told them a dream that he had had. He said to them, "We were making bundles of grain in the field. Suddenly my bundle stood up, and your bundles formed a circle round about it and bowed down to my bundle."

They answered, "Do you mean that you will be king over us?" So they hated him all the more.

He had still another dream that he told to his brothers. He said, "I saw the sun, the moon and eleven stars bowing down to me."

His father scolded him, saying, "What does this dream mean? Does it mean that I, your mother and your brothers are supposed to come up and bow to the ground before you?" But, although Joseph's brothers were jealous, his father did not forget the story.

One day, when Joseph's brothers were a great distance away with their flocks, Israel sent Joseph to see how everything was going.

They saw him in the distance, and before he came close to them they said to one another, "Here comes the great dreamer. Let's kill him, throw him into one of the dry wells and then say that a wild beast has eaten him. Then we will see what happens to his dreams."

But Reuben tried to rescue him, saying, "Let's not kill anyone. Don't shed any blood. Throw him into a well in the wasteland, but don't lay hands on him." His plan was to rescue him from their hands and return him to his father.

When Joseph came to his brothers, they stripped off his multicolored robe and threw him into an empty well.

When they sat down to eat, they looked up and saw a group of Ishmaelites coming from Gilead. Their animals were carrying spices, which they were taking to Egypt. Judah said to his brothers, "What good would it do to kill our brother and cover up his blood? Let's sell him to the Ishmaelites and not touch him, for he is our brother." His brothers agreed. For twenty pieces of silver they sold him to the Ishmaelites, who took him to Egypt.

Joseph's brothers killed a he-goat, dipped Joseph's robe in its blood, and had the multicolored robe sent to their father by way of a messenger. They had the messenger say for them, "We have found this. Take a good look at it: is it your son's robe or not?"

Jacob took a good look at it and then said, "Yes, my son's robe! A wild beast has eaten him! Joseph has been torn apart!" His sons and daughter tried to comfort him, but he kept weeping for Joseph.

## Joseph a Slave

**Genesis 39—40**

Joseph had been taken down to Egypt, and Potiphar, the commander of Pharaoh's bodyguard, bought him from the Ishmaelites.*

Joseph's Egyptian master could see that the Lord was with him for the Lord made anything he did turn out well. So Joseph found favor with Potiphar. Potiphar even put Joseph in charge of his house and servants.

From the moment he made him the steward of his household and put him in charge of everything he had, the Lord blessed the household of the Egyptian for the sake of Joseph. The Lord's blessing was on everything he had—both in the house and in the fields. So Potiphar placed everything he had in Joseph's hands.

But Potiphar's wife took a liking to Joseph and wanted him to commit a sin with her. When Joseph refused, the woman accused Joseph of having done the very thing he would not do. Potiphar believed her, and Joseph was thrown into prison.

While in prison, Joseph showed that he could explain the meanings of dreams. The cup-bearer of Pharaoh was one of the men whose dreams Joseph interpreted.

## Pharaoh's Dream and Joseph's Success

**Genesis 41**

After two years had gone by, Pharaoh

---

*Pharaoh was the title of the king of Egypt.*

had a dream. He seemed to be standing by the Nile River when suddenly seven fat cows came out of the Nile and started eating grassy plants. But all at once, seven other cows that were thin and looked like they were starving came out of the Nile and stood beside the other cows at the edge of the Nile. Then the thin cows ate up the fat cows. After this, Pharaoh woke up.

When he fell asleep again, he dreamed that seven fat ears of grain were growing on one stem. But after them seven ears sprouted which were thin and burnt by the desert wind. Then the thin ears swallowed up the fat, well-filled ears of grain. After this, Pharaoh woke up.

Pharaoh wanted to know the meaning of these dreams and asked who could explain them. The cup-bearer remembered Joseph, and Pharaoh sent for him.

After shaving and changing his clothes, Joseph went to see Pharaoh. Pharaoh said to Joseph, "I have had a dream that no one can explain. But I have been told that when you hear about a dream you can explain it."

Joseph answered, "I am not the one who does it. It is God who will give Pharaoh a good answer."

So Pharaoh told his dream to Joseph.

Joseph said to Pharaoh, "God has told Pharaoh what he is going to do. The seven fat cows are seven years, and the seven fat ears of grain are also seven years—it is the same dream. Again, the seven thin cows are seven years, and so are the seven thin ears burnt by the desert wind. They will be seven years of hunger. This is the message.

"God has let Pharaoh see what he is going to do. The seven coming years will be a time of abundant food in the whole land of Egypt. But after them, seven years of food shortage will start in which all the abundance in the land of Egypt will be forgotten. The fact that the dream was given to Pharaoh twice means that God has firmly decided about this and that he will do it.

"So, let Pharaoh look for someone who is understanding and wise and put him in charge of the farmland of Egypt. Let Pharaoh have him appoint inspectors throughout the land and, during the seven years of abundance, tax the farmland of Egypt to hand over one fifth of the food. Let them store it under Pharaoh's control. In that way, the land will have this food stored up for the seven years of shortage that will be coming."

Pharaoh was pleased with the suggestion, and so were all his officials. So Pharaoh said to his officials, "Can we find anyone else like this, a man in whom God's spirit lives?" Pharaoh then said to Joseph, "After God has shown you all this, no one can be as understanding and wise as you are. You are the person who will be over my household, and my people shall obey your orders. Only as far as the throne is concerned will I be greater than you. Look! I am making you ruler of the whole land of Egypt." Pharaoh took off the ring that held the royal seal and put it on Joseph's hand. He had him clothed in fine linen, with a circlet of gold around his neck. Then he had him travel in the best chariot after his own. Pharaoh also gave Joseph a wife. Her name was Asenath.

Joseph was thirty years old when he began to serve Pharaoh, king of Egypt.

He stored up great amounts of grain, like the sands of the sea—to the point that people stopped keeping track of it, because it was beyond any counting.

Before the years of shortage came, two sons were born to Joseph and Asenath. To his first son Joseph gave the name Manasseh, saying, "God has made me forget all my suffering and my father's entire family." To the second he gave the name Ephraim, saying, "God has made me successful in the land where I was oppressed." The name Manasseh is related to the Hebrew words "he made me forget" and the name Ephraim is related to the words "he made me successful."

At the end of the seven years of abundance, the seven years of shortage began, as Joseph had said. There was hunger in all lands; but throughout the land of Egypt there was bread. When all the land of Egypt began to feel the shortage, the people cried to Pharaoh for bread, and Pharaoh said to everyone, "Go to Joseph. Do whatever he tells you." All the world went to Egypt, to Joseph, to buy grain, because hunger was intense all over the world.

## Joseph's Brothers in Egypt
**Genesis 42–44**

Jacob learned that grain could be gotten in Egypt. So he said to his sons, "Why do you keep looking at one another? I hear that there is grain in Egypt. Go down there, and buy grain for us, so we can stay alive and not die."

Ten of Joseph's brothers went down to buy grain from Egypt. But Jacob did not send Benjamin, Joseph's brother, for he thought, "He might have an accident and die."

Now, Joseph was the ruler of the country and sold grain to all the nations of the world. So Joseph's brothers came up and bowed down before him, with their faces to the ground.

When Joseph saw his brothers, he recognized them but did not let them know who he was. He pretended not to believe their story and called them spies. To prove they were not spies, they told more about themselves.

They said, "Your servants are twelve brothers. We are sons of the same man, who is in the land of Canaan, but the youngest is with our father; and the other is no longer with us."

But Joseph said to them, "You will be tested in this way: If you are honest people, let one of your brothers be held as a hostage. As for the rest of you, go and bring grain to your starving families. But you must come back with your youngest brother. That will prove that you have told the truth, and you will not die."

They said to each other, "We are paying for what we did to our brother, for we saw how disturbed he was when he begged us to free him, yet we would not listen." Since someone was translating for them, they did not realize that Joseph understood. He went out for a moment and burst into tears. Then he returned and chose Simeon to be chained and put in prison.

Joseph gave orders to fill their bags with grain and also to supply them with food for the journey. Although his broth-

ers did not know it, he also told the servants to put each one's money back into his sack.

When the nine brothers returned to Jacob in the land of Canaan, they told him everything that had happened. As they were emptying their sacks, each was surprised to see his purse with the money. Both they and their father began to worry.

But Jacob would not let them return to Egypt. He did not want to part with Benjamin, the remaining son of Rachel. He was afraid that something would happen to him. Only when the grain ran out again did Jacob agree to let Benjamin go with his brothers.

They were surprised at the welcome they received: they were invited to eat at the home of Joseph himself. Since they were afraid of being accused of stealing,

they told the whole story to one of Joseph's servants.

But the servant said, "Don't worry. Your God, the God of your father, permitted you to find treasure in your bags. Your own money was paid to me." Then he brought Simeon out to them.

When Joseph went into the house, they bowed down to the ground in front of him. He asked how they were and then added, "Your father, whom you spoke about, is he still alive?"

As they bowed down, they said, "Your servant, our father, is well. He is still alive."

Then he raised his eyes and, looking at his own mother's son, his brother Benjamin, he asked, "Is this your youngest brother, the one you told me about? May God be gracious to you, my son."

The emotions of his heart went out to his brother, so he suddenly left and went into his room to weep. Then he washed his face and came out. Getting control of himself, he ordered the meal to be served.

They were seated facing him, the eldest in the place for the eldest, and the youngest in the place for the youngest, so they looked at one another in amazement. From the food that was in front of him he distributed portions to them. To Benjamin he gave a portion larger than the portion of any of them—five times as large. They drank and enjoyed his company.

Still without saying who he was, Joseph sent his brothers away with as much grain as they could carry, plus the money they had brought. But he also had his own silver cup placed in the mouth of Benjamin's sack. Then he sent a servant after the group to arrest and bring back the man in whose sack the cup would be found.

The servant began his search, starting with the eldest and finishing with the youngest. He found the cup in Benjamin's sack. The brothers were disturbed and returned to the city.

Judah went with his brothers into Joseph's house, and they threw themselves down in front of him. Joseph said to them, "What have you done?"

Judah answered, "What can we say to my lord? Here we are! We are my lord's slaves."

But Joseph said, "Far be it from me to do such a thing! It is the man in whose possession the cup was found who shall be my slave. The rest of you may go to your father undisturbed."

Then Judah came close to him and said, "I beg your pardon, my lord. May my lord's servant have a word in his ear? If I come to our father without the boy, he will die.

"Besides, I your servant told my father, 'If I don't bring him back to you, you can blame me for the rest of my life.' So please, let me stay here as my lord's slave, instead of the boy, and let the boy go back with his brothers, for how can I go back to my father without having the boy with me? I could not bear to see my father's sorrow."

## Reunion

**Genesis 45–50**

Joseph could not control his feelings any longer. So in a loud voice he said to his servants, "Let everyone leave me." As a result, no one was with Joseph when he told his brothers who he was. He sobbed loudly.

He said to his brothers, "I am your brother Joseph, whom you sold into Egypt. But now do not be sorry and do not hate yourselves for having sold me. God has sent me ahead of you to make it possible for your descendants to stay alive in this land and to save your own lives—to bring about a great rescue.

"It was not you who sent me here, but God, who also made me an advisor to Pharaoh, ruler of all his household and governor over the whole land of Egypt.

"Hurry to your father and tell him, 'This is what Joseph your son says: God had made me lord of all Egypt. Come here to me. You will stay in the land of Goshen so you will be close to me—you with your sons, your grandchildren, your

flocks, your cattle, and everything you have. It is there that I will support you, so that you and your sons won't need anything, though there will still be five years of hunger.'"

Then Joseph threw his arms around his brother Benjamin and wept; Benjamin wept too. Joseph also kissed all his brothers, weeping.

The joyful brothers returned to their father Israel and told him that Joseph was alive. They brought Israel down to Egypt, together with their own wives and children and all their flocks and herds. The descendants of Israel lived in Egypt—in the land of Goshen—for several generations and became more and more numerous.

# THE BOOK OF EXODUS

*Exodus* (which means "going out") is the name of the second book of the part of the Bible called the Pentateuch. The Book of Exodus tells about the most important events in the history of Abraham's descendants: God's rescue of these people (the Israelites) from slavery in Egypt and the covenant (agreement), which God made with Abraham's descendants at Mount Sinai. The covenant was very important for the Israelites and for us.

*Exodus* and the last three books of the Pentateuch also contain laws given by God—some for people of all times and others for the people of Israel at certain points in their history. This is why the Hebrew name for the Pentateuch is the *Torah,* which means "the Law."

Exodus 1

Here is the list of the sons of Israel who, with their families, went to Egypt with Jacob: Reuben, Simeon, Levi and Judah; Issachar, Zebulun and Benjamin; Dan and Naphtali; Gad and Asher. Joseph was in Egypt already.

*Each of Joseph's brothers became the ancestor of a large group, or tribe, named after him. Joseph's sons, Ephraim and Manasseh, also became the ancestors of tribes. Together, these tribes made up the people of Israel. They were also called the Israelites.*

## Slavery in Egypt

Joseph, as well as all his brothers, had died. But the Israelites had such large families and grew so powerful that the land was full of them.

A new king came to power in Egypt. Knowing nothing about Joseph, he said to his own people, "As you see, the Israelites are more numerous and powerful than we are. Let us find a way to handle this situation. Otherwise, they may keep increasing and, if a war breaks out, they may fight on the side of our enemies."

So, to make life hard for the Israelites, they forced them to work building the cities of Pithon and Rameses in honor of Pharaoh. But the Israelites kept growing in numbers as much as Egypt made life hard for them, so the Egyptians continued to worry. Then, they completely made slaves out of the Israelites. They gave them a bitter life with mortar and bricks, and with all kinds of farm work.

## Moses

Exodus 2

Pharaoh was afraid that in a few years there might be so many Israelites in Egypt that they could start a revolution. So he ordered that all Hebrew baby boys be drowned in the Nile River.

A son was born to a family of the tribe of Levi. To save him from being killed, his mother hid him for three months.

When she could no longer hide him, she took a papyrus-reed basket and plastered it with pitch. She put the child in it and set it among the tall grasses at the edge of the Nile. The baby's sister stood a little ways off to learn what the people would do with him.

Now, Pharaoh's daughter went down to the Nile for a swim, while her maid-servants walked along the river bank. She saw the basket in the midst of the grasses and sent a handmaid to fetch it. As she opened it, she saw the baby boy, crying. Pharaoh's daughter was moved to pity for him and said, "This must be one of the children of the Hebrews."

The baby's sister said to Pharaoh's daughter, "Should I go and call someone from among the Hebrew women to nurse the child for you?"

"Please," Pharaoh's daughter answered her.

So the girl went and called the child's mother, to whom Pharaoh's daughter said, "Take this child away and nurse it for me. I myself will pay you."

The woman took the child and nursed him. The child grew. And when she brought him to Pharaoh's daughter, he became her son. She named him Moses.

After Moses grew up, he went out to visit his brother Israelites and saw their life as slaves. An Egyptian was beating one of the Israelites. Moses looked all around, and, not seeing anybody, he struck down the Egyptian and buried him in the sand.

When Moses went out the next day, two Hebrew men were fighting.

To one he said, "Why are you striking your companion?"

But the man answered back, "Who has set you up as judge over us? Are you thinking of killing me as you killed the Egyptian?"

45

Moses was afraid, for he thought, "Clearly, everybody knows about this."

When Pharaoh heard about the matter, he decided to kill Moses. So Moses fled from Pharaoh to live in the land of Midian.

In Midian, a rugged land near the tip of the Sinai Peninsula, Moses met Jethro, a pagan priest. After a while, he married Jethro's daughter, Zipporah, and settled down. They had a son, whom Moses named Gershom.

In those years the king of Egypt died, but the Israelites continued to groan in their slavery. Their cry went up to God, and he listened to their complaints. God had not forgotten his covenant with Abraham, with Isaac and with Jacob, so he watched over the Israelites with concern.

## The Burning Bush

**Exodus 3–4**

Moses had become a shepherd of the flock of Jethro, his father-in-law. One day, he brought the flock to the edge of the wastelands and came to God's mountain, Horeb. The angel of the Lord appeared to him as a blazing fire coming from a thorn-bush.

Moses was surprised to see that the bush was on fire, blazing brightly, without being burned up. So he thought, "Let me go over and take a look at this strange happening. Why isn't the bush burning up?"

The Lord saw him coming to take a look, so God called out from the bush, saying, "Moses, Moses!"

He answered, "Here I am."

God said, "Don't come close to this spot. Take off your sandals, for the place where you are standing is holy ground." Then he said, "I am the God of your father, the God of Abraham, the God of Isaac and the God of Jacob."

Afraid to see God, Moses hid his face.

Then the Lord said, "I clearly see the hard life of my people who are in Egypt, and I hear them crying because of their slave-drivers. I care about their suffering. I will go down to rescue them from the grip of Egypt and bring them up from that land to a good and open land, to a land flowing with milk and honey, to the home of the Canaanites. I want to send you to Pharaoh. You must bring my people, the Israelites, out of Egypt."

But Moses said to God, "Who am I to go to Pharaoh and bring the Israelites out of Egypt?"

He answered, "I will be with you."

Then Moses asked God's name, because he knew that his people would want to know it.

God answered, "I am who am. Tell the Israelites, 'The One Who Is has sent me to you,'

"Go and call together the leaders of Israel and tell them, 'the Lord—the God of Abraham, Isaac and Jacob—has appeared to me to say: I have seen what is being done to you in Egypt. So I intend to bring you from the hard life of Egypt up to the land of the Canaanites, to a land flowing with milk and honey.'

"They will listen to what you say, so with the leaders of Israel you will go up to the king of Egypt and tell him this: 'We

have met the Lord, the God of the Hebrews. Please let us go a three days' distance into the desert to offer sacrifices
to the Lord our God.' Yet I know that
the king of Egypt will not allow you to
go, except by force. I will, therefore,
stretch out my hand and strike Egypt
with all sorts of wonders. And then he
will let you go."

Moses kept raising questions
and objections, while God kept encouraging him. The Lord promised
to work miracles through Moses.
When Moses said that he wasn't a
good speaker, the Lord replied that
Aaron, Moses' brother, could speak for
him. Finally, Moses stopped objecting.

Moses returned to Jethro, his father-
in-law, and said to him, "Please let me
leave and return to my brothers who are

in Egypt; I will see whether they are still alive." Jethro answered Moses, "You may go in peace."

Meanwhile, the Lord told Moses that it was safe to return to Egypt, since everyone who had wanted to kill him was now dead.

The Lord also said to Aaron, "Go into the wasteland to meet Moses." He went and met him at the mountain of God. Moses told Aaron the whole message that the Lord had given him and all the wonders that God had ordered him to work.

So Moses left with Aaron, and they gathered all the elders (leaders) of the Israelites. Aaron repeated the whole message that the Lord had spoken to Moses. Meanwhile, Moses worked miracles while the people watched. The people believed, understanding that the Lord had seen how hard their lives were. So they bowed down in worship.

## Moses and Aaron Go to Pharaoh

**Exodus 5**

Next, Moses and Aaron went to Pharaoh and said, "This is what the Lord, the God of Israel, has said, 'Let my people go to hold a celebration in my honor in the desert.'"

But Pharaoh said, "Who is the Lord, that I should listen to what he says, so as to let Israel go! I don't care about the Lord, so I won't let Israel go."

Moses and Aaron kept pleading, but Pharaoh would not listen. Instead, after they left he gave orders that the Hebrew slaves should be treated even worse than before. This angered the Israelites against Moses and Aaron.

So Moses turned to the Lord and said, "Lord, why have you acted so harshly toward this people? Why have you sent me at all? For, since I came to Pharaoh to speak in your name, he has been harsh toward this people, instead of setting them free."

## The Ten Plagues

**Exodus 6–12**

But the Lord said to Moses, "You will see what I will do to Pharaoh."

Then, through Moses and Aaron, the Lord let one disaster after another happen in Egypt. These disasters were called the "ten plagues of Egypt." Events like these had happened before, but not in this way—one after another.

The first nine plagues were: blood-red water; invasions of frogs, gnats and horseflies; a disease that killed the livestock; sores on people and animals; a destructive hailstorm; an invasion of locusts; three days of darkness. All these struck most of the land of the Egyptians, but not the section where the Israelites lived. Yet, Pharaoh remained stubborn.

Then the Lord said to Moses, "I will strike one more blow at Pharaoh and at Egypt. After that, he will let you leave this place."

The Lord told Moses and Aaron how the Passover should be celebrated.

"Tell the entire community of Israel that on the tenth of this month each man is to obtain a lamb for his family. You shall

keep it until the fourteenth of the month. Then the community of Israel shall kill the lambs in the evening twilight. Someone shall take part of the lambs' blood and apply it on both door-posts and the lintel of each house where it is to be eaten.

"Now, this is the way to eat it: with sandals on your feet, with your staffs in your hands, and in a hurry. This is the Passover of the Lord.

"The same night I will go through the land of Egypt and kill every firstborn, both human and animal. The blood will be a sign on the houses where you are: when I see the blood I will skip over you, so among you there will be no death blow."

The Israelites did just as the Lord had commanded Moses and Aaron.

When Pharaoh, all his officials and all the other Egyptians got up in the night, there was a loud crying in Egypt, for in every house someone had died.

At this, Pharaoh sent for Moses and Aaron in the night and said, "Get up and leave my people—you and the Israelites. You may go and worship the Lord, as you have asked. Take your flocks too, and also your cattle as you have asked, and go. Bring a blessing on me, too."

The Egyptians put pressure on the Israelites to leave Egypt quickly, for they said, "We are all going to die."

Through Moses, the Lord had told the Israelites to ask their Egyptian neighbors for jewelry and clothing. This was to make up for their years of slavery. The Egyptians gave these willingly, for they were eager to see the Hebrews leave.

The Israelites started off from the city

of Rameses. Many people of mixed ancestry went with them, as well as their flocks and herds.

## Departure from Egypt

**Exodus 13–15**

When Pharaoh had let the people go, God did not direct them to the road leading toward the land of the Philistines, although it was the shortest route. God thought, "I'm afraid that, if they see they have to fight, the people might change their minds and return to Egypt."

Rather, God made them take the road leading to the desert, to the Red Sea. The Lord marched in front: in the form of a pillar-like cloud to lead them by day, and in the form of a glowing cloud to give them light by night, so that they could march day and night. The pillar-like cloud by day and the glowing cloud by night never withdrew from its place in front of the people.

Pharaoh was told that the people had left. At this, he and his officials changed their minds about the Israelites. "What have we done?" they exclaimed. "We have freed Israel. They won't serve us any longer." So Pharaoh had his chariots made ready and called up his troops.

Thus, the Egyptians began to pursue the Israelites and caught up with them, camped near the sea.

When Pharaoh was near, the Israelites raised their eyes and saw the Egyptians!

In their panic the Israelites cried out to the Lord. And they said to Moses, "Did you bring us out to die in the desert because there weren't enough graves in Egypt? What good have you done by bringing us out of Egypt?"

Moses answered the people, "Don't panic; if you hold your ground you will see the victory that the Lord will win for you today. The way you see the Egyptians today, you will never see them again. The Lord will fight for you, while you won't have to do anything."

Then the Lord said to Moses, "Order the Israelites to start out. Meanwhile, lift up your staff and stretch out your hand over the sea and divide it, so that the Israelites can go through on dry ground."

The pillar-like cloud in front of them moved around and stood behind them. It came between Egypt's troops and Israel's troops. The cloud was partly dark; so the whole night through, neither side could attack the other.

Moses stretched out his hand over the sea. Throughout the night, with a strong east wind, the Lord swept the sea away, turning it into a dry path, for the waters had separated. Then the Israelites hurried through the midst of the sea on dry ground.

At this the Egyptians rushed after them. All Pharaoh's horses, chariots and horsemen went after them into the heart of the sea.

Then the Lord said to Moses, "Stretch out your hand over the sea, so that the waters will flow back over the Egyptians—their chariots and their horsemen."

Moses stretched his hand out over the sea, and toward morning the sea began to flow back, with the Egyptians running into it. The Lord shook the Egyptians into the sea, and the returning waters flowed over the chariots and the horsemen—that is Pharaoh's entire army. Israel saw what the Lord had done.

The people were filled with respect for the Lord, and they believed in the Lord and in his servant Moses.

Then with the Israelites Moses sang a song of thanksgiving to the Lord. Miriam, the sister of Moses and Aaron, took up a tambourine, and all the women followed her with tambourines and dancing.

The Lord led the Israelites southward, toward Mount Horeb, or Sinai, where he had spoken to Moses from the bush.

## The Journey to Horeb

**Exodus 16–18**

After the people had been walking for a little while, they began to complain about being thirsty and hungry. The Lord worked miracles to provide them with fresh water and something to eat. One miracle was the food called manna, which God began to provide a few days after they had passed through the sea.

In the morning there was a thin coat of dew on the ground around the camp, and after the dew evaporated, something that looked like a flaky dust or frost lay on the ground. When the Israelites saw it, they asked one another, "What is it?"

Then Moses told them, "This is the bread that the Lord has given you to eat."

The Israelites called it *manna*. It was white and tasted like cakes made with honey.

After the Israelites won a victory over the Amalekites, a tribe that had attacked them, they met Moses' father-in-law, Jethro. Moses was reunited with his wife, Zipporah, and with his sons, Gershom and Eliezer.

Jethro said, "Blessed be the Lord, who rescued the people from slavery. Now I realize that the Lord is greater than all gods."

## The Meeting with God at Mount Sinai

**Exodus 19–24**

Three months after the Israelites had left the land of Egypt, they arrived in the wastelands of Sinai and set up camp facing the mountain.

Moses began to climb towards God, while the Lord called to him from the mountain, saying, "This is what you are to say to the Israelites: 'You have seen what I have done to Egypt, and that I have brought you to myself. And now, if you listen to what I say and keep my covenant, you will be my own possession among all other peoples—even though the whole world is mine. You shall be a kingdom of priests and a holy nation for me.'"

God was offering a covenant to the Israelites. A covenant is an agreement. If the people would obey the Lord, he would take care of them and bring them into the land of Canaan.

Moses called together the leaders of Israel and told them what the Lord had asked. The people answered at once and said, "We will do everything the Lord has said."

When Moses told the Lord what the people had said, God said to Moses, "On the third day the Lord will come down upon Mount Sinai, with all the people looking on. Put up barriers in front of the people and warn them: 'Be careful not to move toward the mountain or touch its foot, for whoever touches the mountain must die.' When the ram's horn gives a long blast—then they may move toward the mountain."

When the morning of the third day came, thunder boomed and lightning flashed on the mountain and a heavy cloud hung over it. There was the sound of a powerful trumpet blast. All the people in the camp trembled. So Moses led the people out of the camp to meet God, and they stood at the foot of the mountain. Mount Sinai was all smoke, for the Lord had come down on it in the appearance of fire, and the smoke went up as if from a furnace. The entire mountain shook, and the sound of the trumpet grew more and more powerful. Moses spoke, and God answered him.

As the Lord came down onto the peak of Mount Sinai, he called to Moses, and Moses went up.

Then God declared, "I am the Lord your God, who have brought you out of the land of Egypt, out of that place of slavery."

The Lord continued: "You must have no other god than me.

"You must not make any sculpture, or any sort of figure, of anything that is up in the sky or down on the earth, or in the water under the earth. You must not adore or worship such things, for I, the Lord your God, am a jealous God."

*The Lord was telling the Israelites not to make idols to worship, the way their pagan neighbors did.*

"You must not use the name of the Lord your God in a wrong way, for the Lord will not leave anyone unpunished who uses his name in a wrong way.

"You must keep the Sabbath day in mind so as to keep it holy. During six days you are to work. But during the seventh day, the Sabbath of the Lord, you are not to do any sort of work.

"You must honor your father and your mother, so that you may live long in the land that the Lord your God is about to give you.

"You must not kill.

"You must not commit adultery.

"You must not steal.

"You must not say untrue things about your neighbor.

"You must not even intend to take

your neighbor's house, or wife, or servants, or oxen, or donkeys or anything else that belongs to your neighbor."

All the people heard and saw the thunder claps, the lightning, the trumpet blast and the smoking mountain. So they moved back, shaking with fear.

The Lord said to Moses, "This is what you are to say to the Israelites: 'You have seen that I have spoken to you from heaven. You must not make yourselves gods of silver and gods of gold. You are to make me an altar, and on it you are to offer your sacrifices. I will come to you and bless you.'"

When Moses went and repeated all God's commandments to the people, they all answered together, "We will obey all the commandments that the Lord has spoken." With that, Moses wrote down every commandment of the Lord.

Then on the altar Moses and some of the men sacrificed cattle as offerings to the Lord. Moses took some of the blood and sprinkled it on the altar. He took the book of the covenant and read it for the people to hear. They said, "We will do everything the Lord has said, for we will listen." Then Moses sprinkled the rest of the blood on the people.

*The altar represented God, and blood is a symbol of life. So the sprinkling of blood on the altar and on the people showed that the same life was uniting God and the people. They were now "related" by the same blood. Being related, they had to be loyal to each other. They had to live up to the promises they had made in the agreement called the covenant.*

The Lord said to Moses, "Come all the way up the mountain to me and stay there; let me hand over to you the stone tablets with the law and commandments that I have written to be taught." So Moses and Joshua, his assistant, went up the mountain of God. To the leaders Moses had said, "Wait for us here until we come back to you. Aaron and Hur are with you. Any people who have an argument can ask them to settle it."

When Moses went up the mountain, the cloud covered the top. The brightness of the Lord had come to rest on Mount Sinai. To the eyes of the Israelites, the appearance of the Lord's brightness on the peak of the mountain was like a blazing fire. Yet Moses entered the cloud and went up. And he stayed on the mountain forty days and forty nights.

When the Lord finished speaking to Moses on Mount Sinai, he gave him the two stone tablets of the covenant.

## The Golden Calf

**Exodus 32**

The people saw that Moses was taking a long time to come down from the mountain. So they gathered around Aaron and said to him, "Come on! Make us a god to march before us. We don't know what has happened to that Moses who brought us up from Egypt."

Aaron answered, "Remove the golden rings that your wives, sons and daughters have on their ears and bring them to me." So all the people removed their earrings and brought them to Aaron. He took them from their hands, shaped them in a mold and produced a calf of hot metal.

And they said, "Israel, this is the god who brought you out of Egypt."

Hearing this, Aaron built an altar in front of the calf and said, "Tomorrow we will celebrate in the lord's honor."

The next day they got up early and offered sacrifices. Then they sat down to eat and drink, and got up to celebrate wildly.

Because of this, the Lord said to Moses, "Be on your way—go down! Your people, whom you have brought out of the land of Egypt, are acting wickedly. They have quickly strayed from the way I commanded. They have made themselves a metal calf and have worshipped it and offered sacrifices to it, saying, 'Israel, this is your god, the one who brought you out of Egypt.'"

The Lord added to Moses, "I see clearly that these are stubborn people. So don't stop me. Let my anger blaze and burn them up. Instead, I will make a great nation descend from you."

But Moses pleaded with the Lord, asking, "Why should your anger blaze up against your own people, whom you brought out of the land of Egypt with great power and strength? Why should the Egyptians say, 'It was for a cruel purpose that he brought them out, in order to kill them in the mountains and wipe them off the face of the earth'? Stop being angry. Don't do this harm to your own people."

So the Lord held back from doing the harm he had threatened to do to his people.

Then Moses went down the mountain with the two stone tablets of the covenant. The tablets were covered with writing on both sides.

When Joshua heard the noise the

people were making, he said to Moses, "There are sounds of war in the camp."

But Moses answered, "It does not sound like victory songs, nor does it sound like a sad song of defeat. I hear chanting."

When Moses came close to the camp and saw the calf and the wild dancing going on, he blazed with anger. He threw down the stone tablets he was carrying and broke them at the foot of the mountain. Then he took the calf they had made, burned it, ground it to dust, scattered it on the water, and made the Israelites drink.

To Aaron, Moses said; "What have these people done to you, that you should make them commit such a great sin?"

Aaron answered, "Let my lord calm his blazing anger. You know that the people are sinful. They said to me: 'Make us a god to march before us. We don't know what has happened to that Moses who brought us up from Egypt.' And when I asked them, 'Does anyone have gold?' they took it off and gave it to me. I threw it into the fire, and this calf came out."

The next day Moses said to the people, "You have committed a great sin. So I will go up to the Lord. I want to make up for your sin if I can."

Moses returned to the Lord and said, "In making themselves a god of gold, these people have committed a great sin. I ask you to forgive their sin. If not, I beg you to erase my name from the book you have written."

The Lord answered Moses, "The one who has sinned against me—that is whom I will erase from my book. But now, go and lead the people to the place I have told you about."

## The Renewal of the Covenant

**Exodus 34**

The Lord said to Moses, "Cut two tablets of stone like the other ones. On them I will write the commandments that were written on the other tablets, which you broke."

So Moses cut two tablets out of stone like the others. In the morning he got up early and climbed Mount Sinai, carrying the two stone tablets.

The Lord came down in the form of a cloud, stood beside him there and proclaimed his name: "the Lord."

Moses quickly fell to his knees, bowed his head to the ground in worship, and said, "Lord, if I have won favor in your eyes, please march in our midst."

The Lord answered, "I am making a covenant. In the sight of your whole people I shall work wonders which have never before happened in the whole world or in any nation; and this whole people will see that the Lord's accomplishments are awesome."

The Lord then promised that the Israelites would conquer the land of Canaan to be their own.

## The Ark and the Altars

**Exodus 35–39**

The people of Israel would be on the move for some time. They needed a place to worship the Lord. So God himself told Moses what they should bring with them so they could worship him when they stopped on their journey.

A long wooden box, or chest, was to be built. It would be called the ark of the covenant. The ark would contain the stone tablets, the ten commandments. The box was to have rings attached to it. It would be carried on long poles that were to be slipped through the rings. The golden cover of the ark, would be the Lord's throne. Statues of two golden cherubim facing each other would stand at either end of the ark.

The Lord also told Moses to have the Israelites make a large tent; a table; a lampstand; vestments for Aaron and his sons (who were to be Israel's priests); gold cups, plates, bowls and pitchers for the sacrifices; and two portable wooden altars—one for offerings of incense and the other for burnt offerings. All these, the Israelites would bring with them so they could worship the Lord as they journeyed toward the land of Canaan.

Moses said to the whole community of the Israelites, "Here is what the Lord commands: Take up a collection of offerings for the Lord. Every good-hearted man is to hand in what the Lord deserves: gold, silver and bronze; blue, purple, scarlet, fine linen and goat's hair; rams' skins dyed red; acacia wood; oil for the lampstand; spices for making the anointing oil and the sweet-smelling incense; and jewels for the vestments. Then let all the skilled craftsmen among you come and make everything the Lord has commanded."

Then many of the people brought anything they had—gold ornaments, colorful fabrics, oil, spices or jewels—to the Lord. Craftsmen were chosen and the work began.

# THE BOOK OF LEVITICUS

*Leviticus* is the third book of the Pentateuch. It is named after the tribe of Levi, to which the Hebrew priests and their helpers belonged. Leviticus contains very little history. It is a book of various kinds of laws for all the people and some regulations for the priests and their helpers. Here are some quotes and summaries.

**Leviticus 19–26**

The Lord said to Moses: "Speak to the Israelites and tell them: 'You must be holy, because I, the Lord your God, am holy.

"'You must not be unfair. You must not show that you favor a lowly person, nor take the side of a powerful person. You must not spread gossip against anyone. I am the Lord.

"'You must not hate your brother. You must not take revenge or stay resentful. You must love your neighbor as yourself.'"

The *Book of Leviticus* describes the yearly feasts (holy days) for the people of Israel.

The first feasts mentioned are Passover and Unleavened Bread. Both of these were held in the early spring. Passover recalled God's rescue of his people from slavery in Egypt. The feast of Unleavened Bread followed the Passover. It was an early spring harvest feast. Seven weeks after Unleavened Bread came Pentecost or Weeks, another harvest feast. In the autumn there were more feasts: the Atonement (when a sacrifice was offered for everyone's sins) and the final harvest feast of Booths or Tents.

God asked the Israelites not to plant or harvest their fields every seventh year. This was called the sabbatical year, which means year of rest. The land "rested."

After seven sabbatical years came the fiftieth year, which was called the jubilee. This year took its name from the horn (*jubal*) that was blown at the year's beginning. The jubilee was a time for debts to be cancelled and slaves to be set free.

# THE BOOK OF NUMBERS

*Numbers* is the fourth book of the Pentateuch. It was given this name because at the beginning of the book and again near the end, a census of the Israelites is described.

The stories in the *Book of Numbers* begin in chapter 10, which tells about the Israelites' departure from Mount Sinai. The Israelites spent about forty years in the dry lands south and east of Canaan, and *Numbers* tells something about this time. The book ends with Israel camped in Moab, near the Dead Sea, ready to cross the Jordan River into Canaan.

Like *Exodus* and *Leviticus, Numbers* also contains various laws.

**Numbers 10–12**

In the second year, on the twentieth day of the second month, the cloud rose above the tent of the covenant, so the Israelites left the area around Mount Sinai and went on slowly until the cloud settled down in the wastelands of Paran.

As they moved on, the people began to grumble and complain. They were tired of manna and wanted meat. Moses, meanwhile, was tired of the people.

"Where can I get meat?" Moses asked the Lord. The Lord sent a strong wind into the camp, and with the wind came a huge flock of quail, which the people killed and ate.

But soon, even Moses' sister and brother began to grumble against him.

They said, "Has the Lord spoken only to Moses? Hasn't he spoken to us, too?" The Lord heard this.

Moses was the most gentle person in the world. At once the Lord ordered Moses, Aaron and Miriam to go out to the meeting tent.

Then the Lord came down in a pillar-like cloud and stood at the entrance of the tent. He called to Aaron and Miriam. When they stepped forward, he said, "When someone is a prophet I, the Lord, make myself known to him in visions, I speak to him in dreams. My servant Moses is not like this: he is in charge of my whole household; I speak to him face to face, in plain sight and not through riddles, and he sees my image. How could you dare to talk against my servant Moses!"

When the cloud had left the tent, Aaron looked at Miriam and, to his surprise, she was covered with leprosy! So Aaron said to Moses, "I beg you not to hold against us this sin that we have committed so foolishly." Then, Moses cried out to God, "O Lord, heal her, please!"

The Lord answered Moses, "Let her stay alone for seven days outside the camp. After that, she may come back."

## The Explorers

**Numbers 13–14**

The Lord said to Moses, "Send some men to explore the land of Canaan which I am going to give to the Israelites. Send one leader from each tribe."

So Moses sent them off from the wastelands of Paran, as the Lord had instructed.

They went up into the Negeb and made their way into the land as far as Hebron, then as far as Nahal-eshcol. There they cut a piece of vine with a cluster of grapes, which two of them carried on a pole. They also picked pomegranates and figs.

After forty days they returned from scouting the land. They went to Moses, Aaron and the whole community of the Israelites at Kadesh in the wastelands of Paran and reported to the community, showing them the fruits of that land.

The explorers began by saying that the land looked good, but the cities had strong walls and the people were warlike. Some of them were so tall that they were giants!

But not all of the explorers were so gloomy. One named Caleb had a different opinion.

Caleb said, "We should attack and take over the land, for surely we are strong enough."

But the men who had gone with him said, "We can't attack those people! They're too strong!" And then they began spreading rumors among the Israelites about the land they had explored, saying, "The land that we went to scout swallows up the people who live there. And all the people we saw were huge."

As a result, the whole community began to shout in frustration. They spent the night in tears. Then the Israelites began to protest against Moses and Aaron. The whole community said to them, "Oh, if only we had died in the land of Egypt, or in this wasteland! If only we had died! Why has the Lord brought us into this land? To fall by the sword and have our wives and little ones captured?" So they said to one another, "Let's choose someone to lead us and return to Egypt."

At this, Moses and Aaron fell to the ground face down, in the midst of the whole Israelite community.

The explorer Caleb, and another explorer, Joshua, begged the community to trust in the Lord. The Lord had promised to be with his people, they said. But the people were so angry that they wouldn't listen.

The whole community was thinking of stoning them, when the brightness of the Lord showed itself to all the Israelites at the meeting tent, and the Lord said to Moses, "How long will these people treat me like this? How long will they fail to believe in me, with all the miracles that I worked in their midst? I will strike them with an epidemic and blot them out, but of you I will make a nation greater and stronger than they."

But Moses pleaded with the Lord, saying that surely the people of Canaan had heard about the wonderful way God had rescued his people from slavery in Egypt. If the Lord were to destroy the Israelites now, everyone would say that God had not had the power to lead them into Canaan. Moses begged him to forgive the Israelites.

The Lord answered, "I forgive according to what you have said. But some men have seen my power and the miracles that I have worked in Egypt and the wastelands and still keep testing me. They have tested me ten times. None of those men shall see the land that I promised to their ancestors.

"As for my servant Caleb, since he has a different spirit in him and he follows me with his whole heart, I will bring him into the land which he has explored, and his descendants will own it.

"Tell the Israelites this: 'As I live, I will do to you exactly what you said I was doing. In this very desert your bodies will fall, all of you from twenty years upward, because you have protested against me. Except for Caleb and Joshua, you are not to go into the land where I promised to settle you. And your little ones, who you said would be captured—these I will bring in, and they will know the land you looked down on. For forty years your sons will be shepherds in the wastelands. For forty years you will pay for your sins. This corresponds to the number of days during which you explored that land, forty days: one year for each day. So you will know what it means to turn away from me.'"

Moses told this to all the Israelites, and the people began to wail. In the morning they got up early and began to head toward the mountains of Canaan, saying, "We'll go up to that place the Lord spoke about—because we have sinned."

But Moses said, "Why are you disobey

ing the Lord? You can't succeed. Since the Lord isn't with you, you must not go up, or else you'll be defeated and chased by your enemies. You've stopped following the Lord, so the Lord won't be with you."

Yet, they were reckless enough to set out for the mountains of Canaan. But the ark of the covenant and Moses did not leave the camp. And the Canaanites, who lived in those mountains, came down and fought with the Israelites and chased them back.

## More Wanderings

**Numbers 20–21**

The Israelites moved on, but not towards Canaan. During this time, Miriam, Moses sister, died there in the desert.

There was no water for the community, and the people joined together against Moses and Aaron. "Why have you brought the community of the Lord into this desert?" they asked. "Did you do it so we and our livestock could die here?"

Moses and Aaron moved away from the people and went to the entrance of the meeting tent, where they fell, to the ground face down.

The Lord said to Moses, "Take the staff and with Aaron your brother call the community together. While they watch, speak to the rock. It will let out water."

As God had commanded, Moses took the staff that had been in the Lord's presence. Then Moses and Aaron called the community together in front of the rock, and Moses said to them, "You rebels, listen! Shall we get water for you from this rock?" Then Moses raised his hand and

hit the rock twice with his staff. Water began to pour out. The community drank from it, and so did their livestock.

But the Lord said to Moses and Aaron, "Because you did not have trust in me—that I would show the Israelites my holiness—you shall not bring this community into the land I have given them."

*So, like their fellow-Israelites, Moses and Aaron would not be allowed to enter the land of Canaan. The reason for this is not clear.* *

After some time, the Israelites began to move again, looking for a way to enter Canaan from the east instead of the south. When they came to Mount Hor, Aaron died there and was buried. After a time of mourning for Aaron, they continued on.

Again the people's temper ran short, and they began to speak against God and Moses: "Why have you brought us up from Egypt? To let us die in the wastelands? There isn't any bread or water. This worthless food makes us sick."

So the Lord sent snakes that bit the people. Many died. Then the people said to Moses, "We have sinned by speaking against the Lord and against you. Pray to the Lord, so that he may send the snakes away."

Moses did pray to the Lord for the people. And the Lord said to Moses, "Make a fiery snake and set it up on a pole. Anyone who has been bitten shall stay alive if he looks at it." Moses made a bronze snake and hung it on a pole.

The Israelites who looked at the bronze snake were cured, because they had believed the Lord's promise.

The Israelites came to the land of the Amorites and sent a message to King Sihon, asking him to let them pass through peacefully. The king refused.

Sihon called up his whole army and marched out into the desert against the Israelites. He fought with them at Jahaz. Israel struck him down by the sword and moved into his land.

Then they turned and went up the road leading to Bashan. Og, king of Bashan, marched out with all his army to meet them in battle. The Israelites struck him down and moved into his country.

Then the Israelites camped in the wastelands of Moab, east of the Jordan, across from Jericho.

## Balak and Balaam

**Numbers 22–24**

Balak, the king of Moab, was afraid of the Israelites. So he sent messengers to a prophet named Balaam, who was supposed to be successful at cursing people.

Even though Balak sent a good sum of money, Balaam hesitated. But finally he mounted his donkey and started for Moab.

As Balaam was on his way, the angel of the Lord planted himself on the road. The donkey saw the angel standing on the road, sword in hand, so she tried to leave the road and go through the fields, but Balaam began to hit the donkey to make her return to the road. Then the angel of the Lord took up a position in a narrow passage between two

*For some possible reasons, see the "Parents" section at the end of this book.*

vineyards, where there was a wall on either side. The donkey saw the angel and tried to press herself against one of the walls, squeezing Balaam's foot against the wall in the process, so he began to hit her again.

Then the angel positioned himself in a narrow space where there was no room to turn aside, right or left. The donkey saw the angel of the Lord and threw herself down with Balaam still sitting on her. At this, Balaam's anger flared up, and he began to whip the donkey.

Then Lord enabled the donkey to talk, and she said to Balaam, "What have I done to you? This is the third time that you've beaten me."

Balaam answered her, "You're playing jokes on me. If I had a sword with me, I'd kill you."

Then the Lord enabled Balaam to see the angel standing on the road, sword in hand. He threw himself on his knees and worshipped with his face to the ground.

The angel of the Lord said to him, "Why have you beaten your donkey? Each of these three times the donkey saw me and tried to turn aside."

Balaam answered, "If this displeases you, I will turn back." But the angel said to Balaam, "Go ahead. But you are to speak the words I will tell you to say."

Balak heard that Balaam was coming and went out to meet him. The next morning Balak took Balaam and led him out to see part of the Israelite camp.

Balaam said to Balak, "Let me go apart. The Lord may come my way and meet with me, and whatever he tells me I will tell you." Then he left for a hilltop.

The Lord did come Balaam's way and said, "Go back to Balak, but here is what you are to say...."

Balaam went back and said, "How can I curse someone God has not cursed? Can anyone count the dust of Jacob or number even one fourth of Israel? Oh, may I die the death of a just man! May my end be like theirs!"

At this, Balak said to Balaam, "What have you done to me? I sent for you so you would curse my enemies, and to my surprise you have blessed them!"

But Balaam answered, "Don't I have to say whatever the Lord puts on my lips?"

Balak brought Balaam to different places, where he could see the huge camp of Israel from other angles, in the hope that then the prophet would be able to curse the Israelites. But a second time and then a third, Balaam blessed the Israelites instead of cursing them. Then he spoke a fourth time.

"The prophecy given to Balaam son of Beor, the prophecy of the man whose eyes are open, the prophecy of someone who hears God's words and knows the Most High, someone who sees the vision of the Almighty. I see him, but not yet; I look at him, but not right now. A star will march forth from Jacob and a scepter will spring up from Israel. He will crush Moab."

This was exactly what Balak had not wanted to hear! Balaam and Balak went their separate ways.

## Joshua Leads with Moses

Numbers 27

The Lord said to Moses, "Climb into the mountains over there and look at the land I have given to the Israelites. When you have seen it, you too are to join your departed relatives, just as your brother Aaron did, because in the wastelands of Zin you resisted my orders."

Moses accepted what God had said and asked him to choose a new leader for the community.

The Lord told Moses, "Take Joshua son of Nun and lay your hand on him. Bring him to Eleazar the priest and the entire community. Appoint him as their leader, and share your authority with him, so the whole community of the Israelites may obey him."

Moses did as the Lord had commanded him. He took Joshua and brought him to Eleazar the priest and the whole community. He laid his hands on his head and appointed him to lead the people as the Lord had ordered.

# THE BOOK OF DEUTERONOMY

*Deuteronomy* is the fifth and last book of the Pentateuch. The word "Deuteronomy" means "second law." This book repeats some of the events told and laws listed in the rest of the Pentateuch. At the same time it *adds* to these events and laws, bringing them up to date with the later times in which this book was written.

Most of *Deuteronomy* sounds like an encouraging speech given by Moses to the Israelites waiting to enter Canaan. Moses says that God will bless them if they obey his laws. Near the end of *Deuteronomy,* we read that Joshua was chosen to lead the people into Canaan, and that Moses saw Canaan before he died.

Deuteronomy 29–30

Moses called the people of Israel together and said to them, "You have seen everything that the Lord did to Pharaoh, to all his people and to his whole country, in the land of Egypt.

"Although I had you march through the wilderness for forty years, your clothes did not fall off you in shreds, and your shoes did not drop off your feet in pieces. So you would learn that the Lord is your God, you did not eat any bread, and you did not drink any wine or strong drink. When we arrived here, Sihon, king of Heshbon, and Og, king of Bashan, marched out to fight us and we defeated them.

"You are standing in the presence of the Lord, all of you, to promise to keep the covenant which the Lord your God makes with you today, so as to set you up as a people for himself. He promised this to you. He had also promised this to your fathers—to Abraham, Isaac and Jacob.

"This commandment that I am giving you today is not too much for you. It is not beyond your reach. It is not in heaven, so that someone might say, 'Who will go up to heaven for us and bring it to us, so we can obey it?' It is not beyond the sea either. Far from it—the word is very close to you. It is in your mouth and in your heart, so that you may obey it.

"Look! Today I have set in front of you life and happiness, death and disaster. What I am telling you today will help you to love the Lord your God and to live according to his ways, keeping his commandments. Then you will have life and will multiply, and the Lord your God will bless you in the land that you are going to enter.

"But if your heart turns around and refuses to listen, so that you let yourselves be led astray to worship other gods and serve them, I say to you today that you will not stay long in the land that you are crossing the Jordan to move into.

"This day I call heaven and earth as witnesses: I have set in front of you life and death, blessing and curse. Choose life, so you and your descendants may have it.

"The Lord himself will march before you. He will never leave you. Do not be afraid."

Then the Lord said to Moses, "Go climb Mount Nebo over there, and take a look at the land of Canaan that I am giving to the Israelites. You will die on that mountain and join your relatives, just as your brother Aaron died on Mount Hor. Nevertheless, you may see the land from a distance."

You should love the Lord your God, obey his voice and be attached to him, so that you may stay a long time in the land that the Lord said he would give your fathers—Abraham, Isaac and Jacob."

## Last Days of Moses
**Deuteronomy 31–34**

Moses called Joshua, and in the sight of all Israel he said to him, "Be strong and brave. With these people you will take over the land that the Lord promised to give to their fathers.

So Moses, servant of the Lord, died in the land of Moab, and he was buried there. The Israelites mourned for Moses for thirty days.

Never again did there appear in Israel a prophet like Moses, whom the Lord knew face to face.

So Moses climbed Mount Nebo, and the Lord showed him the whole land. The Lord said to him, "Here is the land that I promised to Abraham, to Isaac and to Jacob, saying, 'I will give it to your descendants.' I have let you see it with your own eyes."

# THE BOOK OF JOSHUA

The *Book of Joshua* tells about some of the battles the Israelites fought to take over the land of Canaan. To today's Christians, it may seem strange that God's people had to gain their land by fighting. But God seems to work with the world as it is. In the thirteenth and twelfth centuries BC, wars were very common.

*Joshua* is the first of what Christians call the Old Testament Historical Books. These books continue the history that began in the Pentateuch.

Joshua 1

After the death of Moses, the Lord said to Moses' assistant, Joshua, son of Nun, "My servant Moses is dead. So now get ready to cross the Jordan, you and all the people, into the land that I am going to give you. I will give you every place where you will walk, as I promised Moses. No one will be able to resist you as long as you live. I will be with you as I have been with Moses. I won't let you down."

## The Two Spies

Joshua 2

The Israelites were still on the east bank of the Jordan River. While they prepared to cross, Joshua thought it would be good to learn more about the people of Canaan and how ready they were to fight.

Joshua sent out two spies with these orders: "Go, inspect the country and especially Jericho." They left.

In Jericho they came to the house of a woman named Rahab and asked to spend the night. But the king of Jericho was told, "Tonight some Israelite men have come to spy on this country."

So the king of Jericho sent these orders to Rahab: "Put out the men who have come to your house, for they have come to spy upon this whole country."

The woman said, "Those men did come to me, although I do not know where they are from, but they left when it was getting dark and the city gates were about to be closed. I don't know where they went. If you follow right away, you will catch up with them."

But she had taken the men up to the roof, where she had covered them with stalks of flax that she had spread out on the roof to dry.

The woman went up to the men on the roof and said, "I know that the Lord has given you this land. We've been stricken with terror because of you. All the people of this land are trembling at your arrival, since we've heard how the Lord dried up the waters of the Red Sea in front of you when you left Egypt. We've also heard what you did to the two kings of the Amorites who were across the Jordan—to Sihon and to Og. As soon as we heard this, our courage melted, for your God is Lord in heaven above and on earth below. So now, since I've been kind to

you, please promise me that you, too, will be kind to my father's family. You must give me a trustworthy sign that you will spare the lives of my father, my mother, my brothers, my sisters and all their families—that you will save us from death."

The men said to her, "If you don't make known this agreement between us, we're ready to die instead of you. When the Lord gives us this land, we will be kind and loyal to you."

She lowered them from the window with a rope, since her house was built into the city wall. She said to them, "Go to the mountains, so those who are looking for you won't run into you. Hide there for three days until they come back. Then you may go your way."

And they told her, "Hang this red cord from the window from which you have lowered us. Then gather your father, your mother, your brothers and the rest of your father's family into the house with you. Anyone who goes outside the doors of your house into the street shall be blamed for his own death, and we will be innocent;

but we shall be blamed for the death of anyone who is inside the house with you if someone touches him. But if you make this agreement known, we are not bound by the promise that you had us make."

She said, "Let it be so." Then they left, and she hung the red cord from the window.

So they went to the mountains, where they stayed for three days, until those who were looking for them returned. Then the two Israelite men came down from the mountains, crossed the river and went to Joshua to report about all their experiences. They told Joshua, "The Lord has given us all this land; the people are trembling at our arrival."

## Crossing the Jordan

**Joshua 3–4**

Joshua said to the Israelites, "Come and hear the instructions of the Lord your God. The ark of the covenant of the Lord of the whole world is going to cross the Jordan ahead of you. So, from among the tribes of Israel choose twelve men—one man from each tribe. As the priests carrying the ark step into the Jordan, the waters flowing down from the north shall stop and stand up like a dam."

So the people packed up their tents to cross the Jordan while the priests carried the ark of the covenant in front of them. The Jordan overruns its banks throughout the whole harvest season, but as the feet of the priests carrying the ark touched the river, the waters stopped flowing down from the north. They stood up like a dam a long distance away, while the rest ebbed away into the Salt Sea.

So the people crossed over opposite Jericho. The priests carrying the ark of the covenant stopped on dry ground in the middle of the Jordan, while all Israel crossed over on dry ground, until the entire nation finished crossing the Jordan.

The Israelites camped at Gilgal, not far from Jericho. This would become Joshua's home base. From Gilgal his troops would go out to attack one city after another.

## Jericho

**Joshua 5–6**

When Joshua was near Jericho, he raised his eyes and saw this vision: a man standing in front of him with an unsheathed sword in his hand. Joshua went up to him and asked, "Are you for us or are you for our enemies?"

He answered, "Neither. I am the commander of the Lord's army, and I have just arrived."

At this, Joshua bowed to the ground in reverence. Then he asked him, "What message has my Lord for his servant?"

The commander of the Lord's army said to Joshua, "Take off your sandals, for the place where you are standing is holy." Joshua did so.

Because of the presence of the Israelites, Jericho's gates stayed closed day and night. No one could go out or in. So the Lord said to Joshua, "You see, I will put Jericho into your hands, together with its king and its brave fighting men. You—all your fighting men—are to circle the city once. Do this for six days. Seven priests will carry seven trumpets before the ark. Then on the seventh day you will circle

priests who were blowing the trumpets, and others followed the ark. As they marched, the trumpets blared. But Joshua gave this order, "Don't shout the war cry until the day I say, 'Shout the war cry.'"

Then he ordered the ark of the Lord to circle the city once. After that, they returned to the camp and stayed there for the night.

the city seven times with the priests blowing the trumpets. At a long blast of the trumpet, have all the people shout a loud war cry. The wall of the city will collapse, and then the Israelites shall attack, each man moving straight ahead."

So Joshua called the priests and said to them, "Pick up the ark of the covenant, and let seven priests carry seven trumpets before the ark of the Lord." To the people he said, "March and circle the city. Let armed troops march in front of the ark of the Lord."

The seven priests marched before the Lord, carrying seven trumpets and blowing them. The ark of the Lord followed. Armed troops marched ahead of the

Early in the morning, the priests picked up the ark of the Lord. The seven priests carrying the seven trumpets marched in front of the ark and blew the trumpets continuously. Armed troops walked ahead of them. Others followed the ark. As the people walked, the trumpets sounded. They circled the city once on the second day, and then they withdrew to the camp. They did this for six days.

But on the seventh day, they got up at dawn and circled the city in the same way seven times. Now, at the seventh time the priests blew the trumpets long and loud, and Joshua said to the people, "Shout the war cry, because the Lord has given you this city." When they heard the blast of the trumpet, the Israelites shouted a loud war cry. The city wall collapsed, and the Israelites attacked the city and captured it.

To the two men who had spied out the country Joshua said, "Go into the woman's house and bring her out to safety with all her family, as you promised her." So the spies went in and brought out Rahab, her father, her mother, her brothers, and the rest of her family. They gave them shelter outside the Israelite camp.

## The Gibeonites

**Joshua 7–10**

Canaan wasn't a nation. Many different peoples lived there, and each city was more or less on its own. Joshua planned to attack them one by one.

After defeating Jericho and a town called Ai, Joshua decided to march farther into the hill-country.

At this point, some men on donkeys came to meet him. They wore old, patched clothes and said they had traveled from a distant land to become friends of the Israelites because of the wonders the Lord had worked in Egypt. The Israelites agreed, and the agreement was sealed with an oath—a solemn promise before God. Three days later, Joshua learned that the Israelites had been tricked! These people lived very close, in the town of Gibeon. Now the Israelites had to keep the promise they had made to be friends of the Gibeonites. They couldn't take over their town.

Then five kings of the Amorites banded together, marched up with all their armed strength, and began to attack Gibeon.

So the people of Gibeon sent messengers to Joshua in the camp at Gilgal, to say: "Don't let your servants down. Hurry to rescue us, because all the kings of the Amorites have come together against us."

So Joshua marched up from Gilgal— he himself and all his brave fighting men.

The Lord said to Joshua, "Don't be afraid of them, for I have given them over to you. Not one of them will be able to stand firm against you."

Joshua marched up from Gilgal during the night and surprised them. The Lord threw them into confusion at the presence of Israel, who roundly defeated them at Gibeon and chased them to the hill of Beth-horon.

When the fleeing Amorites started down the far side of Beth-horon, the Lord hurled huge hailstones at them from the sky. More of them died than were killed by the swords of the Israelites.

Then, calling out to the Lord, Joshua said in the sight of Israel, "Sun, stand still over Gibeon, you, too, moon, over the valley of Aijalon!" And the sun stood still, and the moon stopped for as long as the nation needed to take revenge on their enemies. For about a whole day the sun was in no hurry to set. The Lord fought for Israel.

*Because these are stories that people told for many years, we can't be sure how accurate they are. But like any good collection of stories, the* Book of Joshua *has its message. The crumbling walls of Jericho and the sun standing still both mean that God was taking care of his people as he had promised to do.*

## A Time for Remembering

**Joshua 11–24**

The Israelites fought battle after battle, until they had taken a number of cities.

Then Joshua divided the land among the tribes, as Moses had told him to do. Each tribe was given a section of the country—east or west of the Jordan River. The people settled down to raise crops and pasture their livestock.

When Joshua was old, he called together the leaders of all Israel and said to them, "You have seen everything that the Lord your God has done to all these nations; in fact, the Lord your God fought for you. I have allotted to your tribes the nations that still remain, from the Jordan to the Great Sea on the west. The Lord your God will chase them before you, and you will move into their land, just as the Lord your God has promised.

"You are not to say the names of their gods or serve them or worship them. Instead, you are to be attached to the Lord your God, as you have been to this day. It is because of this that the Lord has driven away strong and powerful nations, and no one has stood his ground before you to this day. One of your men chased a thousand, because the Lord your God fought for you, as he had promised you."

Joshua called all the tribes of Israel to meet at Shechem. He spoke to them in God's name, reminding them that the Lord had called Abraham to stop worshipping many gods and worship him alone; then God had promised the land of Canaan to Abraham, Isaac and Jacob and later had freed the Israelites from slavery in Egypt and brought them to Canaan, where he helped them to conquer one city after another.

Still speaking in God's name, Joshua added, "I gave you a country for which you did not work and cities which you did not build. You live in these, and you are eating from vineyards and olive groves which you did not plant."

Then, speaking for himself, Joshua continued.

"So, fear the Lord and serve him honestly. Get rid of the gods that your forefathers served beyond the river and in Egypt, and serve the Lord. But if you think there is something wrong with serving the Lord, choose today whom you will serve: whether the gods your ancestors served when they lived beyond the River, or the gods of the Amorites in whose country you are now living. In any case, my family and I will serve the Lord."

The people replied, "God forbid that we should leave the Lord and serve other gods! Yes, the Lord our God brought us and our fathers up from the land of Egypt. While we watched, he performed those wonders and guarded us on all the roads we traveled and among all the peoples through whose lands we passed. The Lord also drove away the peoples as we advanced, especially the Amorites living in this land. We, too, will serve the Lord, because he is our God."

That day at Shechem Joshua made a covenant in the name of the people, and he laid down laws and rules for them. Then he took a large stone and set it on end under the oak in the holy place of the Lord. Joshua said to all the people, "You see, this stone serves as a witness against us, since it has heard every word that the Lord has spoken to us. It serves as a witness against you that you should not disown your God."

Then Joshua sent the people home.

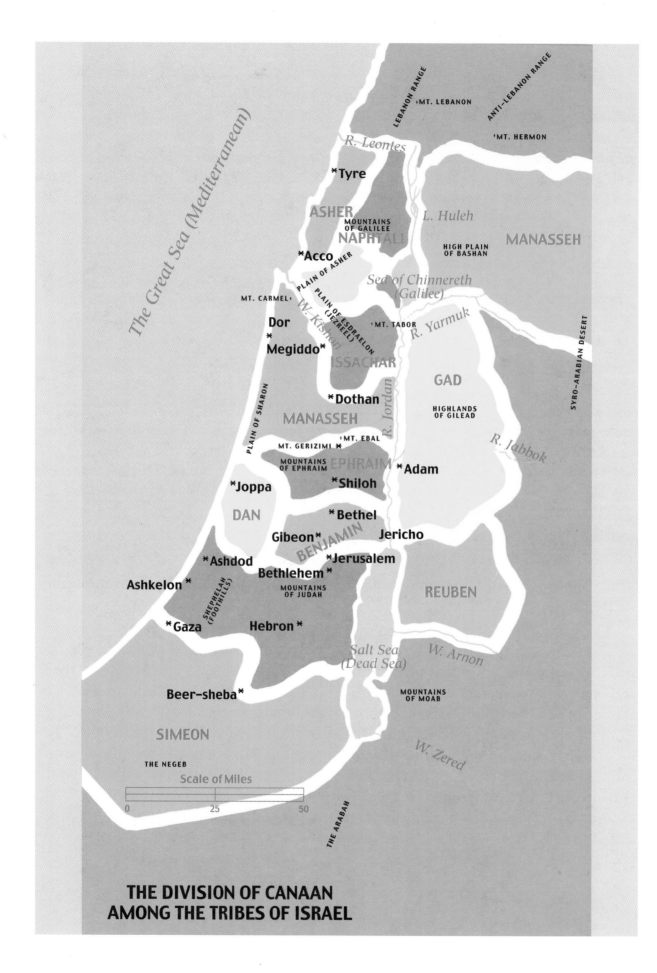

THE NEGEB

Scale of Miles

0    25    50

**THE DIVISION OF CANAAN
AMONG THE TRIBES OF ISRAEL**

## A Backward Glance—Genesis to Joshua

The history of the Israelites in Canaan began long before what is shown in this map. When Abraham entered the land, the Canaanites and various other peoples lived in the cities. But there was much open country, and it was there that Abraham, Isaac, Jacob and Jacob's sons lived with their families. They moved from place to place, looking for good pastures for their flocks and herds *(Genesis)*.

When the Israelites returned to Canaan after living in Egypt for several generations, they began to take over the cities. Then at a certain point they met to divide up the land they had begun to move into *(Joshua)*. The map shows how they planned to divide the country.

How many tribes of Israel were there? There are twelve on the map. Most of them are named for the sons of Jacob. However, there was no "tribe of Joseph." Instead, there were the tribes of Ephraim and Manasseh, named after Joseph's sons. So there were really thirteen tribes. Only twelve tribes show on the map, however, since the tribe of Levi did not inherit farmland but certain cities instead. Levi was the tribe to which the priests and their helpers belonged.

## A Glance Ahead—Judges to 2 Samuel

This map shows the way Joshua and the other leaders intended to divide the land. Not everything worked out as it had been planned, however. The Canaanites and other peoples managed to hold on to several of the cities. Also, the Philistines were settling along the seacoast, gradually taking over parts of the regions claimed by Judah and Dan.

In *Judges* and *1 Samuel* we will see some of the Israelites' struggles to hold onto the land. In *2 Samuel* we will see that they finally succeeded. At the time of David and Solomon, the Israelites would control a territory even larger than what we see in this map.

And after that…. What happened then will be told in *1 Kings* and the books that follow it.

# THE BOOK OF JUDGES

The *Book of Judges* seems to tell about the same period as the *Book of Joshua*. It is the second in the group called the Old Testament Historical Books.

Each tribe of the Israelites was led by its own leaders. But whenever one or more tribes were having trouble with the other peoples living in and around Canaan, they cried out to the Lord, and he inspired gifted persons to lead and rescue his people. These gifted persons were called judges.

The *Book of Judges* is a collection of stories about the judges. One of the main truths about God and his people that the book teaches is this: As long as the Israelites worshipped the Lord and obeyed his commandments, everything went well for them; when they would start to worship other gods, such as Baal, a god of the Canaanites, some nation would begin to give them trouble. Then the Israelites would cry out to the Lord for help, and he would send a judge to save them. After that, there would be peace until the people again began to worship other gods.

**Judges 2**

The people served the Lord as long as Joshua lived and as long as the elders lived who had seen all the wonderful things the Lord had done for Israel. But after them another generation grew up which did not know the Lord or what he had done for Israel.

So the Israelites committed evil in the eyes of the Lord. They began serving the Baals and deserted the Lord, the God of their fathers, who had brought them out from the land of Egypt. They would pray to some of the gods of the neighboring peoples and worship them.

Then the anger of the Lord would flare up against Israel, and he would let them fall into the hands of raiders who robbed them, and into the power of the enemies surrounding them, so they were no longer able to stand their ground before their enemies.

Then the Lord would be softened by their groanings and would raise up a judge for them. The Lord would be with the judge and save them from their enemies as long as the judge lived. But when the judge died, they would fall back and would serve and worship other gods more wickedly than their fathers had.

This was why the Lord did not drive out the rest of the peoples from the land of Canaan. Since the Israelites had not been faithful to him, he left those nations there, as a test and trial for Israel.

## Deborah and Barak

**Judges 4**

*The* Book of Judges *mentions twelve judges and describes what some of them did. One of the most famous was Deborah. She was so much in touch with the Lord that she was called a prophetess—a woman who could speak for God.*

At the time of Deborah, Jabin, king of the Canaanites, was making life miserable for the tribes that lived around the Plain of Jezreel.

Deborah used to sit under a palm tree between Ramah and Bethel in the hill country of Ephraim, and the Israelites would go to her for advice.

One day she sent a messenger to call Barak, son of Abinoam, from Kedesh of Naphtali. She told Barak, "Here is what the Lord commands, the God of Israel: Go, march to Mount Tabor and take with you ten thousand men from the sons of Naphtali and from the sons of Zebulun. I will bring Sisera, Jabin's commander-in-chief, with his chariots and multitudes, toward you, to the brook Kishon, and deliver him into your hands."

Barak answered, "I'll go if you go with me; if you don't go, neither will I."

Deborah replied, "I will surely go with you. However, the glory will not be given to you. The Lord will give Sisera into the hands of a woman." With that, Deborah stood up and left for Kedesh with Barak.

Barak called Zebulun and Naphtali to Kedesh. Ten thousand men followed him, and Deborah went with him.

A Kenite named Heber had left his people, the descendants of Moses' father-in-law, and had come near Kedesh to pitch his tent.

Sisera was told that Barak, son of Abinoam, had gone up to Mount Tabor. So Sisera called up all of his nine hundred armored chariots and his whole army. At this, Deborah said to Barak, "Go! This is the day on which the Lord will give Sisera into your hands. Will the Lord not march before you?"

So Barak came down Mount Tabor with ten thousand men following him. At Barak's advance, Sisera, all his chariots and all his troops were thrown into confusion by the Lord. Sisera got out of his chariot and ran, while Barak chased the chariots and troops. Sisera's men fell by the sword.

As Sisera ran, he came to the tent of Jael, wife of Heber the Kenite. Jabin, king of Hazor, was on friendly terms with the household of Heber the Kenite. Jael went out to meet Sisera and said to him, "Stop here, my lord, stop at my home. Don't worry." So he entered her tent and she covered him over with a blanket.

He said to her, "Please, give me a little water to drink, for I am thirsty." Instead, she opened the skin sack that contained sour milk, gave him a drink and covered him over. He said to her, "Stay at the entrance of the tent. If anyone comes and asks, 'Is there any man here?' answer, 'No.'"

But, when he was sound asleep, Jael took a tent peg. With a mallet in her hand, she tiptoed up to him and hammered the peg through his head, killing him.

Then Barak came along, looking for Sisera. Jael went out to meet him and said, "Go in; I'll show you the man you are after." He went into her tent, and there was Sisera, dead on the ground.

## The Song of Victory

**Judges 5**

That day Deborah burst into song, and so did Barak, son of Abinoam. They sang:

"Listen, you kings! Pay attention, you rulers!

"To the Lord will I sing; I will praise the Lord, the God of Israel.

"O Lord, when you marched out from Seir, when you advanced from the land of Edom, the earth trembled, and the clouds poured down water.

"Mountains shook at the presence of the Lord, the God of Israel....

"My heart is for the leaders of Israel who volunteered for the sake of their people.

"Bless the Lord!

"Wake up, Deborah, wake up! Wake up, strike up a song!

"Up, Barak! And take your prisoners, son of Abinoam.

"Kings came and fought, the kings of Canaan fought at Taanach by the waters of Megiddo.

"From heaven the stars fought from their pathways; they fought against Sisera.

"The brook Kishon swept them away.

"Of all women, may Jael, wife of Heber the Kenite, be blessed.

"Of all women may she be blessed in her tent.

"She stretched out her hand to the peg, and to the workman's hammer...at their feet he lay, collapsed.

"So do all the enemies of the Lord die; and let those who love him be like the sun rising in all its strength."

## The Lord Calls Gideon

**Judges 6**

The Israelites did evil things in the eyes of the Lord, so the Lord let them live under the power of Midian for seven years. For fear of the Midianites, the Israelites prepared for themselves caves and hiding places in the mountains.

This is what would happen: when Israel's crops were growing, Midianites, Amalekites and desert tribes from the East would come marching up, pitch tents on the land and destroy the crops. They would leave no food in Israel, and no sheep, oxen or donkeys. They would arrive as numerous as locusts—they and their camels were beyond counting. So Israel was in great poverty because of Midian, and the Israelites cried out to the Lord.

Then the angel of the Lord came and stood under the terebinth tree that belonged to Joash of the clan of Abiezer. Joash's son Gideon was threshing wheat in the wine press to save it from the Midianites.

The angel of the Lord showed himself and said, "Brave fighter! The Lord is with you!"

But Gideon answered, "Excuse me, sir. If the Lord is with us, why has all this hap-pened to us? Where are all his wonders that our fathers have told us about? The Lord has rejected us and let us fall into the power of Midian."

Then the Lord looked at him and said, "With this strength of yours go and save Israel from the power of Midian."

*As in many of these very old stories, it isn't always clear whether an angel was speaking or the Lord himself.*

Gideon answered, "Excuse me, sir, with what shall I save Israel? You see, my clan is the least important in the tribe of Manasseh, and I am the least important in my father's family."

But the Lord said to him, "I will be with you, so you will strike down all of the Midianites."

Then Gideon said, "If in any way I am your favorite, work a sign for me to see that it is really you who speak with me. Please wait here till I bring out my offering and set it before you."

He said, "I will stay till you return."

So Gideon went in. He prepared a kid goat and with a measure of flour made unleavened cakes. He put the meat in a basket and the broth in a pot, and bringing everything out under the terebinth, he offered it to him.

The angel of God told him, "Take the meat and the unleavened cakes and set them on this rock; then pour the broth on them." He did so.

Then the angel of the Lord reached out with his staff. As soon as the tip of the staff touched the meat and cakes, fire flared up from the rock to destroy them. Then the angel of the Lord vanished from his sight.

That night the Lord said to him, "Tear down the altar of Baal that your father owns. Cut down the sacred pole beside it; and then set up an altar to the Lord on top of the mound, in the right place. Take your father's seven-year-old bull and offer it as a sacrifice, using the wood of the pole that you cut down."

So from among his servants Gideon chose ten men and did as the Lord had told him. Yet, he worked by night, being afraid to do it in daylight because of his father's family and the townspeople.

When the townspeople got up in the morning, they saw the altar of Baal in pieces, the pole beside it cut down, and a bull offered in sacrifice on a new altar.

So they asked one another, "Who did this?"

After making inquiries, they concluded, "Gideon, the son of Joash, did it."

Then the townspeople said to Joash, "Bring your son out and let him die, because he tore down the altar of Baal and cut down the sacred pole beside it."

But Joash answered, "Are you pleading a case for Baal? Let the person who pleads for Baal die before morning. If Baal is a god, let him plead for himself, for it is his altar that has been torn down." That day they gave Gideon the name Jerubbaal.*

―――――――――

*Jerubbaal means "Let Baal plead his case."

All Midian, Amalek and the desert tribes gathered, crossed the Jordan, and set up camp in the plain of Jezreel.

Then the spirit of the Lord came over Gideon. He blew a trumpet and called his clan, Abiezer, to follow him.

He sent messengers throughout Manasseh, and the whole tribe came out to follow him.

He also sent messengers through Asher, Zebulun and Naphtali, and these tribes marched up to meet him.

Then Gideon said to God, "I am going to lay a fleece on the threshing-floor. If dew falls only on the fleece and the rest of the ground stays dry, then I'll understand that you will save Israel through me, as you have said."

When he got up the following day, he pressed the fleece together. The dew he squeezed out of the fleece filled a bowl with water.

Then Gideon said to God, "Excuse me—do not get angry if I speak one more time. Please let the fleece alone stay dry, and let dew fall on the rest of the ground."

And that night God did so. Only the fleece stayed dry, while dew fell on the rest of the ground.

# Gideon's Army

Then Jerubbaal—that is, Gideon—got up early, as well as all the people with him, and set up camp near the camp of Midian.

But the Lord said to Gideon, "The people with you are too many for me to give Midian into your hands. Israel might brag against me, saying, 'It was my own strength that saved me.' So now, shout out this order for the people to hear: 'If someone is afraid, let him leave.'"

Twenty-two thousand men then left the army, and ten thousand remained.

Then the Lord said to Gideon, "Still too many people! Lead them down to the stream, where I will put them through a test for you. The man of whom I tell you, 'This one shall go with you,' shall go with you; and every man of whom I say, 'This one shall not go with you,' shall not go."

So Gideon led the people down to the stream, where the Lord said to him, "Place by themselves all those who lick up the water with their tongues as dogs do, and also all those who kneel down to drink." The result was this: the number of men who licked up the water from their cupped hands were three hundred. All the rest of the people knelt down to drink the water.

Then the Lord said to Gideon, "With the three hundred men who licked up the water I will save you and put Midian into your hands. Let the rest of the people leave, each one for his own place."

The food these people had with them was collected, and so were their trumpets, and then he let every man go. But he kept the three hundred men.

The camp of Midian lay below in the valley.

That night the Lord said to Gideon, "Get up and swoop down on the camp, for I will let it fall into your hands. Or, if you are afraid to swoop down, go down near the camp with Purah, your assistant, and eavesdrop on their conversation. Then your hands will feel strong enough."

So with Purah, his assistant, Gideon went down near the armed men in the camp. Midianites, Amalekites and all the other invading tribes were lying in the valley as numerous as locusts.

Right when Gideon arrived, one man was telling another about a dream. He said, "You see, I had a dream: I saw a cake of barley bread rolling into the camp of Midian; it came all the way to the tent, hit it and turned it over. The tent collapsed."

The other man replied, "This is nothing other than the sword of Gideon, son of Joash, a man of Israel. God will let Midian fall into his hands—the whole camp included."

On hearing about the dream and the explanation, Gideon bowed low.

He returned to the camp of Israel and said, "Up! The Lord has put the camp of Midian in our hands."

He divided the three hundred men into three companies, and to each of them he handed trumpets and empty jars with torches inside.

Then he said to them, "Take your cue from me and do the same. I am going to the edge of the camp, and you are to do exactly as I do. I will blow the trumpet—I and all those with me—and you, too, are to blow the trumpets around the edge of the whole camp. And then you are to shout: 'For the Lord and for Gideon!'"

So Gideon came to the edge of the camp with the hundred men of his company, at the beginning of the middle watch, when the guard had scarcely been changed, and they blew the trumpets and smashed the jars that they held. The three companies blew their trumpets and broke their jars. Then each man held his torch in his left hand and the trumpet in his right, and shouted, "A sword for the Lord and for Gideon!"

Each man stayed where he was at the edge of the camp. The whole camp was filled with of confusion and running and shouting. At the sound of the three hundred trumpets, the Lord turned each man's sword against his companion throughout the whole camp.

The Midianites and their allies fled. Meanwhile, the men of Israel were called up from Naphtali, from Asher and from the whole of Manasseh, and they pursued Midian. Gideon and his men chased many of the scattered and fleeing Midianites into the land across the Jordan.

Thanks to the cooperation of the tribes, it was a great victory—so great that the people wanted Gideon to be their king.

But Gideon answered them, "I won't be your ruler, and neither will my son. The Lord is your ruler."

So the Midianites were defeated by the Israelites, and didn't show their faces again. The country was at peace for forty years.

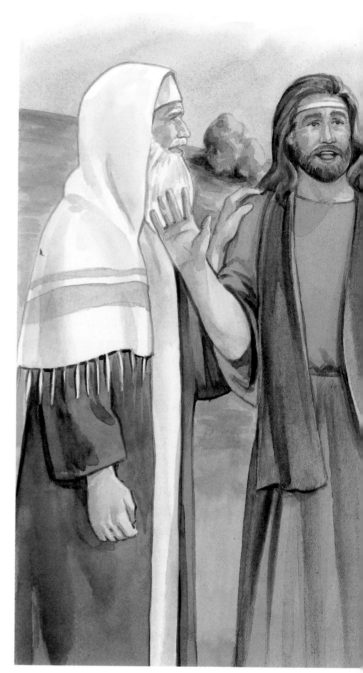

## The Birth of Samson

**Judges 13**

But again the Israelites did what is evil in the sight of the Lord, so the Lord let them fall into the power of the Philistines. They stayed this way for forty years.

his head. The angel added, "He will begin to save Israel from the power of the Philistines."

The woman was happy, because she had not been able to have children. She hurried home to tell Manoah, her husband, who prayed that the Lord would send the angel back, so he could hear the message for himself. The angel returned and repeated the good news.

When the boy was born, they named him Samson. He grew up, and the Lord was with him.

However, Samson didn't seem to know about his mission—to begin to free his people from the Philistines.

## Samson's Riddle

**Judges 14**

Samson went down to Timnah, and in Timnah he noticed one of the Philistine girls. When he came home, he told his father and mother, "I noticed one the Philistine girls. Get her for me, to be my wife."

But his father and mother asked him, "Isn't there any woman among all our own people? Do you have to choose a wife among the Philistines?"

But Samson said to his father, "Get her for me, for she is the one I like."

His parents made the arrangements but were not happy about it. They did not know that the Lord would use these events to begin setting Israel free from the Philistines.

Samson went down to Timnah. At the vineyards of Timnah, a young lion came toward him, roaring. Then the spirit of the Lord came upon Samson, and with

The Philistines had settled along the seacoast, near where the tribe of Dan had also settled. One day an angel of the Lord appeared to a woman of this tribe and told her that she would have a son. The boy was to be consecrated to God before he was even born. No razor was ever to touch

his bare hands he tore it to pieces as if it were a kid goat. But he did not tell his father or mother what he had done.

So Samson went down. He spoke with the woman and liked her.

After some time, when he went back to marry her, he made a detour to see the dead lion and to his surprise he found a nest of bees among the lion's bones. He scraped some honey into the hollow of his hands, and ate it as he walked on.

When he came home to his father and mother, he gave them some honey and they ate it, but he did not tell them that he had scraped the honey from the skeleton of a lion.

When Samson's father had finished making the arrangements for the marriage, Samson held a series of parties, as was the custom. The bride's parents chose thirty young men to be Samson's attendants.

Samson said to them, "Let me ask you a riddle. If you give me the right answer during the week of celebrations, I'll give you thirty linen robes and thirty sets of clothes. But if you can't give me an answer, then you have to give me thirty linen robes and thirty sets of clothes."

They answered, "Ask your riddle, and let us listen."

Then he said to them,
"From a thing that devours
came something to eat;
from a thing that is strong
came something sweet."

They kept trying to figure out the answer. Then they said to Samson's wife, "For our sakes, beg your husband to tell you the answer to the riddle. Otherwise, we will burn down your father's house

with you in it. We see you have invited us to make us poor!"

So Samson's wife began to shed tears and to annoy him, saying, "You hate me instead of loving me. You've asked a riddle to these men from my own country, and you haven't told me the answer."

He replied, "You see, I haven't even told my father and mother. Why should I tell you?"

But she kept annoying him with her tears for the seven days that the celebration lasted. Since she had been bothering him so much, on the seventh day he told her the answer. And she told the young Philistine men.

So on the seventh day before sunset the young men of the city said to him, "What is sweeter than honey and what is stronger than a lion?"

Samson was very angry, for he realized that his bride had told them the answer. He left and went back to his father's house.

## Samson Fights the Philistines

**Judges 15**

Some time had passed, and during the season of the wheat harvest Samson went to see his wife. He brought a kid goat as a present.

But her father would not let him in. He said, "I thought you didn't like her any more, so I gave her to one of your attendants. Isn't her younger sister prettier than she is? Please take her instead."

At this, Samson said, "This time I don't owe the Philistines anything if I do them harm."

So Samson left and caught three hundred foxes. Then he took torches, turned one tail toward the other and tied a torch between every two tails. He lit the torches and let the foxes loose in the Philistines' fields. In that way he set fire to both the bundled and standing wheat, as well as the vineyards and olive groves.

The Philistines asked, "Who has done this?"

And someone answered, "Samson, the son-in-law of the Timnite, because the man took Samson's wife and gave her to one of his attendants."

At this, the Philistines went up and burned down the house with both her and her father inside it.

So Samson said to them, "I will surely take revenge for what you have done." He gave a severe beating to several of them.

Then he went and lived in a cave in the cliff of Etam.

## Samson's Capture and Death

**Judges 16, 21**

Some time later, Samson began to live with a woman named Delilah. The Philistine leaders heard about it and offered to pay Delilah a great deal of money if she could learn the secret of Samson's strength. So Delilah kept trying to find out. Three times Samson made up stories about the secret of his strength, and each time Delilah fell for them.

At last she asked, "How can you say, 'I love you,' when you don't share your thoughts with me? You've teased me three times now, but you haven't told me what makes you so strong."

So, since she was nagging and pressuring him, he grew very much annoyed and told her the truth. He said, "No razor has ever touched my head. If my hair were shaved off, my strength would leave me and I'd be as weak as anyone else."

Delilah realized that he had told her the truth. She sent for the Philistine leaders with this message: "Come over this last time—he's told me his secret." The Philistine leaders came, bringing the money.

When she had gotten him to fall asleep, Delilah signaled to one of the men, who came and shaved the seven locks from his head. Then she said, "The Philistines have come for you, Samson!"

When Samson tried to jump up, his great strength was gone.

The Philistines seized him, blinded him and brought him to Gaza. There they fastened him with bronze chains and put him to work turning the hand-mill in jail.

Meanwhile, his hair began to grow.

One day the Philistines held a celebration in their temple. They said, "Bring Samson to entertain us." So Samson was brought from jail, and he acted like a clown for them. Then they had him stand between the pillars of the temple. Samson said to the boy who was leading him by the hand, "Let me feel the pillars on which the temple rests, so I can lean against them."

The temple was packed with people. All the Philistine leaders were there, and on the roof there were about three thousand people. Then Samson called on God and said, "O Lord, please think of me. Give me strength this once, O God! Let me take revenge on the Philistines for my eyes—just this once!"

With that, Samson took hold of the two main pillars on which the temple rested and pushed himself against them—against one with his right side and against the other with his left, as he said, "Let me die with the Philistines!" He pushed hard, and the temple fell on the leaders and on the rest of the people in it.

His relatives went down, carried him away and buried him in his father's burial place.

*This story and some others in the* Book of Judges *show that people had confused ideas about right and wrong:*

Everyone did what he thought was best.

# THE BOOK OF RUTH

The *Book of Ruth* tells about a young woman from Moab, a country near Israel, and how she was accepted into the Israelite community. She became an ancestor of King David and of Jesus.

This story also shows the goodness of Ruth and the man she would eventually marry.

In the times when the judges ruled, there was a food shortage in the country, and a man traveled from Bethlehem of Judah to live as a foreigner in the country of Moab. He went with his wife and his two sons. The man was called Elimelech. His wife was called Naomi, and his two sons were named Mahlon and Chilion.

Elimelech died, but Naomi outlived him and stayed on in Moab with her two sons. The young men married Moabite wives—one called Orpah, and the other, Ruth. They had lived there about ten years when Mahlon and Chilion also died. Naomi had outlived her two children and her husband.

Naomi decided to return to Bethlehem with her daughters-in-law, since she had heard that the Lord had sent food to his people. So they started out.

But then Naomi said to her two daughters-in-law, "Say good-bye and go back, each of you to her mother's house. The Lord will be kind to you, as you have been kind to the departed and to me. He will grant each of you to find a home by marrying again."

When Naomi insisted, Orpah kissed her mother-in-law good-bye, but Ruth stayed with her.

Naomi said, "Your sister-in-law has returned to her people and to her god. Follow her example and go back."

But Ruth answered, "Don't insist that I leave you. Wherever you go I will go, and wherever you live I will live; your people are my people, and your God is my God. Wherever you die I will die, and there will I be buried. Let not even death separate us." Seeing that Ruth was determined, Naomi gave in.

So they set out and arrived in Bethlehem when the barley harvest was beginning.

## Ruth Meets Boaz

Naomi's husband had had a relative named Boaz, who owned a farm.

Ruth said to Naomi, "If you like, I'll go into the fields and gather up the ears of barley, following anyone who is kind to me." Naomi answered, "You may go, my daughter."

So Ruth went to gather grain in the fields, following the harvesters. She happened to start in the fields belonging to Boaz.

Boaz said to Ruth, "Listen, my daughter. Don't go to gather in any other field. Stay here with my maid-servants. I've ordered the young men not to bother you. When you're thirsty, go to drink some of the water the young men have brought."

Ruth bowed down and said, "How can I have won your favor, when I am from another country?"

Boaz replied, "I've been told about everything you've done for your mother-in-law after her husband's death, and how you left your own father, mother and country to live with a people you didn't know. May your reward from the God of Israel be in full measure, since you have come to take shelter under his wings."

Naomi was happy when she learned that Ruth was gleaning in the fields of Boaz, for Boaz was a good man and a relative of Elimelech's.

## Ruth and Boaz Marry

**Ruth 3–4**

*According to a law of the time, the nearest relative of a man who had died had a right to claim that man's property and marry the widow in order to give the deceased man an heir. Naomi saw that Boaz*

*and Ruth seemed to be suited for one an-other, so she thought of using that law as a reason for them to marry.*

Boaz was very willing to marry Ruth, but there was a closer relative who had to be asked first. Boaz went and sat down by the city gate, where business was done. When he saw the other relative passing by, he called to him.

"Step aside and sit down here," said Boaz. The man stepped aside and sat down. Then from among the elders of the town Boaz called ten men, to whom he said, "Sit down here." And they sat down.

Boaz told his relative that the lands of Elimelech had been put up for sale by Naomi, and that the two of them were first in line to redeem the property. He also reminded the man that, since the property would have gone to Ruth's de-ceased husband, Mahlon, the redeemer's duty would include marrying Ruth and raising an heir who would inherit the re-deemed property.

"I cannot redeem it for myself," his relative said. "Redeem it yourself, since I cannot."

Now, in early times, in order to make official whatever agreement was made in Israel, one party would take off his sandal and give it to the other. So as the relative said to Boaz, "Buy it yourself," he took off his sandal.

At this, Boaz said to the elders, "Today you are witnesses that I am buying from Naomi everything that belonged to Elimelech and everything that belonged to Chilion and to Mahlon, and that I am also acquiring Ruth, the woman from Moab, who once was Mahlon's wife, to be my wife, in order to keep the name of the deceased alive, attached to his property. Today you are witnesses."

And all the people at the gate, as well as the elders, said, "Yes, we are witnesses. May the Lord make the woman who will enter your house to be like Rachel and Leah, who built up the House of Israel."

Boaz took Ruth home, and she became his wife.

When Ruth gave birth to a son, the women congratulated Naomi, saying, "Blessed be the Lord! This child will give you new life in your old age, for it is your daughter-in-law who has given him birth. She loves you and is better for you than seven sons."

Naomi took the child and looked after him. They called him Obed. He became the father of Jesse, who was the father of David.

# THE FIRST BOOK OF SAMUEL

The two books of Samuel are named after the last judge of Israel. Besides being a judge, Samuel was also a prophet.

When the Israelites wanted a king, God chose Saul, and Samuel made him king. After Saul had twice disobeyed the Lord, Samuel found David, the young man whom God had chosen to replace Saul. David would become the most famous king of Israel.

*1 Samuel* tells about Israel's struggle against the Philistines, Saul's jealousy of David, David's friendship with Saul's son Jonathan, and Saul's death.

*The Bible contains some stories of women who were unable to have children until they were helped by God in a special way. In each case, the child that was born had something important to do for God and God's people. One of these women was Hannah, who lived toward the end of the time of the judges. Her famous son was Samuel.*

**1 Samuel 2**

Samuel's mother, Hannah, had prayed for a child for a long time. After Samuel was born, Hannah thanked the Lord, by bringing her young son to the house of God at Shiloh. She left him with Eli, the priest, to serve the Lord at the shrine. He became like another son to Eli.

Every year Samuel's mother would go up with her husband to offer sacrifice. Eli would always bless Elkanah and his wife, saying, "May the Lord give you children to make up for the loan you have made to the Lord." And the Lord did look after Hannah, who gave birth to three sons and two daughters. As for the boy Samuel, he grew up near the Lord.

Eli had grown very old, and his sons, Hophni and Phinehas, were disobeying God's commandments. Eli knew this, and told his sons they were doing wrong, but they wouldn't listen to him. At last a prophet came to Eli with a message from the Lord. He told Eli that his sons would soon die and another priest would take their place.

## Samuel Becomes a Prophet

**1 Samuel 3**

In those days it was not common to receive a message from the Lord. One night Eli was lying in his sleeping place, while Samuel lay in the sanctuary of the Lord near the ark of God. The Lord called Samuel, and he answered, "Here I am."

Samuel, who was probably a teenager at the time, hurried to Eli and said, "Here I am—you called me." Eli said he hadn't called, so Samuel went back to his place. This happened two more times. Then Eli realized that someone really was calling Samuel. It was the Lord himself.

So Eli said to Samuel, "Go and lie

down. When someone calls you, say, 'Speak, Lord. Your servant is listening.'" So Samuel left and lay down in his place.

Then the Lord came and called as before: "Samuel! Samuel!"

And Samuel answered, "Speak, for your servant is listening."

Then the Lord told Samuel that Eli's sons were going to be punished for all the sins they were committing.

Samuel lay down until morning, when he opened the doors of the house of the Lord. He was afraid to tell Eli about God's message. But Eli called Samuel and asked, "Samuel, my son, what is the message that the Lord spoke to you? Please don't hide anything from me." So Samuel told him every word. Then Eli said, "He is the Lord. Let him do what he feels is right."

Samuel grew up. God was with him, and the whole of Israel began to realize that Samuel was a real prophet of the Lord.

## A Disastrous Battle

**1 Samuel 4–7**

At this time, the worst enemies of the Israelites were the Philistines. They lived along the coast of the Mediterranean Sea. Because the Philistines fought fiercely, used war chariots and made iron weapons, the Israelites could not stop them when they pushed into their territory.

At one point, the Israelites decided to bring the ark of God into battle. Eli's sons went along to take care of the ark.

The presence of the ark frightened the Philistines, but in their fear they fought even harder. They won, and many Israelites were killed, including Eli's sons. The ark of God was captured. When Eli heard the news, he died of sorrow.

The Philistines took the ark to one of their own cities, but because strange things began to happen, they soon returned it to the Israelites, who kept it safe on a farm for several years.

Samuel became judge of Israel for life. Every year he traveled from town to town, judging Israel, and then he returned to Ramah, where he lived.*

---

*It seems that Shiloh had been destroyed—perhaps by the Philistines.*

## Israel's First King

**1 Samuel 8–11**

When Samuel was old, some of the leaders of the people went to Ramah to see him and said, "Your sons aren't following in your footsteps. Give us a king to lead us, so we'll be like all the other nations."

Samuel felt that the true king of Israel should be the Lord. When a person was needed to lead the Israelites into battle, the Lord could choose someone to lead them, as he had done ever since the time of Joshua. So Samuel prayed about the matter.

The Lord told him to remind the people that kings can be very demanding. But if the people still wanted a king, Samuel was to let them have their way. When the people still insisted, Samuel went to look for the right man.

He met a tall, humble young farmer from the tribe of Benjamin, and the Lord told him this was the man. His name was Saul. In a private ceremony, Samuel anointed him king. To anoint means to sign with oil. For many years anointing has been a symbol that God is giving power.

A little later, Samuel called the leaders of the people together and introduced Saul to them. They shouted, "Long live the king!"

Some Israelites doubted that Saul could lead an army, but he proved that he could when he saved the city of Jabesh-gilead from the attacking Ammonites.

## Saul's Disobedience

**1 Samuel 13**

The Philistines gathered to fight against Israel: thirty thousand chariots, six thousand horsemen and foot-soldiers who were as numerous as the sands on the seashore.

The people of Israel hid in caves, in the clefts of the rocks, in basements and in cisterns. Meanwhile all Saul's troops were deserting him out of fear.

Saul was supposed to wait for Samuel, who would offer a holocaust (a burnt animal sacrifice) to ask the Lord's blessing for the Israelites in the war. Saul and Samuel had agreed that Samuel would arrive in seven days.

Saul waited seven days, but Samuel failed to arrive in Gilgal. And his men were leaving him one by one.

Then Saul said, "Bring me the holocaust." And he offered the sacrifice himself.

As Saul finished offering the holocaust, Samuel arrived. Saul went out to welcome him.

Samuel saw what had happened and asked Saul for an explanation. Saul explained his reasons for not waiting.

At this, Samuel answered Saul, "How foolish of you! You have not kept the commandment that the Lord your God gave you. Your royal power shall not last."

Samuel left, and Saul with his remaining six hundred men went to join his son Jonathan. So far, no fighting had broken out but the situation was very tense.

## Jonathan's Breakthrough

1 Samuel 14

One day Jonathan, son of Saul, said to his armor-bearer, "Come, let us cross to the outpost of the Philistines."

Between Jonathan and the Philistine outpost lay a ravine with a steep crag on either side of it.

Then Jonathan said, "We'll go over and let ourselves be seen by those people. If they say, 'Stay there while we come to you,' then we'll stay where we are, without attacking them. But if they say, 'Attack us,' then we'll attack, since the Lord will give them into our hands. That will be our sign."

So they let themselves be seen by the Philistines. At this, the Philistines taunted Jonathan and his armor-bearer, "Attack us. We have news for you!"

Then Jonathan said to his armor-bearer, "Come up, follow me. The Lord has given them into the hands of Israel." Then Jonathan climbed up on all fours, followed by his armor-bearer. He lunged into their midst, knocking the Philistines to the ground, while his armor-bearer followed, killing the fallen.

Terror fell on the Philistine camp. Saul's lookouts saw the camp in a tumult, with men rushing here and there.

Saul gathered all the troops under his command, and they marched into battle. Seeing this, some Hebrews who had joined the Philistines decided to side with Saul and Jonathan. And the Israelites hiding in the hill country of Ephraim heard that the Philistines were fleeing and joined in their pursuit. That day the Lord gave Israel a victory.

## The Lord Chooses David

1 Samuel 15–16

Saul disobeyed the Lord a second time. After that, Samuel told him that the Lord had rejected him and had chosen someone else to be king.

The Lord said to Samuel, "Fill your flask with oil. I am sending you to Jesse of Bethlehem. I have chosen one of his sons to be king."

Samuel did what the Lord had commanded. When he arrived in Bethlehem, he invited Jesse and his sons to the sacrifice.

When he saw Eliab, he thought, "Definitely, here in the Lord's presence is his anointed one!" But the Lord said to Samuel, "Pay no attention to his looks and his height, for I have rejected him. A hu-man being chooses according to a person's appearance, but the Lord chooses according to a person's heart."

Jesse brought seven sons before Samuel, but Samuel said to Jesse, "None of these has been chosen by the Lord." So Samuel asked Jesse, "Haven't you any more sons?"

Jesse answered, "There is still the youngest, but he's tending the flock."

Samuel said to Jesse, "Send for him."

Jesse sent word and had him come. He was good looking, with a ruddy complexion and bright eyes. Then the Lord said, "Anoint him. This is the one." Samuel took the jar of oil and anointed him among his brothers. From that day on, the spirit of the Lord was a strong force in David's life.

## David and Goliath

1 Samuel 17

David had been anointed, but Saul didn't know it, nor did he want to think of anyone else becoming king in his place.

The spirit of the Lord had left Saul and an evil spirit had overcome him. So Saul's officials suggested finding someone to play the harp to calm the king whenever he felt disturbed.

One of the servants said, "I have seen a son of Jesse from Bethlehem who can play. He's also a brave fighter. He speaks pleasantly and is handsome. The Lord is with him."

Saul sent messengers to Jesse with these orders: "Send me your son David." So David came to Saul and became his servant. Saul liked David very much.

Whenever the evil spirit seized Saul, David would pick up the harp and play, and Saul would become calm. The evil spirit would leave him.

*The* First Book of Samuel *is a collection of stories from various sources. Now we read another story about how Saul met David.*

The Philistines called up their armies for war, and camped on a hill. Israel camped on another hill. A valley lay between them.

From the Philistine lines advanced Goliath of Gath. He was over nine feet tall. He wore a bronze helmet and was outfitted with a heavy breastplate and bronze shin-guards. The iron head of his spear weighed about fifteen pounds.

Goliath came to a standstill. Then he shouted out his challenge to Israel's troops: "Choose a man, and let him come down against me. If he can strike me down, then we will serve you; and if I strike him down, you shall be our slaves."

Saul and the rest of Israel heard these words of the Philistines and were filled with terror.

Jesse's three eldest sons had followed Saul to the war.

Jesse sent David to bring some food to his brothers in the camp. David arrived when the two armies were marching out in battle formation and hurried to find his brothers. Meanwhile, Goliath came out from the Philistine troops and shouted the same challenge he had given before.

David asked the men standing near him, "What will be done for the man who strikes down this Philistine? Who is this Philistine, anyway, to challenge the army of the living God?"

The soldiers told him that if any man could strike down the Philistine the king would make him rich and give him his own daughter as his wife.

David walked among the troops, repeating his question and getting the same answer every time.

Someone repeated David's question to Saul, who sent for him. David said to Saul, "I, your servant, will go and fight this Philistine."

But Saul said to David, "You can't fight against this Philistine. You're only a boy, while he has been an expert at fighting from his youth."

David answered Saul, "The Lord, who has delivered me from the claws of lions and bears, will deliver me from the power of this Philistine."

At this, Saul said to David, "Go. May the Lord be with you."

Saul outfitted David with his own armor: he put a bronze helmet on his head, made him wear a breastplate and girded David with his own sword. But when David began to walk, he told Saul, "I can't walk with all this on, since I've never tried before." So David took off the armor.

Instead, he picked up his curve-headed shepherd's staff (his crook). From the dry stream-bed he chose five of the smoothest stones, which he put inside his shepherd's bag. Then he walked toward the Philistine, slingshot in hand.

The Philistine steadily drew closer and closer. When he ran his eyes over David, he showed contempt, for David was just a boy—good looking and with a ruddy complexion. So the Philistine said to David, "Am I a dog, for you come against

against you in the name of the Lord of armies, the God of Israel's troops, which you are challenging. This very day the Lord will put you in my hands. I will give the corpses of the Philistine army to the birds of the sky and to the beasts of the earth. All the world will realize that Israel has a God."

me with sticks? Come here! I will give your flesh to the birds of the sky and the wild beasts."

David answered, "You come against me with sword and spear, but I come

When the Philistine started to move toward David, David ran quickly toward him. He put his hand into his bag, took a small stone out of it and hurled it with the slingshot. It hit the Philistine on the forehead. The stone lodged in his forehead, and he collapsed, face down, on the ground.

David had no sword, so he ran up to the Philistine, pulled his sword out of its sheath and finished him off by cutting off his head.

When the Philistines saw that their champion was dead, they fled. At this, the men of Israel and of Judah sprang forward, shouting their war cry, and pursued the Philistines.

It was a great victory, and Saul took David into his service right away. At once a strong friendship formed between David and Saul's son Jonathan.

## Saul's Jealousy

1 Samuel 18–24

When David returned from killing the Philistine, the women came out of the cities to meet King Saul. They danced with tambourines and stringed instruments and sang, "Saul has killed thousands, and David tens of thousands."

Saul became very angry, as he thought, "They have given David tens of thousands, but to me they have given only thousands.

What else can he get? Only the kingship." And from that day on, Saul was jealous of David.

At home the next day, the evil spirit pressed upon Saul, who became frantic. David was playing the harp and Saul was holding his spear. Saul threw the spear, planning to pin David to the wall. But David dodged him. This happened twice.

Saul lived in fear of David because God was with him. So Saul made David commander of a thousand men.

David went out and came in at the head of the troops and succeeded in everything he did, for the Lord was with him. Seeing this, Saul was afraid of him, while all Israel and Judah loved David because he led the troops in and out.

Saul found out that his daughter Michal loved David, so he let David know that he could marry her if he killed a hundred Philistines. Saul thought that David would get killed in the process. Instead, David succeeded again. So he married Michal and became Saul's son-in-law.

Saul was growing more and more afraid of David and spoke to his son Jonathan and his officials about killing him. Jonathan tried to reason with his father, and once he got him to change his mind and promise not to harm David, who had been so good to him.

But soon Saul was after David again. Since David and Michal weren't living in the same house as Saul, David managed to escape.

David gathered a few men who were loyal to him and went into hiding. They lived in the large cave of Adullam. David's brothers and his father's whole family heard about this and joined him there. Around him gathered people who were oppressed, owed debts or were discontented. David became their leader. He had about four hundred men with him.

They began to move from place to place, as secretly as possible, for Saul and his troops kept trying to find them.

Jonathan went to see David and told him, "Don't be afraid. The hand of my father Saul won't reach you. You will become king over Israel, and I'll be second to you. My father Saul knows that too."

They made an agreement, calling on the Lord to witness it.

David and his men were hiding in a desert area. Saul got word of it and went searching for him. Saul came to some sheep pens with a cave behind them and went into the cave for a few minutes. He didn't realize that David and his men were in the back of the cave.

David moved forward quietly and cut off the edge of the cloak that Saul was wearing. But then David's conscience began to bother him. He whispered to his men, "The Lord forbid that I should stretch out my hand against him, for he is the Lord's anointed one." So David would not let his men rise up against Saul. Saul left the cave and started on his way.

Then David went out of the cave and called to Saul, "My lord king!" Saul looked back and David fell on his knees, bowing to the ground to honor him. David asked Saul, "Why are you listening to people who say, 'David intends to harm you'?

"Clearly, this very day you can see that the Lord put you into my hands inside the cave. Someone said that you should be killed, but I said, 'I will not stretch out my hand, for he is the anointed of the Lord.'

"And look, my father, here is the edge of your cloak! You must realize that there is no wickedness or disloyalty in me, for I have not harmed you. Yet you are ready to take my life. Let the Lord judge between me and you, but let not my hand strike at you. Let the Lord stand up for me against you!"

When David finished saying this to Saul, Saul burst into tears. He said, "You are more innocent than I, for you have done good to me, while I have done harm to you. I know now that you will certainly become king and that the kingdom of Israel will last in your hands.

"So now swear to me by the Lord that after my death you will not wipe out my descendants—that you will not erase my name from my father's family."

David swore this oath to Saul, and Saul left for home.

## David among the Philistines

**1 Samuel 27**

Samuel died, and all Israel flocked together and mourned for him. He was buried at his home in Ramah. Meanwhile David went down to the wastelands of Paran.

Even though Saul had been grateful to David for sparing his life, David did not trust him. Soon it became clear that David was right, for he heard that Saul was after him again.

David went down to the Philistines and offered to serve King Achish of Gath by raiding towns of Judah. Achish didn't realize that instead of raiding the towns of his own countrymen, the people of Judah, David was raiding the towns of other peoples who lived farther away.

With David were six hundred men and their families. Achish let the whole community take over a small town called Ziklag.

*By this time, David had married again. As custom permitted, he had two wives, Ahinoam and Abigail.*

## Saul Fears for His Life

**1 Samuel 28–29**

The Philistines camped near Shunem. Saul gathered all Israel and they camped on Mount Gilboa. When Saul saw the Philistine camp, his heart began to beat wildly with terror.

*Saul had outlawed witches because witchcraft is forbidden by the commandments, but now he hoped a witch could tell him the future.*

Somebody found a witch, and Saul went to see her in disguise. He asked her to bring Samuel back from the dead. Samuel appeared—an old man, wrapped in a cloak.

Samuel asked, "Why have you disturbed me by bringing me back?"

Saul answered, "The Philistines are at war with me. God doesn't answer me anymore. So I've called you to let me know what to do."

But Samuel answered, "What's the use of asking me, when the Lord has left you? The Lord has torn the kingdom from your hand and given it to David.

reviewing their troops, David and his men came along with them. The Philistine commanders asked, "What are these Hebrews doing here?"

Achish replied, "You see, this is David, an officer of Saul, king of Israel, who has been under my command one or two years. From the day he came to us until now I have seen nothing to blame him for."

Tomorrow you and your sons will be with me."

Saul collapsed, for Samuel's words had struck terror into him. There was no strength left in him.

The woman offered Saul and his servants something to eat. Then they returned to the troops.

When the Philistine leaders were

But the Philistine commanders disagreed with him sharply and said, "Order the man back. Let him return to the place where you stationed him, and don't let him go into battle on our side. In the middle of the battle he might prove to be our enemy."

So Achish called David and told him that the other commanders didn't trust him. David started back to Ziklag with his companions.

## Amalekite Raiders

**1 Samuel 30**

After three days they reached Ziklag. In the meantime Amalekite raiders had looted the town and burned it down, taking everyone in it captive.

David and his men began to shout and weep. The men were thinking of stoning David, since all of them were angry because of their sons and daughters.

But David found strength in the Lord his God and set out with his six hundred men.

They found the Amalekites, who were celebrating, and caught them off guard before sunrise, attacking their camp and recovering their families and goods.

## The Battle of Gilboa

**1 Samuel 31**

When the Philistines were fighting against Israel, the Israelites fled before the Philistines, and fell and died on Mount Gilboa. The Philistines pressed close after Saul and struck down Saul's sons, Jonathan, Abinadab and Malchishua.

Then the archers hit Saul. He said to his armor-bearer, "Take out your sword and run me through with it, so they may not run me through themselves and make sport of me."

But his armor-bearer refused, so Saul took his own sword and threw himself down on it. When his armor bearer saw that Saul had died, he, too, threw himself down on his own sword and died with him.

That was how on the same day Saul died with three of his sons, his armor-bearer and all his men.

# THE SECOND BOOK OF SAMUEL

*2 Samuel* continues the history found in *1 Samuel.*

At this time, there were two main groups of Israelites: Judah, a large tribe, and "Israel," the other tribes taken together. In *2 Samuel*, David unites the two groups and becomes king of "all Israel and Judah."

*2 Samuel* and other books, such as *1 Chronicles* and *Sirach*, show us that David loved God very much. But David also made mistakes. Whenever he realized he had sinned, he asked God's forgiveness with sorrow and trust.

*The Philistines had been smart in sending David away, since his first loyalty was naturally to his own people, the Israelites.*

**2 Samuel 1**

After rescuing their families from the Amalekites, David and his men rested in Ziklag for two days. They were worried about the battle that was going on many miles away—worried about their relatives and friends. On the third day a man arrived with his garments torn and dust on his head—which was a sign of sorrow.

Coming before David, the man bowed down. David asked him, "Where are you coming from?"

He answered, "I escaped from the Israelite camp."

So David asked him, "How have things gone? Tell me."

The man said that the army had fled from the battle, that great numbers of men were lying dead, and that Saul, too, and his son Jonathan were dead.

David and his men were filled with sorrow. There was much crying and wailing. Then David sang a song to praise Saul and Jonathan.

"O mountains of Gilboa, the pride of Israel has been slain on your heights! How have the heroes fallen!

"May no dew, no rain fall on you, fields of sacrifices, for there the shields of heroes have been thrown away.

"Saul and Jonathan did not separate even in death. They were swifter than eagles, stronger than lions.

"I grieve over you, Jonathan my brother. How have heroes fallen! How have weapons failed!"

## David in Hebron

**2 Samuel 2–4**

Even though Samuel had anointed David as king several years before, this was not the time for him to try to lead the whole people of Judah and Israel. Saul had another son living, and many people of Israel didn't trust David, because Saul hadn't trusted him. So David and his followers went to live in Hebron in the territory of Judah, where the people of Judah made him their king.

During the next few years, some sad things happened:

Abner, the commander of Israel, killed David's nephew Asahel in battle. Asahel's brother Joab took revenge by murdering Abner, even though Abner had asked to come over to David's side.

Saul's son Ishbaal had become king of Israel. One day two of his servants murdered him. David knew that now he might be made king of all Israel, but he felt sad to become king as a result of a murder.

## David King in Jerusalem

**2 Samuel 5–6**

All the tribes of Israel came to David in Hebron and said, "Here we are, we who are your own bone and flesh. While Saul was our king, it was you who led the troops of Israel out and in." David made an agreement with them in Hebron, and so they anointed David king of Israel.

Hebron was within the territory of Judah. To rule a united nation, David needed a capital city that was more central. Jerusalem had a good location, but it was in the hands of a people called the Jebusites.

The king and his men marched on Jerusalem against the Jebusites, who defied David, saying, "You shall never enter here. The blind and the lame will be able to drive you back."

The city had been built on a hill and was well walled, but a tunnel ran down to a spring at the hill's base. David's nephew Joab led a squad up the tunnel to capture the city from inside.

So David occupied the fortress and called it the City of David.

Hiram, king of Tyre, sent messengers to David, together with cedar wood, carpenters and stone masons. They built David a palace.

In Hebron David had taken several wives, as was the custom for kings then. He also took back his first wife, Michal, Saul's daughter, whom Saul had given in marriage to another man. In Jerusalem, David took more wives. Many children were born to him in Hebron and Jerusalem.

David went out to lead the army against the Philistines. As before, he won many victories.

Then David went with his troops to bring the ark of the covenant into Jerusalem, so the city would become the center of worship for the whole nation. They brought the ark up to the city in procession.

David danced before the Lord, turning round and round with full energy. He and the whole House of Israel brought up the ark of the Lord in the midst of shouts of joy and trumpet blasts.

Thus the ark of the Lord arrived in the City of David. It was laid inside a tent that David had set up for it.

After sacrifices had been offered, David blessed the people in God's name and gave everyone some treats to eat. Then all the people went home.

When David went into the palace, his wife Michal came to meet him with a sarcastic remark about how he had looked, dancing in front of the ark.

David answered her, "I was dancing before the Lord. I will lower myself even more."

## The Lord's Promise

**2 Samuel 7–9**

When the king had begun to live in his new palace, he said to the prophet Nathan, "Look at this—here I am, living in a house of cedar, but the ark of God has a tent for a home."

That night God told Nathan that David's son would build his house, even though, he, the Lord, had never asked for one. Also the Lord said that he wanted to make a house—that is, a kingly family, or dynasty—for David, whom he had called from tending sheep to lead his people.

Nathan brought this word of the Lord to David. The king thanked the Lord, who had done so much for him.

David located Jonathan's only son—Meribaal—who was lame from an injury. He was now a young man. David gave him back all of Jonathan's property and invited him to eat at the palace every day.

## The Sword in David's Household

**2 Samuel 11–15**

At one point, David committed a serious sin with a woman and tried to cover it up by having her husband killed. The prophet Nathan went to him in the name of the Lord and told him that because of this, "the sword" would never leave his household.

David asked the Lord's forgiveness, and Nathan told him that God had forgiven him. But violence did come into David's household. The oldest son, Amnon, raped his half-sister and in turn was murdered by her full brother, Ab-

salom. Absolom took refuge with the king of Geshur.* When David eventually let him return home, more trouble began.

No handsome man in the whole of Israel was so highly praised as Absalom. He would stand at the side of the road outside the city gate, and to anyone who had to bring a lawsuit to the king he would say, "If only I were made judge over this country! Then everyone with a lawsuit would appear before me, and I would give that man justice."

When someone would come near to bow down to him, he would reach out, raise him up and kiss him.

So Absalom won the hearts of Israel's citizens.

One day, David found out that Absalom had gathered an army and was marching on Jerusalem. He and his family fled out of the city, with the royal bodyguard and some loyal troops. David left behind in the city five men who might help his cause: two of the priests, their sons and a wise old man named Hushai.

## David's Escape

2 Samuel 16–17

As David and his companions headed toward the Jordan River, one of Saul's relatives, Shimei, came out of a village along the way. He was cursing David, saying, "Off with you, you murderer! The Lord has made you pay for all the blood of Saul's family."

At this, Abishai, Joab's brother, said to the king, "Let me go over and chop off his head."

But the king said, "How does this concern me and you? My own son is trying

---

*A small country east of the River Jordan and Lake Chinnereth.*

to kill me. How much more, then, may a man of Benjamin! Give him no thought and let him curse, for the Lord has told him to. I hope the Lord will repay me with good."

Meanwhile, in Jerusalem, Absalom was consulting two advisors. One urged him to chase David at once. But the other—Hushai—gave many reasons for waiting. And because Absalom listened to Hushai, David and his companions were saved.

Then through the priests' sons, Ahimaaz and Jonathan, Hushai sent information to David about Absalom's plans. The young men had a close call at one point, but a woman hid them in a well, over which she spread a heavy cloth and some corn she was pounding to make flour. When the searchers were gone, Ahimaaz and Jonathan hurried on, caught up with David and urged him to cross the Jordan River before morning. He and all his companions did so.

At Mahanaim, on the other side of the Jordan, they were met by kind-hearted people bringing them beds and food.

## Death of Absalom

**2 Samuel 18–19**

Absalom and his army crossed the Jordan soon after David, and the two armies prepared for battle. David gave orders for Absalom to be taken alive. But Joab ignored the orders. He found Absalom hanging from a tree in which his long hair had gotten tangled. Absalom couldn't defend himself, and Joab killed him.

King David was deeply disturbed, and went up to the room above the city gate, where he broke down, saying, "My son Absalom! My son Absalom! If only I had died instead of you! Absalom, my son, my son!"

But Joab went to the king and said, "Come on! Get up, go out and calm your soldiers. If you don't, not a man will stay with you, and this will be worse for you than all the disasters that have happened to you until now."

So David went outside to greet his victorious troops.

Now, since Absalom was dead, many of the people of Judah who had supported the revolt started talking about bringing the king back. Word of this reached David, so he prepared to cross the Jordan and return to Jerusalem. He sent word ahead of him that he would forgive the other leaders of the plot.

So the citizens of Judah sent word to the king: "Come back, you and all your officials."

The king started on his way back and came as far as the Jordan. Shimei, the man of Benjamin, hurried down with the citizens of Judah to meet King David. When Shimei had crossed the Jordan, he fell down before the king and said, "Let my lord not hold any offense against me. Do not remember the wrong your servant did the day my lord the king left Jerusalem. Here I am today, the first of the whole House of Joseph to come down and meet my lord the king."

At this, Abishai said, "Shall not Shimei be put to death for this, for having cursed the anointed of the Lord?"

But David answered, "How does this concern me and you? Should anyone be

put to death today?" Then the king said to Shimei, "You shall not die."

## Return to Jerusalem

2 Samuel 20–24

Then the leaders of Israel also came to greet the king. They saw that the people of Judah were giving him such a warm welcome, and they wanted to make it clear that David was still king of Israel also. But then an argument started between the people of Judah and the people of Israel. And a new revolt began, led by a man of Benjamin named Sheba.

The people of Israel went away, following Sheba, while the people of Judah stayed with their king from the Jordan all the way to Jerusalem.

Back in Jerusalem, David sent troops out in pursuit of Sheba, who seemed to be even more dangerous than Absalom had been. They found out that Sheba had taken refuge in the city of Abel-beth-maacah. When the people realized that their city would be attacked if they continued to shelter Sheba, they killed him. The revolt was over.

David returned to Jerusalem, and little by little the unrest among the people settled down. Even though David continued to make mistakes, he tried to show his gratitude to God by ruling well.

# THE FIRST BOOK OF KINGS

The history of the kingdom built up by David continues in the *Books of Kings*. In *1 Kings* we see that David's son Solomon became a rich and powerful ruler. But the writer(s) of this history tell us that Solomon began to worship other gods and to take advantage of his position as king by treating his people unfairly. This led to a split between Judah and Israel. Each became a separate kingdom.

1 Kings 1–2

King David was old and had to stay in bed. It was time for one of his sons to take over. David sent for three of his trusted followers and told them to take his son Solomon down to the spring at the foot of the hill on which the city stood and anoint him king at that spot.

The priest Zadok went down with the prophet Nathan, as well as Benaiah son of Jehoiada and the royal guards. They had Solomon ride King David's own mule and led him to the spring of Gihon. The priest Zadok took the flask of oil from the tent of the ark and anointed Solomon. The trumpet was sounded and the whole crowd shouted, "Long live King Solomon!"

They went back up into the city, in the midst of joyful shouting. Solomon took his place on the royal throne, and David's officials promised him their loyalty.

When David was near death, he gave Solomon these orders: "Be brave and show that you are a man. Live according to God's ways, keeping his laws and commandments according to what is written in the Law of Moses. Then you will succeed in everything you do."

David joined his ancestors and was buried in the City of David.

## Solomon's Wisdom

1 Kings 3

The Lord appeared to Solomon in a dream at night and said, "What would you like? Ask me."

Solomon answered, "Lord my God, you have made me king in place of my father David. But being young, I have no experience at leading. I am at the center of your people—a people so great that no one can count them. So give your servant an understanding heart and keen mind to judge your people, to tell good from evil."

The Lord approved these words. He said to Solomon, "Since you have asked for this, and not for a long life for yourself, or for riches or for the lives of your enemies, but have asked for a keen mind to hear law cases, I have done just as you have said: I have granted you a wise and keen mind, so that no one like you has lived before you, and no one like you will come after you.

"But I have also granted you what you have not asked for—riches and glory—so that as long as you live no other king will compare with you."

# The Temple

1 Kings 5–9

The king had a temple built in Jerusalem so the ark of the covenant would have a more suitable resting place. The Temple was a magnificent building of cedar wood from Lebanon, overlaid with gold. It took seven years to build.

Then Solomon called the elders of Israel and all the tribal leaders to join him in Jerusalem to bring up the ark of the covenant from the City of David. The men of Israel gathered around the king, and the priests brought the ark of the Lord to the place for it in the Holy of Holies. Nothing was inside the ark except the two tablets of stone that Moses had placed there at Horeb, where the Lord had bound himself to the Israelites when they came out of the land of Egypt.

When the priests came out of the Holy Place, a cloud and the glory of the Lord filled the Lord's house.

Then, standing before the whole gathering, Solomon raised his hands toward heaven and said, "Lord, God of Israel, listen to the requests of your servant and of your people when they pray in this place."

Solomon then turned to the people and said, "Blessed be the Lord, who has granted peace to his people Israel! Stay with the Lord our God wholeheartedly, living according to his laws and keeping his commandments, as on this day."

## Solomon's Downfall

### 1 Kings 10–11

The queen of Sheba in Arabia came to visit Solomon to see whether everything she had heard about him was true. When she saw Solomon's wealth and listened to his wisdom in judging law-suits, she was completely amazed.

*But Solomon had gotten much of his wealth by taking advantage of the people. He collected very high taxes and made men work on his building projects without paying them. He also married foreign wives, who persuaded him to worship their gods.*

So the Lord said to Solomon, "Since you have kept neither my covenant nor the laws I have given you, I will tear the kingdom away from you and give it to an official of yours. Because of your father David, however, I won't do it in your lifetime. I will tear it out of the hands of your son. And, out of consideration for my ser-

vant David and for Jerusalem which I have chosen, I won't tear away the whole kingdom: I'll let your son have one tribe."

## The Revolt of Israel

### 1 Kings 12–15

And that was what happened. After Solomon's death his son Rehoboam was accepted by the people of Judah as their king. He was supposed to be proclaimed king by the tribes of Israel also, and went to Shechem, where the heads of the northern tribes had gathered. Their leader was Jeroboam son of Nebat, who had once been one of Solomon's officials.

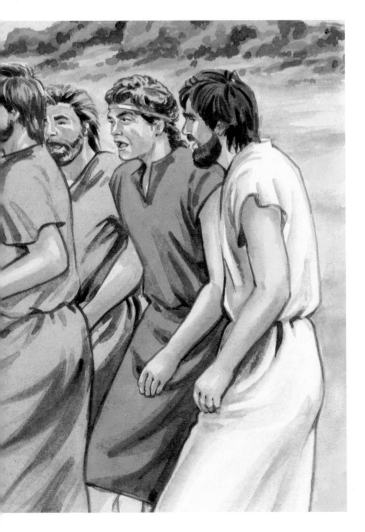

They said to Rehoboam, "Your father made our yoke heavier. Now lighten your father's hard labor and the heavy yoke that he placed on us, and we will be your people."

Rehoboam asked for three days to make a decision. Then he talked with the elders who had been officials of his father, Solomon. They advised him to be gentle and give in to the people's wishes.

But Rehoboam refused the advice the elders had given him, and talked with the men who had grown up with him. He asked, "What is your advice?"

They replied, "This is what you should tell them, 'My little finger is broader than my father's hips. So, if my father loaded you with a heavy yoke, I will add to your yoke. If my father used whips on you, I will use whips that are spiked.'"

When Jeroboam and the other leaders of Israel came back, Rehoboam repeated what his friends had told him to say. And the men of Israel walked out on him. Then they got together and chose Jeroboam to be their king.

Rehoboam wanted to declare war on the tribes that had broken away from him, but a wise man advised him and his friends not to fight the Israelites, who were "their brothers." This time, Rehoboam listened to wise advice.

Meanwhile, Jeroboam was worried about holding onto the northern tribes, which had made him their king.

Jeroboam said to himself, "With things as they are, the kingship could return to the House of David. If the people go up to offer sacrifices in the house of the Lord in Jerusalem, their affections for Rehoboam king of Judah will revive. They will murder me and go back to Rehoboam."

After thinking about this, King Jeroboam ordered workmen to make two young bulls of gold. He had shrines built for them—one near his southern border and the other in the north.

*This wasn't idol worship. Jeroboam seems to have thought of the bulls as thrones for the invisible God—just as the ark of the covenant was. These shrines were Jeroboam's way of keeping the people from going to Jerusalem.*

*But people began to think that the golden bulls were idols. As time went on, they forgot about the Lord.*

Years passed and the two nations continued to go their separate ways. In Judah, the kings always belonged to David's family, because of the promise God had made to David. In Israel, the ruling family changed often and there was much fighting for the throne. Even the capital city changed, until King Omri built the city of Samaria to be his capital.

## Elijah and the Prophets of Baal

**1 Kings 16–18**

Ahab son of Omri was king of Israel in Samaria for twenty-two years. He did what was evil in the eyes of the Lord. He married Jezebel, daughter of the king of Sidon, and went as far as to serve Baal and worship him.

*This was a serious situation for the northern kingdom. It was idol-worship. To help his people, God began to call people to be prophets, just as in earlier years he had called the judges. A prophet is a person who speaks for God.*

Elijah, a prophet from Gilead, invited Ahab to gather the four hundred and fifty prophets of Baal on Mount Carmel for a contest to show which god was the real God. Ahab agreed, and the prophets of Baal gathered on Mount Carmel, together with many other people.

Elijah came forward and said, "How much longer will you hop first on one leg, then on the other? If the Lord is God, stay with him; if Baal, stay with him." But the people did not answer.

So Elijah said to them, "I'm the only prophet of the Lord left, while there are four hundred and fifty prophets of Baal. Let two bulls be given us, and let them choose one of the bulls for themselves, cut it into pieces and put it on the wood, but without lighting any fire. And I'll prepare the other bull and put it on the wood, but without lighting any fire.

"You call on the name of your god, and I'll call on the name of the Lord. The god who answers with fire will be the real God."

"That's fine!" said the people.

Elijah invited the prophets of Baal to have the first turn.

They took the bull, prepared it, and called out to Baal from morning to noon, saying, "Baal, answer us!" But no one heard any answer.

At noon Elijah began to tease them. He said, "Call louder! He may be busy, or having a walk, or out on a journey. Maybe he's asleep."

They kept crying out until the hour of the evening sacrifice. Yet no one answered.

Then Elijah said to the people, "Come to me!" And the people came to him. He took twelve stones, corresponding to the number of the tribes of the sons of Jacob, and built those stones into an altar. Around the altar he dug a deep ditch. He arranged the wood, then cut the bull into pieces and placed them on the wood.

After that, he said, "Fill four buckets with water and pour it on the sacrifice and on the wood." He added, "Do it again." And they did it again.

"Do it a third time," he insisted. And they did it a third time. The water ran down all the sides of the altar. It even filled the ditch.

When the sacrifice was ready, Elijah came forward and said, "O Lord, today show that you are the God of Israel, that I am your prophet, and that it was by your order that I have done all these things. Let these people realize that you, Lord, are the real God. Turn their hearts back."

At this, the fire of the Lord rushed down from the sky and burned up the sacrifice, the wood, the stones and the dust. It even licked up the water from the ditch. All the people saw this and bowed to the ground as they said, "The Lord is the real God, the Lord is the real God!"

## Elijah Flees

**1 Kings 19**

But Ahab's queen, Jezebel, who supported the worship of Baal, sent word to Elijah that she was going to take revenge. Since Jezebel could send troops after him, Elijah left Israel, traveled through Judah, and headed south into the peninsula of Sinai.

At Mount Horeb (Mount Sinai), the Lord encouraged Elijah and told him to anoint Elisha son of Shaphat to be his successor as a prophet.

Elijah returned to Israel, followed the Lord's directions and found Elisha, a rich young farmer. Elijah went up to Elisha and threw his own cloak over him. This was a way of calling him to be his disciple. Elisha became Elijah's follower that very day.

# THE SECOND BOOK OF KINGS

*1* and *2 Kings* used to be just one book. *2 Kings* tells stories of the prophet Elisha and then continues the history of the northern and southern kingdoms—Israel and Judah.

In *2 Kings*, we will see Israel conquered by Assyria and its people scattered. Later we will see the people of Judah taken as prisoners to Babylon, capital city of a new enemy, Chaldea.

2 Kings 2–5

This is what happened when the Lord took Elijah into heaven in the whirlwind.

Elijah and his disciple, Elisha, were walking together, from one place to another. Elisha knew that soon the Lord would call Elijah to himself. Finally they reached the Jordan River.

Elijah took his cloak, made a bundle out of it, and struck the water. The water split open on both sides, and they both crossed over on dry ground. Once they were across, Elijah said to Elisha, "Ask for something I can do for you before I am taken away from you."

Elisha answered, "Let two thirds of your spirit come to me."

*This meant that Elisha wanted to inherit Elijah's ability to speak for God and work wonders, just as a son would inherit his father's property.*

He said, "You've asked something difficult. If you see me being taken away from you, you will have it. If not, you will not."

They were walking along, talking as they went, when suddenly a chariot of fire with horses of fire came between them, and Elijah went up to heaven in a whirlwind.

Elisha was watching, as he cried, "My father! My father! Chariot of Israel with its horses!"*

When Elisha did not see him anymore, he picked up Elijah's cloak, which had fallen off him, started back and stopped on the bank of the Jordan. He took the cloak and struck the water as he said, "Where is the Lord, the God of Elisha?" The water split open, and Elisha crossed over.

Elisha began to work miracles. One of the most famous stories about him tells about his cure of an Aramean general, Naaman. Naaman was not an Israelite. At times the Arameans (Syrians) were enemies of Israel.

After his cure, Naaman asked for a load of earth from Israel to take back to Aram with him.

*It was the belief in those times that gods were "local." Each country or region had its own god. Naaman wanted earth from Israel so he could offer sacrifices to Israel's God.*

---

*Elisha is calling Elijah the guide and protector of Israel.*

## King Ahaz and the Assyrians

2 Kings 16

Difficulties continued for both Israel and Judah. These two kingdoms were no longer powerful, like the kingdom of David and Solomon. And two strong nations, Egypt and Assyria, were conquering smaller countries and making their people serve them or pay them money.

King Ahaz of Judah was tempted to let his country serve Assyria rather than risk being conquered by Israel or Aram. Ahaz didn't trust the Lord to protect Judah. He wanted the protection of a powerful nation. Ahaz did not seem to care that to serve Assyria would also mean worshipping Assyria's gods instead of the Lord.

The prophet Isaiah tried to persuade Ahaz to trust in the Lord. But the result was disappointing.

Ahaz sent messengers to the king of Assyria with this message: "I am your servant and your son. March up and save me from the hands of the king of Aram and from the hands of the king of Israel, who have risen against me with weapons."

Ahaz, therefore, took silver and gold from the house of the Lord and the royal palace and sent them as a present to the king of Assyria. The king of Assyria paid attention to him. He marched on Damascus, captured it and sent it into captivity.

Then King Ahaz went to meet Tiglath-pileser, king of Assyria, in Damascus.

The Assyrians had already set up an altar there in the conquered city. Ahaz sent a model of it back to Jerusalem, so an altar could be built that was exactly like the Assyrian one.

When the king returned from Damascus, he gave orders that, from then on, this new altar, dedicated to pagan gods, would be the altar of sacrifice. The Temple of the Lord had become the temple of pagan gods!

## The Exile of Israel

2 Kings 17

In the twelfth year of Ahaz king of Judah, Hoshea son of Elah became king of Israel in Samaria. In the ninth year of Hoshea, the king of Assyria captured Samaria and led Israel captive into Assyria.

This happened because the Israelites had sinned against the Lord their God, who had brought them up from the land of Egypt. They were living according to the laws of the nations that the Lord had driven away at the coming of the Israelites.

Yet, the Lord had kept warning both Israel and Judah through every prophet, "Stop your wicked way of living and keep my commandments."

*When the Assyrians took away great numbers of the people of Israel and settled them in other lands, they also brought in other peoples and settled them in the territory of Israel. They did this to weaken the nations they had conquered, taking people from their own countries and mixing them with other peoples. This prevented any group from being united enough to revolt.*

The mixture of peoples whom the Assyrians placed in the territory of the old northern kingdom became known as Samaritans. They worshipped the Lord, but not completely the way the people of Judah did.

# King Hezekiah and the Assyrians

**2 Kings 18–19**

When Ahaz king of Judah died, his son Hezekiah became king. He was not at all like his father!

Hezekiah did what was right in the eyes of the Lord, exactly as his ancestor David had done. He put his trust in the Lord. He was attached to the Lord; he did not turn aside from him; he obeyed his commandments, the commandments the Lord had given to Moses.

The Lord was with him. He won victories in war. He stood up to the king of Assyria, and did not become his servant.

The Assyrian army came into Judah, and messengers went to speak with Hezekiah's officials outside Jerusalem. Because the people were looking down from the city wall and listening, the Assyrian commander shouted out in the people's own language.

"Hear the words of the great king, the king of Assyria: Don't let Hezekiah fool you, for he can't save you. Don't listen to Hezekiah, for he is fooling you when he says, 'the Lord will save us.'"

Hezekiah's officials brought him the message. The king did not send back an answer.

The Assyrian commander returned to his king, Sennacherib, who was several miles away with his army. Soon Sennacherib sent a threatening letter to Hezekiah.

"Let the God that you trust not fool you. You know what the kings of Assyria

have done to all the countries, vowing them to destruction. And are you supposed to be saved? Have the gods of the nations saved the countries that my father wiped out?"

Hezekiah received the letter from the messengers. After reading it, he went to the house of the Lord and prayed, "Save us from his hands, O Lord, our God, and let all kingdoms of the earth learn that you alone are God, O Lord!"

Through the prophet Isaiah, the Lord answered Hezekiah's prayer. Isaiah went to Hezekiah with God's message.

"Here is what the Lord says about the king of Assyria:

"'He shall not invade this city, not even shoot an arrow inside it. He shall go back the same way that he came, without having entered this city.'"

That night the angel of the Lord killed a hundred and eighty-five thousand men in the camp of Assyria. When the other men rose in the morning, they saw thousands of corpses. Seeing this, Sennacherib went back to Assyria.

# Manasseh and Josiah

**2 Kings 21–23**

When Hezekiah died, his son Manasseh became king after him. He did the opposite of what his father, Hezekiah, had done.

Manasseh led the people astray by doing evil. Besides the sins which he made Judah commit, Manasseh shed much innocent blood.

Amon, son of Manasseh, also did evil. But Amon's son, Josiah, sincerely tried to please the Lord.

The Temple needed repairs, so Josiah arranged for good workmen to take care of them. He sent Shaphan, one of his officials, to make sure that the workmen received their pay, as well as enough money to buy the materials they needed.

Hilkiah, the high priest, told Shaphan, "I've found the Book of the Law in the house of the Lord." And Hilkiah gave the book to Shaphan, who read it.*

Then Shaphan went and told the king the news. And Shaphan read the book aloud for the king.

When the king heard what was in the Book of the Law, he gave this instruction, "Go consult the Lord for me, for the people, for the whole of Judah about the things in this book that has been found, for the anger of the Lord must be great. Our ancestors failed to listen to the things in this book and to do everything written in it."

_____

*This was probably a manuscript of the* Book of Deuteronomy.

The king sent word for all the leaders of Judah and Jerusalem to meet with him. Then the king went up to the house of the Lord. With him were all the men of Judah and all the citizens of Jerusalem: the priests, the prophets and all the people, both small and great; and he read aloud the things in the book of the covenant found in the house of the Lord, for them to hear.

Then, in the presence of the Lord, the king made a covenant to follow the Lord and obey his commandments and laws with all their hearts and souls and to honor the terms of this covenant as written in the book. And all the people promised to live up to the covenant.

Josiah sent his servants throughout Judah to remove all the idols, altars and objects used for the worship of pagan gods. He even sent men to do the same in the land of the Samaritans—which had once belonged to Israel.

But although Josiah wanted to bring the people of Judah back to the Lord, something happened that put a stop to his projects.

In the land between the Tigris and Euphrates rivers, the Babylonians, or Chaldeans, had become very strong. They had already gotten free from the Assyrians and had begun to conquer parts of the Assyrian empire. Eventually they would conquer Assyria itself.

When Assyria was fighting against the Chaldeans in Aram, the Egyptian king sent troops to help the Assyrians. Because the Assyrians had always been so cruel, Josiah tried to block the path of the Egyptians.

Pharaoh Necho, king of Egypt, marched

up toward the river Euphrates, to support the king of Assyria. King Josiah marched out to stop him, but Necho killed Josiah at Megiddo.

Josiah's officers brought his body from Megiddo and took it to Jerusalem, where they buried him in his own tomb.

Then the people took Jehoahaz, son of Josiah, anointed him and announced that he was king in the place of his father.

Jehoahaz ruled in Jerusalem for three months. Then Pharaoh Necho put him in chains. He made Eliakim, son of Josiah, king and renamed him Jehoiakim, while he took Jehoahaz away to Egypt.

## The Triumph of Babylon

2 Kings 24–25

Jehoiakim ruled in Jerusalem for eleven years. He did evil in the sight of the Lord, the way his ancestors had done. This was when Nebuchadnezzar, king of Babylon, attacked, and Jehoiakim had to send large payments to him for three years.

When Jehoiakim joined his ancestors in the grave, his son, Jehoiachin, became king. Jehoiachin reigned in Jerusalem for three months.

At that time the officers of Nebuchadnezzar, king of Babylon, attacked Jerusalem, and the city came under siege. So Jehoiachin, king of Judah, surrendered to the king of Babylon—he himself with his mother, his officials and his officers. And the king of Babylon put him under arrest.

King Nebuchadnezzar carried away the treasures of the house of the Lord and all the treasures of the royal palace, and took apart all the furnishings of gold that Solomon, king of Israel, had caused to be made. He took Jerusalem into exile. No one was left in the country except the poor.

Nebuchadnezzar took King Jehoiachin into exile in Babylon, together with the king's mother, the king's wives and the powerful people of the country. He also brought seven thousand important people, plus craftsmen, smiths and warriors good for combat as exiles to Babylon.

The king of Babylon made Jehoiachin's uncle, Mattaniah, king in his place, and renamed him Zedekiah.

Zedekiah rebelled against the king of Babylon. As a result, in the tenth month of the ninth year of his rule, on the tenth day of that month, Nebuchadnezzar, king of Babylon, marched upon Jerusalem—he and his whole army. He set up camp beside it and built siegeworks all around it.

The city was under siege until the eleventh year of King Zedekiah. When hunger in the city was severe and the people of the land had no bread, the Chaldeans broke through the city wall. At this, all the soldiers of Judah fled by night through the gate in the angle of the two walls by the king's garden, although the Chaldeans were all around the city.

But the Chaldean troops chased after the king and caught up with him in the wasteland near Jericho. Then all his troops abandoned him. They seized the king and brought him to the king of Babylon, who had him bound in chains and brought to Babylon.

The captain of the bodyguard of the

king of Babylon burned down the house of the Lord and the houses of Jerusalem. Chaldean troops leveled the walls that had stood around Jerusalem. Then the captain led the rest of the people into captivity.

# THE FIRST AND SECOND BOOKS OF CHRONICLES

Up to this point, we have read parts of the Pentateuch, *Ruth*, and a series of six Historical Books that may have been written/edited by the person who wrote/edited *Deuteronomy*. (These books are: *Joshua, Judges, 1* and *2 Samuel, 1* and *2 Kings*.)

*1* and *2 Chronicles*, together with *Ezra* and *Nehemiah*, were written by another author. This author was very much interested in the worship of the Lord in the Temple and also in David as a great leader and a true worshipper of the Lord.

*1 Chronicles* begins with long lists of the early Israelites and their ancestors and ends with the death of David. *2 Chronicles* opens with the kingship of Solomon and closes with the defeat and destruction of Jerusalem (as in *2 Kings*), followed by a promise that people from Judah would someday return home to rebuild Jerusalem and the Temple.

1 Chronicles 28

David called together the leaders of Israel and said, "I wanted to build a house to honor the Lord my God. But the word of the Lord came to me with this message: 'You have been involved in many bloody wars. You should not build a house to honor me. Your son Solomon will build my house, for I have chosen him to be my son. I will be a father to him.'"

*This story of David is an example of what these two books contain. They often give information not found in the* Books of Samuel *and* Kings

*The* Books of Chronicles *also contain some stories that may not be accurate on every point but are important because of the bigger truths that they teach.*

*An example of this is a story about King Manasseh in* 2 Chronicles. *People really don't know whether Manasseh really changed his ways. But his story is important because it reminds us that God can bring good out of bad situations.*

## Manasseh's Change of Heart

2 Chronicles 33

The Lord spoke to Manasseh and his people, but they couldn't care less. So the Lord sent against them the soldiers of the Assyrian king. They captured Manasseh with large hooks, chained him and led him away.

Manasseh asked for the favor of the God of his ancestors, and prayed to him. God answered his prayer and brought him back to Jerusalem and to his position as king. So Manasseh realized that the Lord is God.

# THE BOOKS OF EZRA AND NEHEMIAH

Like *Samuel, Kings* and *Chronicles, Ezra* and *Nehemiah* were once one book. But unlike those other books, *Ezra* and *Nehemiah* may not be completely in the right time order. Although these books are based on writings from the fifth and fourth centuries B.C., some dates may not have been copied correctly. (Remember that for hundreds of years, the books of the Bible were copied by hand.)

In *Ezra* and *Nehemiah* Abraham's descendants are called by a different name. We have read about them first as "Israelites" and later as "people of Judah." Here, they are called "the Jews" or "the Jewish people." This name comes from "Judah." After their exile in Babylon, the people who returned to Judah were called Jews. Their ways of living their religion developed to help them face the difficulties of their times. The religion of the Jewish people after the Exile and even today is called "Judaism."

The books called *Ezra* and *Nehemiah* center around the problems that the Jewish people faced when they returned to Jerusalem from exile. The Samaritans and other peoples who were living in the area tried to prevent the Hebrews from practicing their religion. The heroes of these two books protected the people from their enemies and helped them to be faithful to the Lord, both in worship and in daily life.

*Many of the people of Judah who had been taken away to Babylon hoped to return to Jerusalem. The prophets Jeremiah and Ezekiel had encouraged them to hope for this. And at last Cyrus, a Persian general, conquered the Chaldeans. Cyrus told the peoples conquered by the Assyrians and Chaldeans that they could return to their own countries and worship their own gods. The Jewish people were included in this policy.*

Ezra 1–2

In the first year of Cyrus king of Persia the Lord stirred up the spirit of Cyrus, who sent this message throughout his empire: "The Lord, the God in heaven, has given me all kingdoms on earth. But he himself has given me an order to build him a house in Jerusalem, which is in Judah. If someone from his people is among you, may God

be with him and let him go up to Jerusalem and build the house of the Lord, the God of Israel."

So the heads of families of Judah and Benjamin, the priests and Levites, all those whose spirit God stirred up, got ready to go to build the house of the Lord in Jerusalem, and their neighbors helped them with articles of silver, with gold, goods and animals.

The returning exiles found their family homes in ruins and their fields overgrown with weeds and brush. They began building new homes and trying to plow the fields.

## The Temple

Ezra 3–7

The foundations of the Temple of the Lord were yet to be laid. So they contributed money for stone-workers and carpenters, and in the second month of the second year after they arrived, they set to work. When the builders had begun to lay the foundations of the Temple of the Lord, the priests with trumpets and the Levites with cymbals praised the Lord. And they sang the refrain: "For he is good, for his love for Israel is forever."

When the foundations of God's house were laid, many old priests, Levites and heads of families who had seen the former house, wept loudly, but many others raised joyful shouts.

However, the Samaritans, Ammonites and others tried to block the building of the Temple, and they succeeded for almost twenty years. Then the prophets Haggai and Zechariah urged the people to finish the construction. You might like to read what Haggai told the people.

When the Temple was finished, they held a joyful celebration.

Over half a century later, Ezra, a priest and an expert in the law of God, came from Babylon to instruct the people.

## Nehemiah

Nehemiah 1–4, 8

At some point—before or after Ezra—Nehemiah arrived, with the Persian king's permission, to protect his people from enemy attacks by rebuilding the walls of Jerusalem. Nehemiah kept his plans secret until it was time to begin the project. He didn't want Sanballat, governor of Samaria or Tobiah, governor of Ammon, to know what was happening, since they had already been making trouble.

One day, the people set to work all together, each on a particular section of the wall. In the book named after him, Nehemiah describes what happened.

When Sanballat learned that we were rebuilding the wall, he flared up with anger, and began to laugh. And Tobiah the Ammonite, said, "Even if they were to rebuild it, if a fox were to climb up, it would tear down their stone wall."

The wall had been built up to half its height when Sanballat, Tobiah, the Arabs, the Ammonites and the Ashdodites plotted together to come and attack Jerusalem. At this, we prayed to our God. Then, for fear of them, we set a guard to protect the workers.

When the Samaritans and others learned that the people were waiting behind the wall with bows, swords and spears, they decided not to attack.

All of us returned to the wall, each one to his own work. But from that day on, half of my men were busy with the work, and half of them, wearing breastplates, were holding spears, shields or bows.

The wall was finished in fifty-two days. When all our enemies heard of it, all the nations around us were amazed, for they realized that this work had been God's doing.

Gates were built for the city, and at last the people felt safe inside it.

One day the people gathered to hear Ezra instruct them in God's law. When the law was read to them, they realized that they had not kept it well. They began to weep.

All the people were in tears as they had heard the precepts of the Law. So Nehemiah, the governor, Ezra, the priest, and the Levites who were teaching the people told them, "Today is holy to the Lord your God: you mustn't be sad or cry."

*It was a new beginning for the Jewish people. Instead of being united in serving a king, they were united in serving the Lord, as in the days of Joshua.*

# THE BOOK OF TOBIT

*Tobit* is a story about the family of a good-living Israelite who had been taken to Nineveh by the Assyrians and became a good servant of the Assyrian king, while he also stayed loyal and kind toward his fellow Israelites. The purpose of the story is to show that God is pleased with people who help others.

As the book opens, Tobit introduces himself, his wife Anna and his son Tobiah. The focus of the story then moves to Tobit's cousin Sarah and back to young Tobiah. But the real hero of the *Book of Tobit* is the archangel Raphael, whose name means "medicine of God."

Tobit 1–3

After I had been captured by the Assyrians, when I was brought away into exile I came to Nineveh. Since I kept my heart set on my God, he granted me favor in the eyes of Shalmaneser. I used to buy all sorts of things that the king needed. In fact, I used to travel to Media and buy things for him there, until he died; and in Media I gave some bags containing ten talents of silver to Gabael, to keep for me.

I gave money to my people many times. I gave my bread to the hungry and my clothes to the naked. Whenever I saw some fellow Israelite dead and thrown behind the wall of Nineveh, I would bury him.

Gradually Tobit became blind from a white film that had formed in his eyes. These new troubles had an effect on his disposition. He became suspicious and short tempered.

By then my wife Anna was working for hire, making cloth for women. One day, she finished weaving and sent the cloth to the people who had ordered it. They gave her full pay and added a kid goat for the family meal. When she came into the house, the kid began to bleat. So I called to her and asked, "Where has this little kid come from? It may be stolen property. Give it back to its owners, for we have no right to eat anything stolen."

She answered, "It has been given to me as a gift on top of my wages." But I would not believe her, and insisted that it should be given back to its owners.

Then she said to me, "Now, where are your good deeds? Where, your works of mercy? How miserably you are doing!"

My heart sank into sorrow and I broke down with moans. Then I began to pray with groanings:

"You are just, Lord, and so are all your actions. All your ways are love and faithfulness. So, Lord, you must be concerned about me, for I prefer death to life, since I have been insulted. Lord, let me leave for the final dwelling place, for I would rather die than live and experience such torment."

On the same day Sarah, the daughter

of Raguel, a relative of Tobit's, was also insulted. One of her maid-servants accused her of having killed each of the seven young men who had married her one after another. These young men had been killed by a demon—each of them on the night of their wedding. Sarah, too, prayed to die rather than to live with insults.

Both prayers were heard by God, and Raphael was sent to bring healing to both of them.

## Tobiah Starts on His Journey

**Tobit 4–6**

Tobit remembered the money that he had left with Gabael at Rages in Media, and said to himself, "I have just prayed for death. Why not call my son Tobiah and tell him about this money before I die?"

So he called his son Tobiah and said, "Bury me with dignity. Give your mother an honorable life and do not abandon her as long as she lives; do what she likes and never sadden her in anything.

"Do works of mercy as long as you live and don't walk paths of wickedness, for people who act faithfully will succeed in what they do, and to those who do what is right the Lord gives good things.

"And now, my son, I will tell you that I have entrusted ten talents of silver to the keeping of Gabael, Gabri's brother, at Rages in Media. Look for some reliable person to travel with you. We will pay him when you come back. Go and get that money."

Tobiah went out to look for a traveling companion and came back almost at once with a young man who called himself Azariah. Tobiah did not know that this young man was really the archangel Raphael.

Tobit questioned "Azariah" and was pleased with his answers.

Then Tobit sent them on their way, asking God to bless them.

Tobiah kissed his parents good-bye and set out with the angel and the family dog. That evening they camped by the river Tigris.

Tobiah went down to the river to wash his feet. When a huge fish leaped up from the water as if to swallow his foot, he screamed. But the angel told him, "Grab the fish and get control of it!" So Tobiah grabbed the fish and pulled it up on the land. Then the angel said to him, "Break the fish open and take out its gall, heart and liver. They come in handy as medicine." Tobiah broke the fish open and collected the gall, heart and liver. Then he roasted and ate part of the fish. He salted the rest.

The two of them traveled on until they drew near to Media. Then Tobiah asked, "Brother Azariah, what kind of medicine is contained in the heart and liver of the fish, and particularly in the gall?"

He answered him, "If you burn the heart and liver in the presence of a man or woman bothered by a demon or evil spirit, the trouble will disappear. The person will be free from it forever. As for the gall, if you smear it on someone's eyes that have a white film on them and blow on the film, the person will be cured."

## Tobiah Meets Sarah

**Tobit 7–9**

When he had entered Media, Raphael said, "Brother Tobiah, tonight we will stop over at Raguel's. This man is a relative of yours and has a daughter named Sarah. She is his only child, and you, rather than any other man, are her closest relative with the right to marry her. The girl is level-headed, brave, and very beautiful; her father is an honorable person."

*Raphael suggested marriage because at that time it was the custom for relatives to marry, in order to keep property within the same family.*

But Tobiah protested. Even though he had never met Raguel or Sarah, he had heard about her and about the seven bridegrooms who had died on their wedding night. He was afraid to take the risk.

"I am the only son my father has," he said. "I refuse to die and thus bring my father and mother down to the grave in grief over me."

Raphael answered, "Don't think about this demon anymore. Marry her, for I know that she will be given to you as your wife tonight. When you go into the bridal chamber, take some of the liver and heart from the fish and put them on the incense that will be burning there. The odor will spread, and when the demon smells it, he will leave and never again come near her. Then pray, both of you, asking the Lord to have mercy on you and keep you safe."

Tobiah felt better then. In fact, by now he was eager to meet Sarah.

Raguel, his wife Edna and their daughter Sarah were happy to meet Tobiah also. They prepared a big meal for the two travelers.

Before they began to eat, Tobiah asked Raguel to let him marry Sarah. Raguel warned him about what had happened to the other bridegrooms. But Tobiah insisted.

So Raguel called his daughter to him. He took her by the hand and gave her to Tobiah, saying, "Receive her according to the Law. May the Lord give both of you peace and good things."

Then he ordered a sheet of paper to be brought and he wrote out the marriage certificate. After that, they began to eat and drink.

That night, when Tobiah and Sarah were alone, Tobiah did as Raphael had told him. He took the liver and heart of the fish out of the bag he was carrying and placed them on the incense that was burning in the bedroom. Then he and Sarah stood and prayed to the Lord, asking him to bless them and let them grow old together.

Meanwhile, Raguel and some of his servants had gone outside to dig a grave for Tobiah!

In the morning Tobiah and Sarah were

both in good health, so Raguel held a wedding party for them—which, according to custom, lasted two weeks. Since Tobiah knew that his father would be worrying, he asked Raphael to go on to Rages. Raphael did so and came back not only with the money but also with Gabael himself, who wanted to meet his young cousin.

## Happy Homecoming

**Tobit 11**

After the close of the fourteen-day wedding celebration, Raguel gave to Tobiah his wife Sarah and half of all his own possessions. "Farewell, my son!" he said. "Go your way safe and sound. May the Lord give happiness to you and to your wife Sarah, and may I see your children before I die."

So Tobiah set out from Raguel's house, full of joy, blessing the Lord of heaven and earth for having turned his journey into such a success.

When they had come close to Nineveh, Raphael suggested that they hurry ahead to greet Tobit, leaving Sarah and her servants to travel more slowly.

Anna was sitting down, gazing along the route her son had taken. She saw him coming and said to his father, "Here he is! Your son is coming with the man who went with him."

Before Tobiah reached his father, Raphael said, "I feel sure that his eyes will be opened. Plaster them with the gall of the fish. The remedy will shrink and thus peel off the white spots from his eyes, so your father will recover his sight."

Anna hurried up and, hugging her son, said to him, "I have seen you, my son! Now I can die." And she wept. Tobit came stumbling out of the courtyard door.

Tobiah went up to his father and applied the remedy as Raphael had told him to do. Tobit could see again!

He threw himself on Tobiah's neck and in tears said to him, "I have seen you, my son, the light of my eyes!"

Tobiah told his father that his journey had been a success, that he had brought the money, that he had married Sarah daughter of Raguel, and that Sarah was about to arrive— she was already at the gates of Nineveh.

Full of joy and blessing God, Tobit set out for the gates of Nineveh to meet his daughter-in-law. The citizens were amazed to see him walking and moving about in all his strength with no one leading him by the hand. Tobit told them that God had been merciful to him and had opened his eyes.

Tobit came up to Sarah and blessed her, saying, "Welcome, my daughter! Worthy of praise is God who brought you to us!"

That was a day of celebration for all the Jewish people of Nineveh.

## Raphael Reveals Himself

**Tobit 12–13**

When all the celebrations were over, Tobit called Raphael, in order to pay him what he deserved for all he had done for them. But they were in for a surprise.

Raphael said, "I'll tell you the whole truth without hiding anything from you.

At one and the same time God assigned me to heal both you and your daughter-in-law Sarah. I am Raphael, one of the seven angels who wait on the Lord."

At this, the two of them were amazed and bowed down before him. But he said to them, "Don't be afraid. Peace to you! Praise the Lord on earth and give recognition to God. I am about to return to the One who sent me."

With that, he rose above them, and they couldn't see him anymore. Then they began to praise God and to thank him for his great deeds.

# THE BOOK OF JUDITH

The *Book of Judith* is another story with a message. This message is the greatness of God's love and power.

Many of the details of this story do not seem to match the history and geography of the Holy Land. They seem to be *symbols,* telling us truths that are not related to historical facts. For example, the enemy army comes from *Assyria,* one of the cruelest nations of ancient times. (Assyria was the nation that conquered Israel, the northern kingdom.) But the enemy king is called *Nebuchadnezzar.* That was the name of a cruel ruler of the Babylonian empire. In this book, "Assyria" and "Nebuchadnezzar" are symbols of evil. Judith is also a symbol. The name "Judith" means "Jewish woman." The message is that with God's help people can defeat the powers of evil.

The story of Judith reminds us of the Israelites' victory at the time of Deborah. The enemy commander was killed by a woman. Since women aren't usually as strong as men physically, this kind of victory shows God's power acting to save his people.

*As the story opens, Nebuchadnezzar asks various peoples—including the Jewish people—to help him fight a war. But they refuse. So after Nebuchadnezzar has won the war, he sends an army under a general named Holofernes to destroy the Jewish people unless they surrender to Assyria. Among the cities to attack is Bethulia, described as being on a mountain overlooking a plain near Dothan.*

**Judith 2–7**

Holofernes commanded his army to close in upon Bethulia so as to first capture the routes into the hill country and then fight the Israelites. In the narrow valley near Bethulia they advanced as far as the spring.*

---

*\*The spring was part of the people's water supply. The enemy intended to cut off this supply.*

The Israelites were greatly disturbed at the sight of the great numbers of Assyrians. Each man took up his fighting gear. They lit signal fires on their towers and stayed alert all through the night.

On the second day Holofernes had all his mounted soldiers spread out below the Israelites in Bethulia. Then he began to check out the paths leading up to the city, making a tour of the springs and taking charge of them.

The Assyrians did not try to attack the city. They took the easier course of waiting for the citizens of Bethulia to surrender or die of thirst.

The Assyrian foot-soldiers, chariots and horsemen stayed camped around the city for thirty-four days, so the people of Bethulia were left with no water.

Then the people, including young men, women and children, gathered before the leaders of the city, and cried out at the top of their voices, "Let God judge between you and us about how you have hurt us by refusing to talk peace with the Assyrians. Invite them in. Yes, we will become slaves, but our lives will be spared and we will not have to see the death of our infants, wives and children." Then they cried out loudly to the Lord God.

Uzziah (the ruler of the city) said to them, "Cheer up, brothers! We will hold on for five more days. In these days the Lord our God will certainly turn his mercy to us once again.

"But if we are given no help before these days are up, I will do as you say."

## Judith Turns to the Lord

**Judith 8–9**

What Uzziah had told the people was reported to Judith. She was a widow—young and religious.

Judith was very beautiful. Her husband Manasseh had given her gold and silver, servants and maids, livestock and lands. No one could say anything bad about her, for she had great reverence for God.

Judith sent one of her maid-servants to call the leaders of the city. When they arrived, Judith told Uzziah that she was disturbed by what he had said. It was almost like commanding God, Judith reminded the leaders.

"Who do you think you are—to be laying down conditions for God? Let's call on him to help us while we wait with trust.

"Tonight wait at the gate. I'll go out with my maid, and the Lord will visit Israel through my hand. But you mustn't ask what I am planning, for I won't tell you anything before what I'm going to do has been done."

Uzziah and the leaders replied, "May you go in peace, and may the Lord God go before you." Then they left her and went back to their posts.

On her part, Judith prayed, crying out to the Lord with a powerful voice:

"My God, my God, listen to me, to this widow! Look at the Assyrians! Yes, they feel powerful with their army: they brag about their horses and riders. They rely on their shields, spears, bows and slings. Yet, they do not recognize that you are the Lord who crushes wars.

"Give my hands the strength I want. Your strength doesn't consist in great numbers. Far from it—you are God to the lowly, helper to the oppressed, protector to the powerless, shelter to the outcast, savior of those without hope.

"Lord of heaven and earth, King of your whole creation, you are the God of all power and might, and there is no one else, except you."

## Judith Carries Out Her Plan

**Judith 10–16**

Then Judith made herself as beautiful as possible with makeup and jewelry. She and her maid-servant set out for the city gates. By now it was night.

The city leaders waiting at the gates were very much impressed by her beauty and prayed that the Lord would help her accomplish whatever she intended. Then the gates were opened, and Judith walked down towards the valley with her maid.

An advance guard of the Assyrians came to meet her. They asked, "What people are you from? Where are you going?"

She replied, "I am Jewish, but I am fleeing from them because they are sure to be conquered by you. So I come to appear in person before Holofernes, to give him information and let him know how he can conquer the whole hill country without losing any of his men."

Some of the soldiers escorted Judith and her maid to Holofernes' tent. When Judith appeared in front of him and his aides, they all marveled at her beauty. Holofernes said to her, "Feel comfortable, woman. Don't be afraid, for I have never

been harsh with anyone who has chosen to submit to Nebuchadnezzar, king of all the earth."

After flattering Holofernes, Judith told him that in a few days he should be able to safely attack the city of Bethulia. She said she would pray to God every night around midnight near the spring below the city and would let Holofernes know when the time was right to attack. Holofernes agreed.

So Judith and her maid-servant spent each day in the tent that Holofernes had given to them. Every night, around midnight, they would leave the camp and go to pray at the spring. The maid-servant always carried a bag for food, since Judith had explained that as Jewish women they could eat only certain foods that they prepared themselves. The soldiers did not question them, because

Holofernes had given orders to leave them alone.

On the fourth day Holofernes gave a banquet for his chief officers and asked Judith to join them. The meal lasted several hours, and Holofernes became very drunk. His men carried him into the section of his tent that he used as a bedroom. All the officers left. Only Judith and her maid remained. Judith prayed and entered the sleeping area.

Judith went to the bedpost that was close to Holofernes' head and took down his sword. She came near the bed, grasped his head by the hair, and said, "God of Israel, give me strength!" With that, she struck his neck twice with all her strength and cut his head from his body.

She came out and handed Holofernes' head to her maid, who put it into the bag she was carrying. Both of them went out together, as they usually did for prayer. After passing the edge of the camp, they headed uphill for Bethulia.

Judith shouted to the guards, "Open the gate! God, our God, is with us! He still acts with strength in Israel!"

As the watchmen heard her voice, they rushed down to the gate and called the city leaders.

In a loud voice, Judith said to them, "Praise God—give praise! Praise the God who this very night has smashed our enemies by my hand."

Then she showed them the head, which she took out of the bag, saying, "Here is the head of Holofernes, commander-in-chief of the Assyrian army. It was by the hand of a woman that the Lord

struck him! Certainly, my appearance led him to his ruin, but he committed no sin with me."

Amazed, the people bowed down in adoration of God and said with one spirit, "Blessed are you, our God, who this very day have destroyed the enemies of your people!"

Judith said, "Brothers, listen to me! Take this head and hang it on the walls. And when the sun has risen, pretend that you are getting ready to march down toward the plain against the Assyrians. They will go to the camp to awaken the commanders of their army, who will rush into Holofernes' tent. Since they won't find him, they will be filled with panic."

They did as Judith suggested. The Assyrians' second in command went to tell Holofernes.

He found him dead, with his head gone. At this, he screamed as he burst into tears, sobs and cries. Then he went into the tent where Judith had been staying and did not find her. So he rushed out and shouted, "Those slaves have deceived us! One Jewish woman has shamed the House of Nebuchadnezzar. Holofernes is lying there on the ground, but without his head."

When the leaders of the Assyrian army heard the news, their morale was badly shaken. And their wailing rose strongly throughout the camp.

The ordinary soldiers were amazed when they heard what had happened and began to run, fleeing along every path. The Israelites rushed after them like a river.

Uzziah sent messengers to nearby cities, and all their men, too, went out to chase the Assyrians. It was a complete victory.

Joakim, the high priest, and the leaders who lived in Jerusalem came to see the good things that the Lord had done for Israel, and especially to meet Judith.

When they saw her, they all blessed her with one voice as they said, "You are the glory of Jerusalem, the great pride of Israel, the great joy of our people. You have done all this by your own hand—you have done good for Israel—and God has been pleased by this. May you be blessed by the almighty Lord forever."

And all the people answered, "Amen!"

The women flocked to see her. They blessed her, and some of them danced for her. Then, leading all the women as they danced, she marched at the head of a procession, while the men of Israel followed, carrying their weapons.

As they marched, Judith led them in a song of thanksgiving to God. They walked all the way to Jerusalem, where they offered sacrifices of thanksgiving to the Lord.

For three months, the people celebrated at the Temple in Jerusalem, and Judith stayed with them.

At the end of this time everyone returned home, and Judith went to Bethulia, where she was shown honor throughout her life. She died in Bethulia after having set her maid-servant free and was buried in the burial cave of her husband Manasseh.

During Judith's lifetime and for many years after her death, no one terrorized the Israelites again.

# THE BOOK OF ESTHER

Like *Tobit* and *Judith*, the *Book of Esther* is more concerned with telling a story than with giving historical data. One important message of the story is that if people have a great need for help that only we can give, we have a responsibility to do what we can.

The story takes place in Susa, a leading city of the Persian empire. The king seems to be the ruler whom history calls Xerxes I. It is uncertain how many of the other persons in the story really existed, but the author did know something about the Persian empire, which makes a colorful background for Esther's act of courage.

Esther 1–2

The Persian king, Xerxes, decided to replace his queen, since she had disobeyed him. He gave orders for hundreds of young women to be brought to his palace, so he might choose a new queen. The girl he chose was Esther, an orphan who had been raised by her cousin Mordecai, a palace official. Mordecai told Esther not to let anyone know she was Jewish—in other words, a foreigner.

In those days, two officers of the palace guard planned to harm King Xerxes. Mordecai learned about this and told Queen Esther, who informed the king for Mordecai. When the report was checked out and found to be true, the two men were hanged on a gallows tree, and the event was written down in the records of the kingdom.

## Haman Seeks Revenge

Esther 3–4

Later on, King Xerxes gave power to Haman, a descendant of Agag, by giving him a rank above all his companions. All royal officials knelt and bowed down to Haman, because this was the order that the king had given about him. But Mordecai would not kneel and bow down.

This made Haman very angry. When he found out that Mordecai was Jewish, he decided to have all the Jewish people in the Persian empire killed. He and his friends cast lots to choose a day for this to happen. The lot fell to the thirteenth day of the twelfth month. Then Haman went to convince the king that all Jews should be killed.

Haman said to King Xerxes, "In all the provinces of your kingdom there lives a people different from all others because of their laws. They do not follow the laws of the king. If it is the king's pleasure, let it be written that they have to be destroyed."

The king took off the ring with his seal on it and gave it to Haman, saying, "The people must be treated as you think best."

On the thirteenth day of the first month, everything that Haman commanded was written to the governors of all the provinces and to the leaders of all the people. This was written in the name of King Xerxes and sealed with the royal signet ring. So, through messengers, letters were sent to all provinces of the king ordering the death of all Jews, young and old, including children and women, on one day: the thirteenth day of the twelfth month.

Meanwhile, the law was made public in the palace of Susa, where the king and Haman sat down to drink as the city of Susa went into a state of shock.

Mordecai came to know everything that had been plotted. He put on sackcloth and ashes and went out into the midst of the city, raising his voice in a loud, bitter cry.

Word of the letter had not reached Queen Esther, but she learned from her servants that Mordecai was wearing sackcloth. This meant that something serious had happened.

Esther sent Hathach, one of her menservants, to ask Mordecai what was wrong. When Hathach returned, he told her what had happened and gave her a copy of the letter. He also told Esther that Mordecai wanted her to pray for help and then speak to the king, in an attempt to save her people from death.

Then Esther sent Hathach back to Mordecai with this message: "All the king's servants and all the people in the king's provinces know that for any man or woman who goes in to the king in the inner courtyard without being invited, there is only one law—death. The only exception is when the king reaches out toward someone with his scepter; that person will live. For thirty days I have not been invited to go in to the king."

Esther's words were reported to Mordecai. Mordecai ordered this answer to be brought back to Esther: "Don't think you will escape just because you live in the royal palace. If you don't say anything at a time like this, rescue for the Jews will come from somewhere else, but you yourself will die. Who knows? Perhaps you became queen exactly for a time like this."

Then Esther ordered this answer to be brought back to Mordecai: "Go and gather all the Jews in Susa. You must fast for me: you must not eat anything day and night for three days. I, too, will fast with my maid-servants in the same way. After this, I will go in to the king, although it is not according to the law. If I die, I die."

## Esther Approaches the King

**Esther C–D, 5**

Mordecai did as Esther had directed him. He prayed to the Lord, saying, "Lord King, you rule over everything and you know everything. You know, Lord, that it was not out of pride or love of glory that I refused to bow to proud Haman. No, I acted this way so as not to place the honor given to a man above the honor given to God. And now, God of Abraham, have mercy on your people."

All Israel cried out with all their strength, for their death was before their very eyes.

Queen Esther, too, turned to the Lord for security: "My Lord, you are our King, you alone! Help me, for I am alone and have no helper other than you. I am going to take my life in my hands.

"Make yourself known at this time of trouble. King of gods and holder of all power, give me courage in the presence of the lion. Put gracious words into my mouth and change his sympathies for our enemy into hatred, so that Haman may be destroyed along with everyone who thinks the same way he does."

On the third day, after she had prayed, she took off the clothes she had worn for prayer and put on fine garments. She took two maid servants with her, leaning on one while the other followed, lifting her train. She was blushing slightly and had never looked more beautiful. But she was very much afraid.

After going through one door after another, she came before the king. He was seated on his royal throne, wearing his full robes of state, which were covered with gold and precious stones. When he lifted his head, his face was red with the reflection of the jewels, and he glared at Esther in anger.

At this, the queen turned pale and fainted, collapsing onto the maid beside her. But God changed the king's feelings into tenderness, so that he jumped up from his throne and took her in his arms until she came around. Then he began to calm her, asking, "What happened, Esther? I'm your brother. Don't be afraid! You won't die, for our order is for ordinary people. Come closer." Then he raised the golden scepter, rested it on her neck, kissed her, and said, "Tell me."

Then she said to him, "My lord, I saw you looking like an angel of God, and my heart hesitated with fear, for you are im-

pressive, my lord—yet your face is full of kindness."

"What's bothering you, Queen Esther?" the king asked. "Even if you ask for as much as half the kingdom, it shall be given to you."

Esther answered, "If it is the king's pleasure, let the king come today with Haman to a banquet I have prepared."

The king answered, "Fetch Haman quickly to respond to Esther's wish."

So with Haman the king attended the banquet which Esther had prepared. Over the wine the king said to Esther, "Whatever you ask shall be given to you."

In answer Esther invited the king and Haman to a second banquet, which would take place on the next day.

Haman went out full of joy. But as soon as he saw Mordecai in the outer courtyard, Haman was seized by a fit of anger.

Haman went home and boasted to his wife and friends about the banquet to which the queen had invited only two persons—the king and himself.

"But all this is not enough for me," he said, "as long as I see Mordecai around."

His wife and friends said to him, "Let a seventy-five foot gallows be prepared, and tomorrow say to the king, 'Let Mordecai be hanged on it.' Then go with joy to the banquet with the king." The proposal met with Haman's approval, and he had the gallows tree prepared.

## Honors for Mordecai

**Esther 6**

That night the king wasn't able to sleep, so he ordered the history of his years of rule to be brought and read to him. It

was recorded there how Mordecai had alerted the palace about two officials who were planning to harm the king. At this, the king asked, "Was anything done to honor Mordecai for this?"

"Nothing has been done for him," the servants answered.

"Who is out there in the courtyard?" the king asked.

Haman had come into the outer courtyard to tell the king that Mordecai should be hanged. So the king's servants answered, "Haman is here, waiting in the courtyard."

The king ordered them to let him in. Then the king asked Haman, "What should be done for a man whom the king wants to honor?"

Haman thought to himself: "Whom else can the king want to honor except me?"

Haman told the king that the person to be honored should be allowed to wear some of the king's finest clothes and a royal crown. He should be seated on the king's favorite horse and led through the streets by one of the king's highest officials, who would shout: "This is how a man is treated when the king wants to honor him."

Then the king said to Haman, "Right away take the fine clothing and the horse, as you have said, and do this for Mordecai. Don't leave out anything of what you have said."

So Haman took the fine clothing and the horse, had Mordecai dressed up, led him through the city square, and called out before him, "This is how a man is treated when the king wants to honor him."

Later in the day, a very sad Haman returned to the palace for the banquet prepared by Queen Esther.

## The Jews Are Saved

**Esther 7–9**

On this day, too, the king told Esther, "Whatever you ask, Queen Esther, it shall be granted."

Then Queen Esther said, "O King, if I am in your good favor, and if it is your pleasure, let me be granted my own life, and my people's lives. For I myself and my people are to be destroyed."

At this, King Xerxes asked Queen Esther, "Who and where is the person that intends to do this?"

Esther answered, "The enemy is this wicked Haman."

The king was furious. When his servants told him that Haman had built a tall gallows tree for Mordecai, the king told them to hang Haman himself on it.

That same day the king took off his signet ring, which he had gotten back from Haman, and gave it to Mordecai.

There was still the decree against the Jewish people to deal with. According to law it could not be changed or done away with. All the king could do was ask people to help the Jews fight back. So King Xerxes left Mordecai and Esther free to write whatever document they felt would undo the effects of the original letter and to seal it with the king's seal. This they did.

*The* Book of Esther *states that this was the origin of the Jewish feast day called Purim. Its name comes from the Persian word for lots—since lots had been cast by the enemies of the Jews in order to establish that date.*

# THE FIRST BOOK OF MACCABEES

*1* and *2 Maccabees* are the last Historical Books of the Catholic Old Testament. They tell about events that happened around two hundred years before Jesus' death and resurrection. Their name comes from an important person in both books: Judas Maccabeus. "Maccabeus" was Judas' nickname. It means "hammer."

During the years of the Persian empire, the Jewish people had enjoyed peace. But in the fourth century B.C., the Greek army, led by Alexander the Great, conquered the Persian empire and Egypt. Alexander died young, and the generals of his army took over the lands they had conquered.

For about 130 years the Jews were governed by the Greek rulers of Egypt. They were free to follow their own religion, as they had been under the Persians. But when the Jews came under the control of the Greek kings of Syria, things changed. One king in particular—Antiochus IV—wanted to force the Jews to give up all their religious beliefs, laws and acts of worship and to adopt those of the Greeks. Some Jewish people were willing to do this, but others stayed loyal to their religion. Great trouble began.

*1 Maccabees* tells about the wars that the loyal Jews fought to free themselves from the persecution of the kings of Syria.

After defeating Egypt, Antiochus marched against Israel. He went up to Jerusalem with many troops and boldly made his way into the Temple. He took away the golden altar, the seven-branched candlestick, the table for the sacred bread, the bowls, the cups, the golden censers and the golden decorations that had been over the front of the sanctuary. Then he set out for his own country, taking everything with him.

There was great sorrow throughout Israel.

After two years the king sent one of his commanders to Judah. He arrived in Jerusalem with many troops and spoke in such a friendly way that the people trusted him. But suddenly the troops attacked the city and killed many of the people. They looted the city, set it on fire, and tore down its buildings and the walls around it. Women and children were taken captive.

Then King Antiochus told his entire empire that they were all to become one people, so each nation was to give up its own customs.

The king sent messengers to announce in Jerusalem and in all the cities of Judah that people were not to offer sacrifices in the Temple, or to rest and worship on the Lord's day or to keep copies of the law of the Lord in their homes.

The king also gave orders for the Greek god Zeus to be worshipped in the Temple. He said that the people were to be forced to eat pork and other foods forbidden by their religion. Throughout the country, sacrifices had to be offered to Greek gods.

But many people in Israel stood firm, and refused to eat unclean things. They were willing to die—and they did die. Terrible sufferings had come upon Israel.

## Mattathias and His Sons

**1 Maccabees 2**

It was at that time that Mattathias left Jerusalem and went to live in Modein. Mattathias was a priest and the father of five sons: John, Simon, Judas, Eleazar and Jonathan.

The king's officers who were forcing the Jews to worship pagan gods came to the town of Modein to have people offer sacrifices. Many Israelites came forward to them, but Mattathias and his sons kept back. Then the king's officers said to Mattathias, "You are a leading citizen in this town. So be the first to come forward and obey the king's command. You and your family shall be honored with silver, gold and many rewards."

In answer, Mattathias cried out, "Even if all the nations under the king listen to him and break away from the religion of their ancestors, I with my sons and brothers will live according to the covenant of our ancestors. May heaven help us and keep us from breaking with the Law and the commandments! We will not obey the king's orders."

He had just finished speaking, when another Jew came forward to offer sacrifice on the altar in Modein, in accord with the king's command. When he saw this, Mattathias burned with zeal. Rushing forward, he killed him at the altar. He also killed the king's officer who was forcing the sacrifice, and he pulled down the altar.

Then Mattathias shouted out, "Let everyone who loves the Law and supports the covenant follow me." With that, he and his sons headed for the mountains, leaving everything they owned behind in the town.

Many men, women and children who wanted to be faithful to their religion went out into the wastelands, with the idea of living in caves.

The king's men, as well as the troops stationed in the City of David inside Jerusalem, were told that people who would not obey the king's command had gone to hideouts in the desert. So they rushed after them, and when they found them, they took up battle positions, to fight with them on the Sabbath. They warned, "Come out and obey the king's orders, so you will stay alive."

But the Jewish people said, "We will neither come out nor carry out the king's orders. To do either would be to break the laws about the Sabbath."

At this, the king's troops attacked them. But the Jews did not fight back. They died with their wives, children and livestock—about a thousand people.

When Mattathias and his friends heard about this, they mourned for them deeply. They said among themselves, "If we act as our brothers have, and fail to fight against the pagans for our lives and laws, they will soon root us out of the earth." So that very day they decided, "If anyone attacks us on the Sabbath, let us fight back. Let's not die as our brothers did in their hideouts."

Men joined Mattathias and his sons and friends in the mountains. They began to carry out guerrilla raids against the king's officers and the people who supported them.

After a short while, however, Mattathias became ill and it was clear he was going to die. He encouraged his sons to keep fighting.

"Here is your brother Simon," he said. "Listen to him always; he'll be like a father to you. Judas Maccabeus has been a brave fighter since he was a boy; he'll be your commander and carry on the war against the foreign peoples. You must bring to your side everyone who lives up to the Law."

With that, he blessed them. Then he joined his ancestors. He was buried in the burial place of his ancestors in Modein, and all Israel went into mourning for him.

## Judas Maccabeus Begins to Fight

1 Maccabees 3–8

So Judas, known as Maccabeus, became his successor. All his brothers and all his father's followers backed him up and, in high spirits, they began to fight for Israel.

The author of *1 Maccabees* often inserts songs of praise into his account. Here is part of one about Judas.

He was like a lion, like a lion's cub roaring for prey.

Those who broke the Law shrank in fear of him, not knowing what to do.

He brought sorrow to many kings, but joy to Jacob.

His memory will be blessed forever.

The number of Judas' followers grew, and since they had captured some weapons during their raids, they soon dared to face an army in battle. Their first two victories were over troops led by the king's officers, Appolonius and Seron.

Then the king sent a larger force under Gorgias. Judas and his men went to

Mizpah, an ancient place of prayer, to fast and pray.

Hearing that Gorgias was planning to attack them by night with horsemen and foot soldiers, Judas and his men made their way over the hills in the dark and circled around the enemy camp in order to surprise its guards on the far side. The Jews still did not have good weapons, but Judas encouraged them.

"Don't be afraid of their numbers," he said. "Don't shrink when they attack. Remember how our ancestors were rescued at the Red Sea, when Pharaoh pursued them with such power. Let us raise our voices to heaven [to God] and hope that he will destroy this army. Then all nations will know that there is Someone who rescues Israel."

The battle with the camp guards was fierce, but the Jews won. And when Gorgias' other soldiers came and saw their camp in ruins, they were so stunned that they turned around and fled.

The following year, Judas and his men defeated a still larger force under Lysias.

Then Judas and his brothers said, "Let's go purify the sanctuary and dedicate it." So the whole army was brought together, and they went up to Mount Zion. When they saw that the gates had been burned down and that weeds were growing in the courts as if in a forest, they lay flat on the ground and mourned.

Then they built a new altar like the other one. They also made new vessels for worship, and brought the seven-branched candlestick, the altar of incense, and the table into the Holy Place. They offered incense on the altar and lit the lamps of

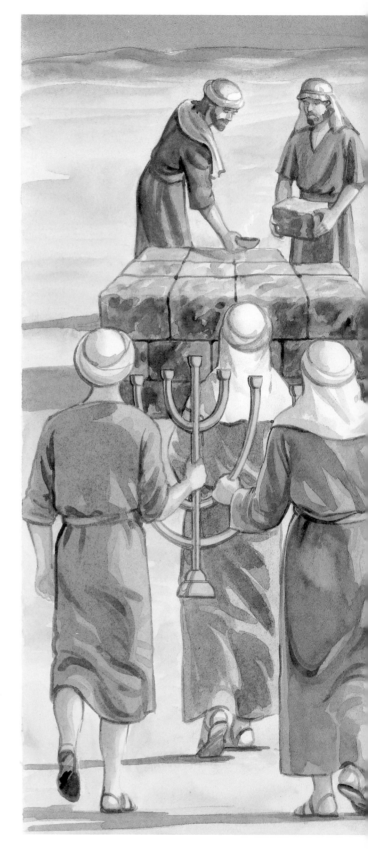

the seven-branched candlestick, which gave light in the Holy Place.

*This joyful event is remembered by Jewish people every year in December, with the celebration called Hanukkah.*

More battles followed, and the Jews continued to win. Then the new king, Antiochus V, called up a large army. Even elephants were used, since men could shoot arrows or fling spears from small towers mounted on the elephants' backs.

This battle could have ended in disaster for Judas, but fortunately the king was called back to Syria to defend his throne. His commander, Lysias, made peace with the Jewish forces.

## Jonathan Succeeds Judas

1 Maccabees 9–12

Soon, however, Syria had a new king—Demetrius—who sent other commanders into Judah. One of them, Nicanor, was defeated, but when Judas faced Bacchides, he had too few men. While he was pursuing one wing of the enemy army, the other wing swung around behind him. Judas was killed in battle. In great sorrow, Jonathan and Simon buried him in Modein.

After Judas' death a terrible persecution broke out. So all Judas' friends joined together and said to Jonathan, "Since your brother Judas died, no man acts as he did, leading campaigns against our enemies, against Bacchides in particular, and also against those of our own nation who are against us. So today we have chosen you to succeed him as our ruler and our leader and to fight our battles."

That day Jonathan became the leader in place of his brother Judas.

Jonathan showed that he, too, was a brave leader, but the situation in Syria also helped him. King Demetrius was fighting for his throne, so he sent a letter to Jonathan asking for peace.

Jonathan moved to Jerusalem. He ordered master workmen to rebuild the walls around Mount Zion.

Meanwhile, Alexander, Demetrius' rival for the throne, also wanted to have Jonathan on his side, so he offered Jonathan the title of high priest. Jonathan accepted it.

Jonathan was a good leader both in war and in negotiations for peace. He led the Jewish people for several years, until he was betrayed, imprisoned and murdered.

## Peace under Simon

1 Maccabees 13–16

Simon was the one brother left. (Eleazar had died in the battle with Lysias. John had been killed in an ambush.) When Simon offered to lead the nation, the people accepted with joy. Simon became high priest, military commander and eventually ethnarch—king of his own people.

The land of Judah was undisturbed as long as Simon lived, for he looked after the concerns of his nation, and people were happy with his rule.

But Simon and two of his sons were murdered by Simon's son-in-law, who wanted to rule the nation himself. Simon's other son, John, was warned in time. He stopped the revolt and made himself the leader of the nation. John's descendants ruled until the Romans conquered Judah in 63 B.C.

# THE SECOND BOOK OF MACCABEES

*2 Maccabees* does not continue where *1 Maccabees* leaves off. Instead, *2 Maccabees* tells about some events that happened before the persecution began, then repeats information that is found in *1 Maccabees* but goes into more detail. It also focuses more on certain persons—for example, Judas Maccabeus. The author brings his book to an end before the death of Judas.

2 Maccabees 2–7

These matters were written by Jason of Cyrene in five books. We shall try to sum them up in a single book. Surely, for us who have taken on this hard work of summarizing, this is no easy job but a matter of sweat and sleepless nights. But, knowing that many will be thankful, we will do this with pleasure.

Well then, when the Holy City was in perfect peace and the laws were still carefully kept, thanks to the devotion of the high priest Onias and to his hatred for evil, even the kings themselves began to honor the Temple and add to its beauty with the finest gifts.

But then people who were jealous of the priest Onias and greedy for money and power began to cause trouble. One of them, named Simon, spread lies against Onias and had him killed. Jason, Onias' brother, bought the high priesthood for himself by bribing King Antiochus. Then Jason began to introduce pagan customs into Jerusalem. Later, Simon's brother, Menelaus, bought the high priesthood for himself and had Jason removed.

It was after this that the persecution by Antiochus began.

The author tells about some heroic people who died for what they believed. For instance, there was an elderly man named Eleazar who was asked to disobey the religious laws regarding food. Eleazar had made up his mind to obey all the religious laws of his people. So he refused to eat, even when some old friends asked him to simply pretend he was disobeying the laws. But he had an answer for his friends.

"Pretending isn't worthy of our age," he said. "Many young people might suspect that ninety-year-old Eleazar had gone over to paganism. They themselves might go astray through my fault. Meanwhile, I would win dishonor. And even if I were to avoid human punishment for now, I won't escape God's hands whether I'm alive or dead. If I leave this life now as a man, I'll show myself worthy of my age and I'll leave a noble example for the young."

While he was being beaten to death, he groaned, "In my body I'm suffering

great pain, but in my soul I'm happy to do this because of my reverence for God."

So that was how this man died, leaving by his death an example of virtue not only for the young but also for many of his people.

The author also tells about seven brothers who were arrested with their mother, tortured and killed. The author speaks about their strong belief in the resurrection of the dead.

The mother kept encouraging each of them, saying, "The Creator of the universe designed the human race. In his mercy he will once again give you both your breath and your life, since for the sake of his laws you are paying no attention to yourselves."

The mother died after her sons.

## Judas Gathers an Army

**2 Maccabees 8–10**

Meanwhile, Judas Maccabeus and his companions were quietly slipping into the villages and inviting their relatives to join

them. In that way, they enrolled men who were loyal to Judaism and raised a fighting force of six thousand.

Judas entered cities and villages when he was least expected and sent many of their enemies fleeing. Usually he carried out this kind of raid at night. He was becoming famous.

With the Lord guiding them, Maccabeus and his companions reconquered the Temple and the city. The purification of the Temple took place on exactly the same date on which the Temple had been made unholy by the foreigners. For eight days they joyfully celebrated.

## Judas Prays for the Dead

**2 Maccabees 12**

*One of the best known passages from 2 Maccabees is the following one. It shows faith in a place of purification after death. The scene is a battlefield on which a number of Judas' men had fallen.*

The men with Judas came to take away the bodies of those who had been killed, to send them to be laid to rest with their relatives in the family burial places.

But under the tunic of each of the dead men they found religious objects dedicated to idols, although the Law forbade the Jews to wear these. So it was clear why they had fallen.

At this, all the men began to pray that the sin might be erased.

Then, taking up a collection, Judas sent about two thousand silver coins to Jerusalem for the offering of a sacrifice for sin. He acted honorably and rightly indeed, since he was thinking about the resurrection. For, if he had not expected that those fallen men would rise, it would have been strange and senseless to pray for dead people. If, however, he was considering that there is a great reward waiting for people who have fallen asleep with devotion to God, the idea was holy and good. He made up for those dead men's sins, so that they might be freed from them.

## The Holy Dead Pray for Their People

**2 Maccabees 15**

*Another time, before a battle, Judas told his men about a marvelous dream he had had. This dream shows belief that the dead can pray for us:*

Here is the kind of vision he had: the former high priest Onias—an honorable and well-born man of gentle ways, graceful speech, educated from childhood in everything good— was spreading his arms wide and praying for the whole Jewish community.

Then there appeared a man with a white head and serious manner, and Onias said, "This is a true lover of the brothers, who prays much for the people and for the holy city—Jeremiah, the prophet of God."

*The author of 2 Maccabees does not tell the whole story of Judas and his brothers. He ends his book while Judas is still alive:*

I have finished my story. If I have done it with a beautiful skill for writing, that is exactly what I wanted; if, instead, I have done it poorly—that was all I was able to do.

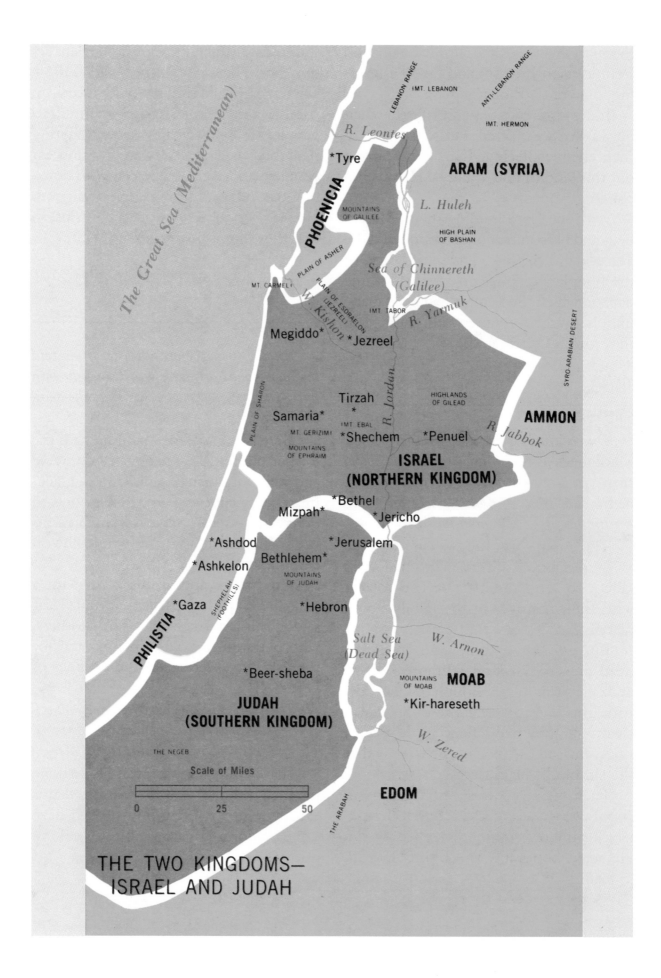

THE TWO KINGDOMS—
ISRAEL AND JUDAH

## A Backward Glance—Kings to Maccabees

This map shows the kingdoms of Israel and Judah in the tenth century B.C. after they split apart and before they began to grow smaller as a result of wars.

As we have seen, the northern kingdom, called Israel, was conquered by the Assyrians toward the end of the eighth century B.C. Many of its people were taken away to other parts of the empire, while various peoples were brought in to take their place. Soon a mixed religion resulted. The Samaritans did worship God, but their religion was different from that of the people of Judah.

In the early sixth century B.C., the southern kingdom, Judah, was conquered by the Chaldeans of Babylonia. All the people except the poorest were taken away to Babylon or fled into Egypt. When the Persians conquered Babylon and let people return to Judah if they wished to, some went back to rebuild Jerusalem and the Temple. They faced many hardships.

Little by little, conditions improved for the Jewish people (the inhabitants of Judah). The Persian rulers let them follow their own religion and laws. Even after the Persians were conquered by the Greeks, life seems to have gone smoothly for the people of Judah until the persecution by Antiochus IV. That persecution led to the Maccabean revolt and eventually to independence for Judah.

With the *Books of Maccabees,* the Historical Books of the Old Testament end.

## The Books of the Prophets and the Wisdom Books

The "writing prophets" lived during the period we have just reviewed. These men (or sometimes their disciples) wrote down messages from God that they told to the people. Often these messages were about being faithful to God—worshipping only him and no other gods. But the prophets also spoke and wrote about being just (fair) to each other. There was much lying and cheating going on in Israel and Judah—as in other nations.

During this period, there were also wise men or sages among the Jewish people. The sages gave good advice on many subjects. Much of it was written down in the Old Testament Wisdom Books.

The Prophetical and Wisdom Books help us understand how God wants us to live. They also help us to understand the Historical Books better.

# THE BOOK OF JOB

*Job* is another book that tells a story, but this book is different from the books we have been reading. With Job, we come to a section of the Old Testament called the *Wisdom Books*. These books teach us how to please God and/or get along well with others.

The *Book of Job* asks a question that no one in this world can completely answer: "Why does God let good people suffer?" In the *Book of Job,* the main character wonders about this. His "friends" say that suffering is sent to persons who have done wrong (and that, therefore, Job has committed sins). But Job says he has not committed any serious sin. He accepts his suffering, more or less, but insists that he is innocent and that God knows it. In the end God appears and says that Job makes more sense than his friends.

In the New Testament, when we read that Jesus suffered to save us from our sins and that Paul invited his friends to join their sufferings to those of Jesus, we can begin to understand that God can bring good things out of suffering. But there is much that we don't know, and like Job we may have to stop questioning and simply trust the Lord.

Although Job is said to have lived around the time of Abraham, this book was probably written in the third or fourth century B.C.

**Job 1—42**

In the land of Uz, there lived a man named Job. He was a good man who respected God and avoided sin. He had seven sons and three daughters, and his property included seven thousand sheep, three thousand camels, five hundred pairs of oxen, five hundred donkeys and very many servants.

One day when the sons of God came to serve the Lord, the Enemy (Satan) came with them.

*"Sons of God" probably means the angels, who were sometimes called by this name.*

The Lord said to the Enemy, "Have you noticed my servant, Job? There isn't anyone else in the world like him. He respects me and avoids sin."

The Enemy answered, "You have blessed his work, and he owns many things. But reach out and touch what he has and I'm sure he will insult you."

Then the Lord said to the Enemy, "Everything he has is in your power. But do not harm the man himself."

So the Enemy went out, away from the presence of the Lord.

Then, the story continues, the Enemy sent raiders to kill his servants and take his thousands of sheep, camels and donkeys. But in all his sorrow, Job didn't say anything bad about God.

"It is the Lord who gives and the Lord who takes away," Job said. "May the name of the Lord be blessed."

Then the Enemy went back to the Lord and asked permission to harm Job himself. He wanted to prove that this would make Job insult God.

The Lord said, "He is in your power, but don't kill him."

So the Enemy went out and covered Job with boils from the bottoms of his feet to the top of his head.

Then Job said, "We have accepted good things from God. Should we not accept the bad, too?"

Job's "friends" came and tried to make him admit that he was being punished by God for doing or thinking something wrong. But Job would not agree with them. He knew he was not guilty of serious sin.

Yet, Job did want to know why he was suffering, so God spoke to him out of a storm.

"Do you really want to put me in the wrong so you can be right?" God asked. "So, then, show your power and your glory."

"My words have been thoughtless," said Job. "I have nothing more to say."

Then the Lord blessed Job more than before: he had fourteen thousand sheep, six thousand camels, a thousand yoke of oxen and a thousand donkeys. He lived to an old age, and saw his children's children.

# THE BOOK OF PSALMS

The *Book of Psalms* is a collection of prayer-songs that were written at different times, by different people. Some psalms go back to about 1,000 B.C. Others were written later, but all of them before the time of Jesus. Many of the psalms are labeled: "of David," but probably not all of these are David's. Perhaps David collected psalms or had someone make a collection for him.

The *Book of Psalms* is one of the Wisdom Books, since the psalms contain important truths, and knowing these truths helps us to become wise.

Jews and Christians often pray the psalms, especially the psalms that praise God or express sorrow for sins or some other need for help.

Here are selections from some of the better known psalms.

## A Teaching Psalm

**Psalm 1**

Happy is the person who does not follow the advice of wicked people, but instead finds joy in the law of the Lord and repeats God's law day and night.

This person is like a tree planted by a stream—which gives fruit at the right time and whose leaves do not dry up.

It is not the same with the wicked. They are like straws that the wind takes away. The future of the wicked will end in ruin.

## God's Goodness to All

**Psalm 8**

O Lord, our God, how great is your name over all the earth. Your praise echoes above the sky.

When I see your sky, the work of your fingers, the moon and stars that you set in place, what are we humans that you think about us?

Yet you have put us in charge of everything you have made. O Lord, our God, how great is your name over all the earth!

## God's Love for Each of Us

**Psalm 16**

Guard me, O God, for I have come to you for safety. I bless the Lord who has given me advice. My conscience has taught me even at night.

My heart is glad and my soul is happy. You will show me the path to life—to lasting happiness at your side.

## God's Goodness

**Psalm 23**

The Lord is my shepherd. There is nothing that I need. He makes me lie down in green pastures. He leads me along quiet streams. He makes me feel refreshed.

I don't fear any harm, even when I go through a dark valley, because you are with me. Your rod and your staff give me courage.

You prepare a table for me while my enemies are watching. You have poured oil on my head. My cup is flowing over.

May happiness and love be with me all the days of my life, and may I live in the Lord's own house forever.

## Praise of God's Goodness

**Psalm 100**

Praise the Lord, all the world! Serve the Lord with joy. Come before him with joyful shouts. The Lord made us, so we are his people, the flock he cares for.

Go through his gates with an offering of thanksgiving. Go through his courts with a song of praise. Give thanks to him and bless his name.

The Lord is good. His loving-kindness is everlasting and his faithfulness lasts forever.

## Longing for God

**Psalm 42**

As the deer thirsts for streams of water, so my soul is thirsty for you, my God. Day and night I have had no food but tears.

My soul, why are you sad? Why are you moaning within me? Hope in the Lord. I will still praise him—my savior and my God.

## A Call to Praise God

**Psalm 150**

Praise God in his holy place. Praise him in the heights of his power. Praise him for his mighty deeds—in a way that fits his greatness.

Praise him in the midst of trumpet blasts. Praise him with lyres and harps. Praise him with tambourines. Praise him by dancing. Praise him with strings and pipes.

Praise him with clashing cymbals. Praise him with crashing cymbals. Let everything that breathes praise the Lord—Alleluia!

# THE BOOK OF PROVERBS

*Proverbs* is a typical Hebrew Wisdom Book. It contains advice about living in a way that agrees with God's law and pleases other people.

Most of the book is made up of short sayings. Each saying is not usually connected with what comes before or after it. But there are also longer sections about particular subjects. The book is made up of seven main sections, which seem to have been written at different times. The whole book is called the Proverbs of Solomon, and it is quite likely that some parts of it really do come from the wise sayings of the famous king.

*A key expression in the wisdom books is: "Fear of the Lord is the beginning of wisdom." "Fear of the Lord" doesn't mean being afraid, as if God might want to hurt us. "Fear of the Lord" is a healthy respect for God because he is God.*

*Here are some verses from different chapters of the* Book of Proverbs:

## Proverbs 1

The beginning of knowledge is the fear of the Lord. Fools look down on wisdom and self-control.

If sinners try to tempt you, do not go along with them. Pull your foot back from their path, for their feet are running toward ruin.

## Proverbs 3

*Sometimes the author speaks of wisdom as if it were a person.*

Happy is the person who has discovered wisdom. She is a tree of life to those who hold on to her. Everyone who grasps her is made happy.

## Proverbs 6

*The author encourages people to work hard.*

You lazy person, go to the ant. Look at what she does, and grow wise. She has no commander, supervisor or king, but she stores up food at the harvest.

*Further on, the author uses numbers to emphasize what he wants to say.*

There are six things that the Lord dislikes and seven that he hates: proud eyes, a lying tongue, hands that shed innocent blood, a heart that plans sin, feet eagerly running to do evil, someone who tells lies about another person and someone who stirs up quarrels among brothers.

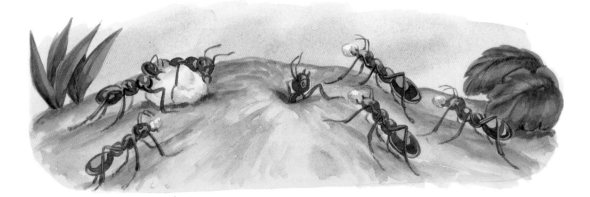

## Proverbs 8

*In this chapter, wisdom is again presented as a person. "She" speaks about having been with God at the creation of the world. Then she asks everyone to pay attention to her.*

"So now, children, listen to me! Happy are the people who follow my ways. The person who finds me finds life and wins favor from the Lord. Whoever does not find me hurts himself and whoever hates me loves death."

## Proverbs 11

*Most of the following proverbs may have been composed by Solomon himself.*

Doing what is right leads to life, but someone who wants to do evil goes to death.

## Proverbs 13

Someone who despises God's law must pay for it, but a person who respects God's commandment is rewarded.

## Proverbs 15

A gentle answer turns away anger, but a rough word stirs it up.

The eyes of the Lord are everywhere, watching those who do wrong and those who do right.

It is better to have little but with fear of the Lord than to be rich but full of anxiety.

## Proverbs 16

It is better to have a little that was gained fairly than a large income that was gained unfairly.

Pride goes before disaster and self-importance before a fall.

Someone who pays attention to God's word finds joy; the person who trusts the Lord is happy.

## Proverbs 19

Someone who helps the poor lends to the Lord, and God will repay that person for the good done.

Listen to advice and accept corrections, so you may be wise in the end.

# THE BOOKS OF ECCLESIASTES AND THE SONG OF SONGS

The name of King Solomon is connected with both of these books. The author of *Ecclesiastes* calls himself a king and David's son. This suggests that he is Solomon. The *Song of Songs* has a second name: "Song of Solomon."

But because of the form of Hebrew used in these books and for other reasons, experts say that *Ecclesiastes* and *Song of Songs* were written much later than Solomon's time—in fact, after the Exile—maybe in the third century B.C. (People at that time liked to name their writings after famous men.)

*The name* Ecclesiastes *(or in Hebrew* Quoheleth*) means a preacher or speaker at a religious service.*

*Here is a famous part of the book:*

**Ecclesiastes 3**

There is a time for everything that happens in this world—a time for being born and a time for dying; a time for planting and a time for pulling up the plant.

There is a time for crying and a time for laughing, a time for being sad and a time for dancing.

There is a time for ripping and a time for mending, a time for keeping quiet and a time for speaking.

There is a time for loving and a time for hating; a time for war and a time for peace.

*The author is not very cheerful. He keeps saying that most things people do are useless. But he ends the book with an important reminder: "Fear God and keep his commandments. This is everything."*

## A Difficult Book

**Song of Songs 2**

*The* Song of Songs *is a collection of love poems in which a woman seeks and celebrates her true love.*

*Some experts think this book is about the love between God's people and God himself.*

*This is one of the easier parts, in which the woman speaks about the man she loves:*

Listen! There comes my beloved, leaping over the mountains, jumping over the hills.

My beloved is like a young deer. There he stands behind our wall, looking through the windows.

He speaks and says to me, "Come away, my darling. Look! The winter is behind us and the rains are over. The flowers have appeared."

# THE BOOKS OF WISDOM AND SIRACH

These two books were written late in Old Testament times—*Sirach* in the early second century B.C., and *Wisdom* even closer to the time of Jesus. Both books talk about wisdom and its importance, but there are great differences between them.

*The* Book of Wisdom *was written by a man who said he was King Solomon. He wrote in Greek instead of Hebrew and may have lived in a city where the people spoke Greek. He was interested in many things, including life after death.*

**Wisdom 2–3**

God formed human beings to live forever. He made them in the image of his own nature. But by the devil's hatred death came into the world, and people who are on his side experience it.

But the souls of upright people are in the hand of God and no suffering will touch them.

They are in peace.

## Advice from Jesus ben-Sira

Sirach 6, 21, 30

*Unlike the author of* Wisdom, *the author of* Sirach *is known. In the introduction, his grandson says his name was Jesus ben-Sira. He wrote less than 200 years before Jesus Christ.*

A loyal friend is a strong shelter. Someone who finds a friend like this finds a treasure. Anyone who fears the Lord has a good friendship, because one's friend is just like oneself.

Run away from sin as if from the presence of a snake, for if you get close to it, it will bite you. Its teeth are like a lion's. They can kill you.

Joy gives length to one's life. Sadness has destroyed many people. There is nothing to get from it.

# THE BOOK OF ISAIAH

This is the beginning of another large section of the Old Testament: the Prophetical Books, or books of the prophets. A prophet is someone who speaks God's message. Some of the prophets are called "major," because the books by or about them are long. The major prophetical books are *Isaiah, Jeremiah, Ezekiel* and *Daniel.* The other Prophetical Books are called "minor."

The *Book of Isaiah* is the longest book in the Bible. About half of it seems to have been written by Isaiah himself, or by his disciples, around the time when Judah was in danger from the Assyrians. The rest of the book was written later by one or more persons who lived during the Exile in Babylon and perhaps after the people's return to Judah.

Isaiah's story does not begin in the first chapter of the book but in chapter six. There, he tells about a vision that he had in the Temple.

In the year King Uzziah died, I saw the Lord seated on a high throne. Above it there were seraphs* waiting on him. They each had six wings. With two, each one covered his face, with two he covered his legs, and with two he flew.

One to another they cried out, "Holy, holy, holy is the Lord Almighty. His glory fills all the earth."

At their voices the Temple was filled with smoke. Then I said, "I am lost! I am a man with unclean lips living in the midst of a people with unclean lips. Yet I have seen the King, the Almighty Lord."

Then one of the seraphs flew to me with a burning coal in his hand, which he had taken from the altar with a pair of tongs. As he touched my mouth with it, he said, "Look— this is touching your lips, so your guilt will be taken away and your sin forgiven."

Then I heard the voice of the Lord say, "Whom shall I send, and who will go on a mission for us?"

And I answered, "Here I am. Send me."

## The Prophecy about Emmanuel

*Isaiah's mission was hard, because he had to keep telling the people that they were not loyal to God and were disobeying his commandments.*

One of the kings of Judah who disobeyed God was Ahaz. He refused to trust God, even when Isaiah brought him a message from the Lord.

This was what happened: Rezin, king of Aram (Syria), and Pekah, king of Israel, decided to attack Jerusalem. Ahaz was afraid and decided to ask for help from

*Angels.*

Assyria. This would mean not only payment of heavy taxes called tribute but—much worse—an obligation to worship the Assyrian gods instead of the Lord.

The Lord said to Isaiah, "Go out with your son to meet Ahaz near the upper reservoir and say to him, 'Don't worry or let your heart weaken. If you don't stand firm, you won't stand at all.'"

Then the Lord went on to say to Ahaz, "Ask the Lord your God to give a sign."

*The Lord wanted to show Ahaz that he would protect Jerusalem.*

But Ahaz answered, "I won't ask for anything. I won't test the Lord."

At this, Isaiah said, "Listen, you house of David: is it so little for you to wear out men's patience, that you have to wear out God's patience, too? But even so, the Lord himself will give you a sign: a young woman is going to have a son, and she will call him Emmanuel."**

*Isaiah did not succeed with King Ahaz, as* 2 Kings *tells us. But Isaiah kept trying to call the rest of the people back to the Lord. And he announced that someday a king from David's family would bring joy and peace.*

The people walking in darkness will see a bright light. Light flashes on people who

---

** *"God with us."*

have been living in gloom. You bring great joy. People are happy in your presence with the same joy that they have at harvest time.

For a child is born for us—a boy is given to us, on whose shoulders leadership rests and whose name is wonderful advisor, powerful God, everlasting father and prince of peace.

*Isaiah used images to show that this child would truly bring peace:*

The wolf will stay with the lamb and the leopard will lie down with the kid. Both the cow and the bear will eat grass, and their little ones will lie down together. The lion will eat straw like a cow.

The baby will play beside the snake's den, and the small child will reach his hand out to the scorpion's home. The earth will be filled with the knowledge of the Lord as the water fills the sea.

## Hope for the Exiles

**Isaiah 40**

*In chapter 40 of the* Book of Isaiah, *we find the words of another author or authors. "Second Isaiah" wrote more than a century after the original Isaiah. "Second Isaiah" encouraged the Jews in Babylon to hope that someday they would go home to rebuild Jerusalem.*

A herald's voice can be heard: "Make a level road for the Lord through the wastelands! Make a straight highway for our God through the desert! Let every low spot be filled in and every mountain and hill leveled. Let the rough ground become a plain, and the mountain ranges split into a broad valley. That is how the greatness of the Lord will show itself, and all living things will see it. The Lord has said this."

Zion, messenger of good news, climb to the top of a tall mountain. Jerusalem, messenger of good news, raise your voice strongly. Raise it without fear.

Say to the cities of Judah, "Here he is—your God! Here comes the Lord. Like a shepherd, he takes care of his flock. He carries the lambs in his arms."

## The Servant of the Lord

**Isaiah 52 – 53**

*Four sections in this part of the* Book of Isaiah *are called the "servant songs." They tell about a mysterious "servant of the Lord," who suffers for the people of Israel.*

*Here is the most famous of the servant songs. You will see images in it, because the servant songs are a form of poetry.*

My servant will succeed: he will be honored. The people were shocked because his appearance had been made less than human. Just so, he will startle many.

He sprang up in his presence like a small plant or like a root sprouting from dry soil. He was not handsome for us to look at, not impressive for us to delight in.

Despised and left aside by human beings, he suffered and was trained in hardships. He was someone from whom we hide our faces. We looked down on him and thought nothing of him.

Yet, he was the one who underwent the hardships we should have had, who carried the sufferings we deserved, while we thought he had been beaten by God and disgraced. He was stabbed for our faults, crushed for our sins. His punishment made us whole, and healing came to us through his bruises.

All of us had wandered away like sheep. We had each taken our own course, and the Lord caused the guilt of us all to pounce upon him. He was wronged and disgraced, yet he did not open his mouth. Like a lamb taken to be killed for the market and like a sheep that is silent when its wool is to be shorn off, so he did not open his mouth.

After his cruel death, he was placed in a grave among wicked people, even though he had done nothing wrong and no lie had been on his lips.

Yet it was the Lord who had chosen to crush him with hardships, who had had him suffer. If his life is laid down as an offering, he will see disciples and live long, and the plan of the Lord will succeed through him.

# THE BOOK OF JEREMIAH

Jeremiah lived and prophesied somewhere between the times of Isaiah and "Second Isaiah," and in a different situation. In Isaiah's time, the people had been asked to trust that God would save them from the Assyrians. At the time of "Second Isaiah," they would be called to trust that the Lord would bring his people back to Jerusalem.

But in Jeremiah's time—when Jerusalem was about to be conquered by the Chaldeans—the people had the wrong kind of trust. They thought that the Lord would keep them safe no matter how they lived. Jeremiah spent most of his lifetime warning them: unless they began to love and obey the Lord, they would be conquered and taken into exile.

Besides telling us what Jeremiah said, this book also gives some details of his life.

Jeremiah 1

This is the story of Jeremiah, son of Hilkiah, one of the priests living in Anathoth in the territory of Benjamin. The word of the Lord came to him in the time of Judah's king Josiah, and it kept coming through the time of Judah's king Jehoiakim, until the eleventh year of Judah's king Zedekiah—until Jerusalem was taken into exile.

*Jeremiah was less than thirty when the Lord called him to be a prophet. At his time, people paid more attention to older men because of their experience. So when God called him, Jeremiah objected.*

The word of the Lord came to me with this message: I knew you before I formed you; before you came out of the womb I made you a prophet for the nations.

At this I said, "Ah, Lord! See, I'm not a speaker at all. I'm only a boy."

But the Lord said to me, "You must not say, 'I'm only a boy.' You must go to whomever I send you and say whatever I tell you to. Don't be afraid of them, for I am with you to rescue you, says the Lord."

With that, the Lord put out his hand and touched my mouth, as he said to me, "You see, I am putting my words into your mouth."

## The Temple Sermon

Jeremiah 7

*Back in the time of Isaiah, the Lord had promised to protect the people of Jerusalem because their Temple was dedicated to him. But in Jeremiah's time people seemed to think it was God's duty to protect them no matter how badly they lived, since he had protected their ancestors. Jeremiah tried to get them to open their eyes before it was too late. He told them not to think they were safe simply because God's Temple was in their city.*

This message came to Jeremiah from the Lord: "Stand at the gate of the house of the Lord and announce this message: Hear the word of the Lord, you people of Judah who come to worship the Lord.

This is what the Lord Almighty says, the God of Israel: Improve the way you live. If you do, I will let you stay here. Don't depend on words that trick you and say: 'This is the Temple of the Lord, the Temple of the Lord, the Temple of the Lord!'

"Instead, if you really improve the way you live, if you really are fair to each other, not taking advantage of strangers, orphans and widows or shedding innocent blood, or worshipping other gods, then I will let you stay in this place—in the land that I gave to your fathers.

"You steal, you murder, you commit adultery, you tell lies in court, you offer sacrifices to Baal and you follow other gods. After that, you come into my presence in this house of mine and you say, 'We are safe! We can do all those things again.'

"Go to my shrine in Shiloh, and see what I have done to it because of the wickedness of my people. Now, since you have refused to listen to me, I will do the same to this Temple, and I will drive you away from here."

## The Potter

**Jeremiah 18**

The Lord found other ways to warn his people. Once Jeremiah visited a potter, who was making pots and jugs out of clay, shaping them on a spinning horizontal wheel.

This word came to Jeremiah from the Lord: "Go down to the potter's, and there I will tell you my message." So I went down to the potter's, and there he was, working at the wheel. Now, if the object—whatever he was making with the clay—was spoiled, he started all over again and remade it into another object, as he thought best.

Then this message of the Lord came to me: "House of Israel, can't I do with you what this potter has done? What the clay is in the hand of the potter—this is how you are in my hand.

"Tell the people of Judah and the citizens of Jerusalem: This is what the Lord says: If I have announced that I will destroy a nation but that nation stops doing evil, I change my mind about destroying it. Stop doing evil—each one of you. Improve your actions."

## Jeremiah Complains

**Jeremiah 20**

*People wouldn't listen to Jeremiah, so he became discouraged and complained to the Lord:*

You talked me into this, Lord, and I let you do it; you put pressure on me, and you won.

Everyone is making fun of me, so I said, "I'm going to forget about the Lord. I'm not going to speak in his name anymore."

But deep inside me, trapped in my very bones, there's something like a burning fire. I keep trying to hold it in, but I just can't.

*Yet even though Jeremiah suffered much, he was sure the Lord was with him. So he continued:*

Sing to the Lord, praise the Lord, for he has saved the life of a miserable man from the hands of wicked people.

## The New Covenant

**Jeremiah 31**

*Jeremiah also announced that after the people's exile in Babylon they would return to their homeland. He spoke of a new covenant between the Lord and his people.*

Times will be coming, says the Lord, when I will make a new covenant with the people of Israel and the people of Judah. It won't be like the covenant that I made with their ancestors, when I took them by the hand to lead them out of the land of Egypt. They have broken that covenant with me, says the Lord.

This is the covenant that I will make with the people of Israel after those times: I will plant my Law within them and write it in their hearts, so I will show that I am their God and they will show that they are my people.

## Jeremiah in the Mud

**Jeremiah 37**

After the Chaldeans had placed Jerusalem under siege, Jeremiah's enemies decided to silence him. They told King Zedekiah that the prophet's warnings were lowering the army's morale. Zedekiah did not have the courage to argue, so he let Jeremiah's enemies have their way.

They took Jeremiah and lowered him with ropes into a water tank in the court of the guard. There was no water in the tank—only mud—so Jeremiah sank into the mud.

Ebed-melech, a servant at the royal palace, heard that Jeremiah was a prisoner in the water tank. He told the king, "These men have caused harm by doing that to the prophet Jeremiah. He's going to starve to death, since there isn't any food left in the city."

So the king told Ebed-Melech, "Take thirty of my men and pull Jeremiah out of the tank before he dies." Ebed-Melech took the men with him and they pulled Jeremiah out of the water tank with rags and ropes.

King Zedekiah respected Jeremiah and secretly spoke with him about the future of Judah. But the king did not have the courage to disagree with the other leaders of the people and surrender to the Chaldeans. Jerusalem continued to hold out, even though people were dying of starvation and disease.

After the Chaldeans broke through the city wall and destroyed Jerusalem, some men of Judah forced Jeremiah to go to Egypt with them. He was old by then, and that was where he died.

# THE BOOKS OF LAMENTATIONS AND BARUCH

These two short books tell about the sadness of the people of Judah over the destruction of Jerusalem. Each of these books also expresses hope and trust in God, in spite of all the people's sufferings.

*The Book of Lamentations was probably written by different authors—much or all of it, in Babylon during the Exile. It was written as poetry. Here is part of its most hopeful section:*

### Lamentations 3

This is what I remember and why I am hopeful: the love and kindness of the Lord have surely not run out; his tenderness of heart has surely not ended. Every morning they are fresh and new.

"My portion is the Lord," says my soul. "This is why I hope in him."

To someone who trusts in him, to a soul who seeks him, the Lord is good.

Let us raise not only our hands but also our hearts to the God in heaven.

## Encouragement from Baruch

### Baruch 5

*The Book of Baruch is named after a scribe who wrote down Jeremiah's prophecies. But it is thought to have been written much later than the time it speaks about. Here the Lord encourages Jerusalem:*

On your feet, Jerusalem! Stand on the heights! Look at the horizon toward the east and see your children. They have been gathered from sunset to sunrise by the command of the Holy One, and they rejoice that God remembers them.

They departed from you on foot, driven by their enemies, but God will bring them home to you, carried in honor.

# THE BOOK OF EZEKIEL

Ten years before the destruction of Jerusalem and the Temple, Nebuchadnezzar took a large group of Hebrews away to Babylon. One of them was a young priest named Ezekiel. There in Babylon Ezekiel was called to be a prophet. The Lord asked him to warn his people that soon Jerusalem and the Temple would be destroyed.

After that, God asked Ezekiel to encourage the people to look to the future with hope. They may have thought that God had left them when the Temple was destroyed. Instead, he was very much with them and was going to bring them back to their own land.

**Ezekiel 1–2**

I was living as an exile beside the river Chebar when the heavens opened, and I saw visions of God.

From the north a stormy wind came, with a great cloud and flashing fire, which made everything bright on all sides. In the midst of the fire there seemed to be four animals.

Each had four faces, and each had four wings. The four of them had the faces of humans, and toward the right the faces of lions; the four of them also had the faces of oxen toward the left, and the faces of eagles. Two wings of each one joined another, and the other two covered their bodies. The animals looked like fiery coals, burning torches. Bright fire moved among them and lightning went out from the fire. The animals looked like lightning as they ran back and forth.

As I watched the animals, for each of the four figures I saw a wheel on the ground. When the animals moved, the wheels moved beside them; and when the animals lifted off from the ground, the wheels, too, lifted off.

I heard the noise of their wings when they moved. It was like the roaring of the open sea, like the voice of the Almighty—a loud noise like the sound of an army.

Above the sky over their heads, there was the shape of a throne and a figure that looked human. From his waist up was what looked like polished bronze, and this appeared to be like fire. From his waist down was what looked like fire, sending out rays of light all around him that resembled a rainbow. This was how the brightness of the Lord appeared to me. I bowed down at the sight.

Then I heard a voice, telling me, "Stand up, son of man; I will speak to you." As he spoke, the spirit filled me and brought me to my feet. So I listened.

He said to me, "Son of man, I am sending you to the Israelites. They and their fathers have been sinning against me to this very day. As for you, son of man, you must not fear their words, even though rebels are at your side."

## Ezekiel Makes a Prophecy in Actions

**Ezekiel 12**

*The people who were in exile with Ezekiel did not want to believe that Jerusalem and the Temple were going to be destroyed. They felt that God would never let his city be destroyed (even though the people had been disobeying the commandments and worshipping pagan gods.) God had Ezekiel try different ways of warning them, so they wouldn't be completely stunned. Close to the time of the actual destruction, the Lord asked Ezekiel to act out King Zedekiah's escape from the city.*

The word of the Lord came to me with this message: "Son of man, pack up your belongings. Take them outside in the daylight, while the others are watching. Then in the evening, while they are watching, set out. Make a hole in the wall and carry your belongings through it. While they watch, leave in the darkness of night, carrying your belongings on your shoulders. Cover your face. I have made you a warning for the people of Israel."

I did as he had told me. By daylight I took out my belongings as if for a journey, and in the evening I dug a hole in the wall. In the darkness I took away my belongings, carrying them on my shoulders, while the people watched.

Early the next morning the word of the Lord came to me with this message: "Son of man, the people of Israel have asked, 'What are you doing?' Answer them: 'This is what the Lord says: I am a warning for you about Jerusalem and all the people of Israel in it. What I have shown in actions will be done to them. They will go away into exile as prisoners. Their leader will carry his belongings on his shoulder in the darkness of night and go out through the wall in which they will make a hole. He will cover his face, for he shall not see the country with his own eyes.'"

*After King Zedekiah had been captured by the Chaldeans, they blinded him. Ezekiel was foretelling this when he prophesied that the leader would not see the country.*

*One day, word came that all these things had really happened. Jerusalem and its Temple had been destroyed and the king had been captured and blinded. At that, the exiles in Babylon became very depressed. They felt that the Lord could no longer be with them, since his Temple was gone. Many of them did not yet understand that God is the ruler of the whole universe and is not limited to living in one place.*

## Ezekiel Encourages His People

**Ezekiel 37**

*After the destruction of Jerusalem, Ezekiel's job was to encourage his fellow-exiles. Like Jeremiah, Ezekiel promised that the Lord would make a new covenant with his people.*

*Ezekiel encouraged the people in many ways. For example, he told them about this vision of the dry bones, which stood for their nation.*

The hand of the Lord came upon me, and through the spirit the Lord took me outside and placed me in the middle of a plain, which was full of bones. He had me walk around the whole edge, so I saw that there were many bones on the surface of the plain and that they were very dry.

Then he asked me, "Will these bones live, son of man?"

I answered, "Lord, you are the One who knows these things."

So he said to me, "Say to them, 'Dry bones, listen to the word of the Lord.'"

I did as I had been told. As I spoke, there was a noise, followed suddenly by a great racket. Bones were coming together. As I watched, tendons appeared on them. Flesh was growing and skin was spreading over them. But there was no spirit in them.

So he said to me, "Say to the spirit, 'This is what the Lord says: Come, spirit, from the four winds and breathe upon these people who are dead, so they may live.'" I did as he had told me, and they came to life and sprang to their feet. It was a huge army.

Then he said to me, "Son of man, these bones are the whole people of Israel. You see, they keep saying, 'Our bones have grown dry, there is no hope for us, we are lost.' So tell them, 'This is what the Lord says: My people, I am going to open your graves and lift you out of them and bring you to the land of Israel. And when I have opened your graves and lifted you out of them, you will realize that I am the Lord. I will place my spirit in you so that you will live, and I will lead you to rest in your own land. And then you will realize that I, the Lord, have said so and I have done it.'"

# THE BOOK OF DANIEL

The *Book of Daniel* is very different from the books of *Isaiah*, *Jeremiah* and *Ezekiel*. It does not contain the writings of a prophet or his followers. Instead, it tells stories about a Hebrew named Daniel, who is shown as living up to his Jewish religion while serving the Chaldean and Persian kings in Babylon.

These stories show that God rewards people who are faithful to him. Probably this book was written at the time of the Maccabees, to encourage people to be faithful to their religion no matter what might happen to them.

King Nebuchadnezzar first attacked Judah and began demanding money from King Jehoiakim. Several young men of Judah were taken away to Babylon. Among these were Daniel, Hananiah, Mishael and Azariah. Each of them was given a new name: Belteshazzar, Shadrach, Meshach and Abednego.

God had given these four young men knowledge and understanding of all kinds of writing and of wisdom. He had also given Daniel understanding of all kinds of visions and dreams. On every subject that the king asked them about, he found them ten times better than all the magicians in his kingdom.

## Nebuchadnezzar's Dream

In the second year of the reign of Nebuchadnezzar, the king had a series of dreams. His spirit became so anxious that he found it hard to sleep. So the king had his magicians called in to explain his dreams.

The magicians said, "O king, live forever! Tell your servants the dream and we will explain the meaning."

In answer the king said to the magicians, "If you fail to let me know the dream and its meaning, you shall be killed and your houses turned into a heap of ruins; but if you explain the dream and its meaning, you will receive presents, gifts and positions of honor. So explain the dream and its meaning to me."

But the magicians insisted that first the king must tell them what the dream was. Nebuchadnezzar became angry at this and ordered that all the wise men in his kingdom be killed. This would include Daniel and his friends.

Daniel went home and told his companions, Hananiah, Mishael and Azariah about the problem, so that they could pray to God for mercy. Then in a vision during the night the mystery was made clear to Daniel. And he blessed God.

Daniel went to Arioch, whom the king had told to execute the wise men of Babylonia. "Present me to the king," he said. "I will explain the meaning of the dream."

Arioch rushed Daniel into the king's presence, saying, "I have found a man from the captive people of Judah who will explain the meaning."

The king asked Daniel, "Can you really let me know what I saw in my dream and its meaning?"

Daniel replied, "No wise men or magicians can explain the mystery you are inquiring about. But in heaven there is a God who reveals mysteries.

"Your dream and the vision you had were like this: There was a huge statue. Its head was of solid gold; its chest and arms, of silver; its belly and upper legs, of bronze; its lower legs, of iron; its feet, partly of iron and partly of clay. Then, as you were watching, a stone got loose and hit the statue on its feet of iron and clay, smashing them. Immediately, iron, clay, bronze, silver and gold were smashed together and became like straw. The wind whirled them away, and no trace of them could be found. But the stone that had hit the statue grew into a great mountain and filled the whole earth. That was your dream."

Then Daniel explained the meaning of the dream. The head of gold represented Nebuchadnezzar and the kingdom of the Chaldeans. Each of the other metals represented another kingdom that was to come later. The last of these kingdoms would be so weak that it would break apart.*

*This meant the kingdom of Antiochus IV, against which the Maccabees would revolt.

King Nebuchadnezzar was pleased with Daniel's explanation. He promoted Daniel and his three friends.

## The Fiery Furnace
**Daniel 3**

King Nebuchadnezzar had a golden statue made that was ninety feet high and eighteen feet wide. He set it up in the plain of Dura, in the province of Babylon. Then King Nebuchadnezzar sent messages to all the officials in the provinces, to come for the dedication of the statue.

All the officials came. As they were standing in front of the statue, a herald called out loudly, "This is an order to you: as soon as you hear the sound of the horns, pipes, lyres, zithers, harps, bagpipes and stringed instruments, you are to bow to the ground in front of the statue of gold that King Nebuchadnezzar has set up. Anyone who does not do this shall be thrown at once into a furnace of blazing fire."

So, as soon as all the people heard the sound of horns, pipes, lyres, zithers, harps and stringed instruments, they bowed to the ground in front of the statue of gold that King Nebuchadnezzar had set up.

But some Chaldeans reported to Nebuchadnezzar that Hananiah, Mishael and Azariah (Shadrach, Meshach and Abednego) had not bowed down to the statue.

Blazing with anger, Nebuchadnezzar immediately sent for Shadrach, Meshach and Abednego and told them, "If you do not bow down to the ground, you shall be thrown at once into the furnace of blaz-

ing fire. And what god can rescue you from my hands?"

Shadrach, Meshach and Abednego replied to the king, "Your Majesty, if our God can rescue us from the furnace of blazing fire and from your hands, may he do so. And if he will not, please know, O King, that we will neither worship your gods nor bow down before the statue of gold you have set up."

Nebuchadnezzar gave orders for the furnace to be heated seven times hotter than usual. Then he ordered some strong men from his army to bind Shadrach, Meshach and Abednego and throw them into the furnace of blazing fire.

They were immediately bound and thrown into the furnace of blazing fire. But they walked among the flames, singing to God and blessing his name.

An angel of the Lord descended to join Azariah and his companions and throw the blazing flames out of the furnace. He turned the air of the furnace into a moist, whispering breeze, so the fire did not touch them at all.

Then inside the furnace the three of them glorified God, saying, "Lord, God of our fathers, you are worthy to be blessed and praised."

King Nebuchadnezzar stood up in astonishment. He asked his officials, "Didn't we throw three men bound into the fire?"

They answered, "Certainly, O King!"

Yet he continued, "Look! I see four men. They are unbound and walking unharmed in the midst of the fire. The fourth looks like a son of the gods."

With that, Nebuchadnezzar came closer to the mouth of the furnace and

called, "Shadrach, Meshach and Abednego, servants of God the most high, come out."

Shadrach, Meshach and Abednego immediately came out from the midst of the fire. Everyone saw that the flames had had no power over them. The hair on their heads had not been burnt and their clothes had not been scorched. Not even the smell of smoke had come out with them.

"Blessed be the God of Shadrach, Meshach and Abednego!" said Nebuchadnezzar. "He sent his angel and rescued his servants who trusted in him."

## The Writing on the Wall

**Daniel 5**

*Another well-known story from the* Book of Daniel *is about the end of the Babylonian empire. This story shows the importance of reverence for sacred vessels (cups, plates, bowls and pitchers used in worship).*

King Belshazzar gave a splendid feast for his princes—one thousand of them.

While they enjoyed the wine, Belshazzar ordered that the vessels of gold and silver taken away from the Temple of Jerusalem by Nebuchadnezzar should be brought in for the king, his princes, his wives and his entertainers to drink from. The vessels were immediately brought in, and the king, his princes, his wives and his entertainers began to drink from them. As they drank the wine, they praised their gods of gold, silver, bronze, iron, wood or stone.

Right then, the fingers of a human hand appeared from nowhere, writing on the whitewashed wall of the royal palace near the candlestick.

At this, the king turned pale and his thoughts began to terrify him. Crying out loudly, he sent for the wise men of Babylonia and said to them, "Whoever reads this writing and tells me its meaning shall be dressed in purple, with a chain of gold round his neck. He shall be the third authority in the kingdom."

At this, all the king's wise men went in, but they couldn't read the writing and tell the king its meaning. Then King Belshazzar was very much afraid.

But the queen remembered Daniel and suggested calling him. The king sent for him at once.

Daniel was brought into the presence of the king. The king told him, "If you can read the writing and let me know its meaning, you shall be dressed in purple, with a chain of gold round your neck. You shall be the third authority of the kingdom."

Then Daniel said, "Keep your gifts for yourself, O King, or give your presents to someone else. But nevertheless I will read the writing. You have exalted yourself above the Lord in heaven. You have brought in the vessels of his house for you, your princes, your wives and entertainers to drink from. You have praised gods of silver, gold, bronze, iron, wood or stone, who can neither see, nor hear, nor know anything, and meanwhile you have failed to honor the God to whom all your actions belong.

"It was right after this that the hand was sent by him. Now the writing is this: *Mene, Tekel* and *Peres*. And here is the meaning of the writing: *Mene:* God has counted your kingdom, and brought it to an end; *Tekel:* you have been weighed on the scales, and found wanting; *Peres:* your kingdom has been divided and given to the Medes and Persians."

That night Belshazzar, the Chaldean king, was killed, and Darius the Mede took over the kingdom.

## The Lions' Den

Daniel 6

Darius decided to appoint one hundred and twenty governors to be over the whole kingdom, and above them, three vice-presidents, one of whom was Daniel. Daniel soon so outshone the governors and other vice-presidents that the king thought about putting him in charge of the whole kingdom.

So the vice-presidents and governors tried to find some fault against Daniel, but they could find nothing because he was an upright man. Then they said, "We can't find anything to accuse Daniel of unless we find something in his religion."

After this, they hurried excitedly to the king, and said, "King Darius, live forever! All the officials of the kingdom have decided on a royal decree: anyone who within thirty days offers prayers to any god or man other than yourself should be

The men went to the king and reminded him about the law they had tricked him into signing. Then they told him that Daniel had broken it. The king became upset, because he liked Daniel, but according to the customs of his empire, he could not change the law he had signed.

By order of the king they brought Daniel and threw him into the lions' den. The king said to Daniel, "May the God whom you have been worshipping so faithfully save you." Then a stone was brought and placed over the mouth of the den, and the king sealed it with his own ring and with the rings of his princes.

The king went to his palace. He spent the night without eating or sleeping. He got up with the first light of dawn and hurried to the lions' den. When he came to the den, he called out sadly, "Daniel, servant of the living God! Has your God, whom you have worshipped so faithfully, been able to save you from the lions?"

At this, Daniel answered, "O King, live forever! My God sent his angel, who muzzled the mouths of the lions so that they didn't hurt me, because in God's judgment I have been found innocent."

The king was glad and gave orders for Daniel to be brought up out of the den.

Right away king Darius wrote to all the peoples living everywhere in the world: "Great peace to you! I have written a decree that urges people to tremble with fear before the God of Daniel, for he lives forever and his lordship never comes to an end. He works signs and wonders in heaven and on earth. He has saved Daniel from the lions' claws."

thrown into the lions' den. O King, sign this decree so that, as a law of Medes and Persians, it cannot be changed." King Darius signed the decree.

As soon as Daniel knew that the decree had been signed, he went to his house, where in his upper room he had some windows facing in the direction of Jerusalem. This was where three times every day he would fall on his knees and praise and pray to his God.

Some men came rushing in and found Daniel in prayer to his God.

# THE BOOKS OF HOSEA AND JOEL

While *Isaiah, Jeremiah, Ezekiel* and *Daniel* are called the "major prophets," because the books by or about them are long, there are twelve other prophets called "minor." The books by or about these men are shorter.

The minor prophets spoke and wrote at various times between the eighth and third centuries B.C. Unlike the books of the major prophets, those of the minor prophets are not arranged according to time order.

Hosea wrote at the time when many people of the northern kingdom (Israel) were worshipping idols and treating poor people unfairly. In God's covenant with Israel, God's rights and the rights of the poor were very important. So Hosea called the northern kingdom unfaithful to the Lord. He compares the nation to a wife who is not loyal to her husband.

*Joel* was probably written much later than *Hosea.* In Joel's time only the kingdom of Judah remained. In the first part of the book, the prophet describes an invasion of locusts as if it were the invasion of an army. He called on the people to be sorry for their sins so that God would help them. He also foretold a future time when God's Spirit would be very active in the world.

*Speaking for God, Hosea calls Israel God's child:*

**Hosea 11**

Israel is a child and I love him. I called my son out of Egypt. But the more I called, the further away he went.

How could I give you up, Israel? My heart is troubled. I am the Holy One and I am with you. I will not come to you in anger.

## Joel—the Locusts

**Joel 2**

They charge like horses in war. Rumbling like chariots they leap down the mountains. Like crackling flames they devour the fields.

They charge like warriors and scale the walls like soldiers, each of them holding its own course. They leap upon the city, run upon its walls and enter the windows like thieves.

# THE BOOKS OF AMOS AND OBADIAH

The prophet Amos was the earliest of the "writing prophets." He came after Elijah and Elisha, who were "prophets of action." Amos began writing before Isaiah did. He had been a shepherd and farmer in Judah, but the Lord called him and sent him to Israel. He went to Bethel and spoke out against the wrongs that were being done in the northern kingdom.

Obadiah wrote much later—after the Exile—and his words were directed against the people of Edom, who had been cruel toward the people of Judah. *Obadiah* is only one chapter long. Nothing is known about its author.

Both Amos and Obadiah spoke about the Day of the Lord—a time when God would reward and punish, according to how people had lived.

Notice the poetic language of both prophets. They give God's message in images.

*Amos called on the people of the northern kingdom to be loyal to the Lord and stop making life hard for the poor.*

**Amos 2, 5**

This is what the Lord says: "They [Israel] have sold the innocent person for money and the poor person for a pair of sandals. They have pushed the heads of the weak into the dust and shoved the rights of the oppressed to one side."

*Speaking for God, the prophet promised punishment. (This punishment would come when Assyria conquered the northern kingdom and took the people away to other lands.) The prophet invited the people to turn to the Lord so they could avoid being punished for their sins.*

The One who made the Pleiades and Orion,* who turns deep darkness into dawn and blackens day into night, who calls up the waters of the sea and pours them all over the earth—his name is the Lord.

Seek good and not evil, so you may live. Then the Lord God will be with you.

## The Shortest Old Testament Book

*The author of the* Book of Obadiah *says that Israel (Jacob and Joseph) will destroy Edom (Esau).*

The day of the Lord is near for all the nations, but on Mount Zion there will be some who escape.

The house of Jacob will become fire and the house of Joseph a blaze, while the house of Esau will become straw which they will set afire and burn up. The Lord has spoken.

Those who have been saved shall climb Mount Zion and will rule Mount Esau. The kingdom will belong to the Lord.

*Groups of stars.

# THE BOOK OF JONAH

This book does not contain the writings of a prophet but a story about him. A prophet named Jonah lived around the time Isaiah began to speak God's message. However, this story about Jonah was written much later. The story's purpose is to teach that God loves all peoples. Here is almost the complete book.

The word of the Lord came to Jonah, son of Amittai: "Get ready. Go to Nineveh, that great city, and tell it that I can see its wickedness very clearly."

But instead, Jonah got ready to flee to Tarshish away from the presence of the Lord. He went down to Joppa, where he found a ship sailing to Tarshish. He paid the fare and got on, intending to escape from the presence of the Lord.

But the Lord sent a strong wind over the sea, and such huge waves rose up that the ship was almost breaking. The sailors were afraid, and each one cried out to his own god. They threw as many things as they could into the sea to lighten the load.

Meanwhile Jonah had gone down below and lay there sound asleep. So the deck officer went to him and said, "Get up and pray to your god. Maybe God will be concerned about us and we won't die."

The sailors said to one another, "Let us cast lots and see whose fault this storm is." They cast lots, and the results pointed to Jonah. So they asked him, "Where are you from?" He answered, "I am a Hebrew, a worshipper of the Lord, the God in heaven who made the sea and the dry land."

The men were terrified and asked him, "What have you done?" (He had told them that he was running away from the Lord.)

They saw that the sea was growing wilder and wilder, so they asked him, "What shall we do with you to get the sea to calm down?"

He answered, "Take me and throw me into the sea, so the sea will calm down, for I know it is my fault that you have to face this storm."

But the men rowed, intending to bring him back to land. Yet they could not, because the sea grew wilder and wilder. Then they called on the Lord and said, "We beg you, O Lord, we beg you! May we not die because of this man's life. Do not charge us with murder, for you, O Lord, have acted as you pleased."

With that, they took Jonah and threw him into the sea. Then the sea lost its fury. The men were filled with great respect for the Lord, so they offered a sacrifice to him and made promises.

## Jonah's Prayer

The Lord had a huge fish ready to swallow Jonah. And Jonah was in the belly of the fish three days and three nights.

While he was in the belly of the fish, Jonah prayed to the Lord his God. He said, "I called to the Lord when I was in trouble, and he answered me. In the center of the land of death I cried for help. You heard my voice. When you threw me into the heart of the sea, when the surgings surrounded me and all your waves broke over me, I said, 'I have been driven out of your sight. If only I can see your holy Temple again!'

"You, O Lord my God, brought up my life from the pit. As my life was fading away from me, I remembered the Lord. My prayer came to you in your holy Temple. I will do what I have promised. The Lord saves."

Then the Lord told the fish to spit Jonah onto the shore.

## Jonah Goes to Nineveh

**Jonah 3**

For the second time, the word of the Lord came to Jonah: "Get ready and go to Nineveh, that great city, and announce

to it what I tell you." In obedience to the Lord's command, Jonah got ready and went to Nineveh.

Nineveh was a very large city. It took three days to walk through it.

So Jonah entered the city and walked one day's journey. He cried out this message: "After forty days Nineveh will be destroyed!"

The Ninevite citizens believed God: they called for a fast and, from the richest to the poorest among them, they all put on sackcloth.

The news came to the king of Nineveh, who rose from his throne, took off his fine robes, covered himself with sackcloth, and sat in ashes. And he gave this order to be shouted out by heralds throughout Nineveh:

"Humans and animals, herds and flocks, must neither eat nor drink. Let humans and animals be covered with sackcloth. Let them earnestly cry to God and each one stop doing evil. Who knows? God may change his mind and stop burning with anger against us. Then we shall not die."

Seeing from their actions that they had stopped doing evil, God changed his mind. He did not punish them.

# The Plant and the Worm

Jonah 4

Jonah was very angry about this. So he prayed, "O Lord! Wasn't this what I thought all along in my own country? This is why I hurried off to Tarshish! I knew that you are a tender-hearted God, patient, full of love and kindness. You change your mind about punishing people. O Lord, since this is so, please take my life from me, for I would rather die than live."

The Lord replied, "You are really angry!"

Jonah left the city and sat down to the east of it. There he built himself a shack and sat in its shade, while he watched to see what would happen to the city.

The Lord God made a plant grow up over Jonah's head to protect him from the sun. Jonah was very happy about the plant.

The Lord also sent a worm. At dawn the next day, the worm began to eat the plant, which withered. As the sun rose, God sent a hot east wind; the sun beat down so hard on Jonah's head that he wanted to die. He said, "I would rather die than live."

The Lord replied, "You are so upset about a plant that didn't cost you any work. You did not make it grow. It came up in one night and went away in another night. And I, instead—shouldn't I be concerned about Nineveh? Shouldn't I care about this great city where there are over a hundred and twenty thousand human beings who can't tell their right hand from their left, not to mention the many cattle?"

*The Lord's reply is the point of the story. God is the father of all peoples and loves them. Jonah knew this, but he didn't want the Lord to forgive the Ninevites.*

# THE BOOKS OF MICAH, NAHUM AND HABAKKUK

These three books come from two different times in the history of God's people. Not much is known about these three prophets, except that they lived in the southern kingdom, Judah. Micah, who came from a place in the countryside of Judah, told the people how upset the Lord was with their lying and cheating. He lived at the time of Isaiah, while Nahum and Habakkuk lived at the time of Jeremiah.

*Micah foretold that the Messiah (David's famous descendant) would be born in Bethlehem:*

**Micah 5–6**

From you, Bethlehem, Ephrathah—small among the families of Judah—will come someone for me who will be king in Israel. He will shepherd [his brothers] with the strength of the Lord. He will be peace.

*Further on, Micah summed up the practical teaching of all the prophets:*

You have been told what is good and what the Lord asks of you: to be fair, to love goodness and to act humbly toward your God.

## The Cruel City Will Fall

**Nahum 3**

*Nahum foretold the destruction of Nineveh, capital of the cruel Assyria. Here is the end of the* Book of Nahum:

Are your shepherds sleeping, king of Assyria? Are your best soldiers sleeping? Your people are scattered over the mountains. There is no one to bring them together. All who hear the news clap their hands. There was no one in the world whom your wickedness did not sweep over.

## The Enemy's Success Will Not Last

**Habakkuk 3**

*Habakkuk also writes about Judah's enemies (perhaps the Assyrians or Babylonians). He dares to ask the Lord why these enemies have such power. Then he makes an act of trust in God. He knows that the Lord will make everything turn out right:*

Even if the fig tree does not blossom and there is no fruit on the vines, even if the flock disappears from its pen and there are no cattle in the stalls, even then will I rejoice in the Lord and be glad in God my savior.

# THE BOOKS OF ZEPHANIAH AND HAGGAI

Zephaniah brought God's message to the people of Judah just before Jeremiah began his long ministry. This was soon after the time of King Manasseh, who had encouraged the worship of idols. Zephaniah called the people to turn back to the Lord.

Haggai lived two hundred years later. He was one of the exiles who returned to Jerusalem from Babylon. He encouraged the people to keep rebuilding the Temple.

*Several of the prophets foretold the Day of the Lord—a time when God will come to judge the rightness or wrongness of what people do. Zephaniah described that day like this:*

**Zephaniah 1–3**

The great day of the Lord is near and coming quickly. It is a day of pain and unhappiness, of darkness and gloom and thick, black clouds, a day of trumpets and noise. Silver and gold will not save people.

*Zephaniah went on to encourage the people of Judah and "all the poor of the earth" to keep God's law so they would be saved. He looked forward to happier days and spoke about "the poor of the Lord," whom God would guide as a shepherd:*

On that day all people will call out to the Lord. You will not need to be ashamed because of the ways you have offended me, for I will take away those who are proud. I will leave a people who are poor and needy. They will trust in the Lord to take care of them. They will graze in their pastures and rest with no one to bother them.

## Haggai's Call to Rebuild the Temple

**Haggai 1**

*The people who returned from exile had to rebuild their homes and clear the land before they could farm. Meanwhile, they seemed to forget about God's house.*

The word of the Lord came through the prophet Haggai: "Think about your lives. You're planting much, but harvesting little. You're wearing clothes, but you're never warm. You're earning money, but there are holes in your purses.

"Go, bring wood and rebuild my house. My house is a ruin, while each of you is concerned about his own house. It's because of you that the sky has held back the dew and the earth has held back its crops."

# THE BOOKS OF ZECHARIAH AND MALACHI

Zechariah was another prophet sent by God to encourage the exiles to rebuild the Temple. He began giving the Lord's messages to the people at the same time that Haggai did, but *Zechariah* is much longer than *Haggai* and talks about more things. *Zechariah* has two distinct parts and is believed to be the work of two prophets. The first describes some of his visions and encourages the people to rebuild the Temple. The second foretells the coming of a leader (the Messiah?).

Malachi probably lived a few years later than Zechariah, just before the time of Ezra and Nehemiah. "Malachi" means "my messenger." It may not have been the prophet's real name. Malachi was worried about the way sacrifices were being offered in the Temple, since there was some carelessness and lack of reverence.

*This is from the first part of* Zechariah:

### Zechariah 2, 9

The Lord says, "Break into cheers and be happy, daughter of Zion,* because I am coming to live among you. When that day comes, many nations will become my people, but I will live here with you."

All you peoples, be quiet in the presence of the Lord, because he is coming from the holy place where he lives.

*Here is a famous prophecy from the second part of* Zechariah:

Burst into great joy, daughter of Zion, into happy shouts, daughter of Jerusalem! You see, your king is coming to you. He is lowly and riding on a donkey. Chariots and horses and the fighter's bow will be banished** from Jerusalem. He will speak about peace to the nations. He will rule from one sea to the other and from the river to the farthest parts of the earth.

## A Pleasing Sacrifice

### Malachi 1

*Malachi foretold a time when sacrifices pleasing to the Lord would be offered day and night:*

"From sunrise to sunset my name is great among the nations, and everywhere gifts are offered to my name and a pure offering," says the Lord.

*With the* Book of Malachi, *the Old Testament ends.*

---

* *The people of Jerusalem.*

** *He will end war.*

# INTRODUCTION TO THE NEW TESTAMENT

The New Testament is the second part of the Christian Bible. It is made up of the four Gospels, the *Acts of the Apostles,* letters written by early Christians and the *Book of Revelation.*

The Gospels hold a special place in the New Testament, because they tell us about the life and teachings of Jesus. Jesus is the center of Christianity. Two thousand years ago, he, who is God, like the Father and the Holy Spirit, came to live among human beings. He showed us what God our Father is like. He did this by the way he lived and by what he taught, but especially by dying, rising and sending the Holy Spirit to live in us, teach us, make us holy and help us live as children of the Father.

It's important to read the New Testament in order to know Jesus and how to be like him. And through Jesus we come to know the Father, who calls us to live with him forever. We also come to know the Spirit of love, who gives us guidance and strength as we try to live as good Christians and Catholics.

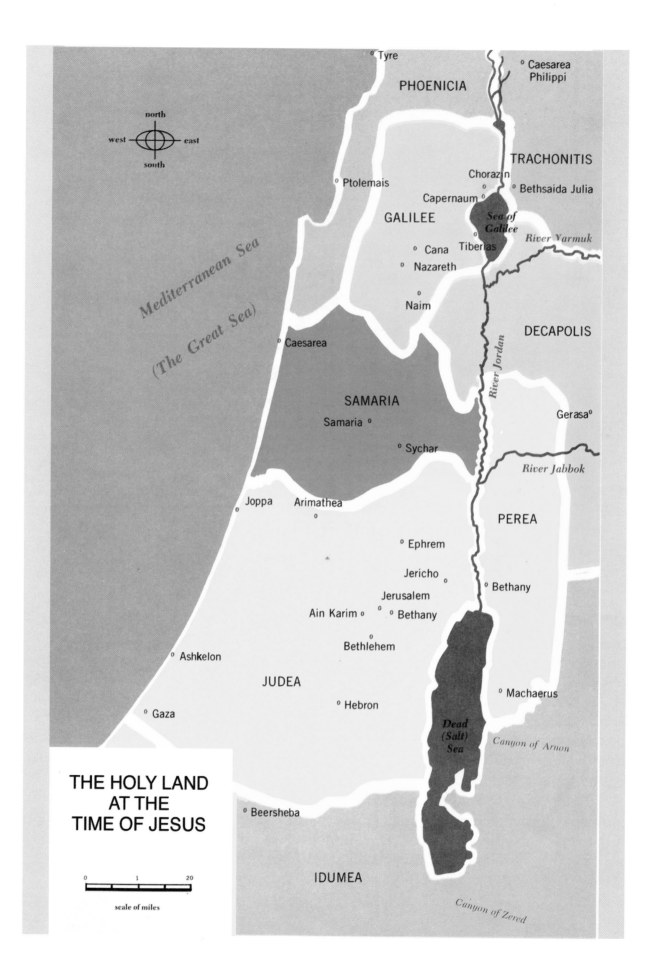

THE HOLY LAND
AT THE
TIME OF JESUS

scale of miles

# A BACKWARD GLANCE—

## The Years Between the Testaments

The descendants of Simon's son John ruled Judah as kings and high priests until 63 B.C., when a Roman general, Pompey, conquered Judah and made it part of the Roman empire. After a few years the Romans set up as ruler in the Holy Land a man named Herod, whose family came from Idumea, the old land of Edom. Herod ("the Great") was given the title "king of the Jews." After his death, his kingdom was divided among his sons. One of them, Herod Antipas, ruled Galilee and Perea at the time of Jesus. But Herod Antipas had limited power. The real rulers were the Romans.

## The Holy Land at the Time of Jesus

The map shows the way the Romans had divided the Holy Land at the time of Jesus. They called the whole territory "Palestine." It consisted of five sections, the most Jewish of which were Judea, Galilee and Perea. Samaria was the home of the Samaritans, and Decapolis was chiefly the home of Greek-speaking gentiles (non-Jews).

There were many different Jewish groups in the Holy Land at the time of Jesus. Some of the most important were the Pharisees, the Sadducees and the Zealots.

Jesus often had discussions with the Pharisees. These were lay people who appreciated God's law so much that they made other laws to help people obey it. They wanted to bring holiness into everyday life. At times they and Jesus had discussions because the Pharisees did not always agree with Jesus' explanation of God's law.

The Sadducees belonged to the upper class in Jerusalem. Some of them came from priestly families. They tended to cooperate with the Romans for the sake of peace.

Some copyists and students of Scripture (called scribes or lawyers) were Pharisees; others, Sadducees.

The Zealots were people who wanted to drive the Romans out of the Holy Land by fighting them.

It seems that the persons who eventually asked for Jesus' death came from the high priest's family and other leading families in Jerusalem. They were afraid that Jesus would try to make himself king and that the Romans would punish the whole Jewish nation for this.

# THE GOSPEL AS TOLD BY MATTHEW

"Gospel" means "Good News," and the Good News is Jesus. The four Gospels are very important, because they tell us what God has done in and through his Son, Jesus, the heart and center of what we believe and how we live as Catholics and Christians.

Each of the Gospels tells us truths about who Jesus is and what he did and taught. The Gospels were written several years after Jesus' resurrection (from about thirty to sixty years, with *Mark* probably first and *John* last). Before the material in the Gospels was collected, the events, stories and teachings were told over and over again by the members of the early Church when they gathered to talk, pray or celebrate the Eucharist.

Some of the stories about Jesus and teachings by him are repeated in the Gospels written by Matthew, Mark and Luke. These three Gospels are called *synoptics*. This word comes from the Greek language and means "at a glance." When a person glances at the synoptic Gospels, all three look very much alike, because many stories and teachings are almost the same in each one. But there are also differences between the synoptics, and these differences are important. The differences help us learn more about the writers and the life of the early Church. Also, some sections of *Matthew* are not found in *Mark* and *Luke*. The same is true for *Luke* and to some extent even for *Mark*, the shortest. So to really learn about Jesus, it's important to get to know each of the Gospels well.

The first synoptic Gospel is *Matthew*. It is named after an apostle, but Matthew may not have been involved in any stage of its writing. The final editor is unknown.

*The* Gospel As Told by Matthew *shows connections between Jesus and the Old Testament. It begins with a list of Jesus' ancestors, including David, through his legal father, Joseph. This information was important for Jews who were becoming Christians. They could see Jesus as David's descendant, the Messiah.*

## The Birth of Jesus

**Matthew 1**

This is the way Jesus Christ was born. When his mother Mary had been promised to Joseph, but before they began to live together, she was found to be carrying a child through the power of the Holy Spirit.

Joseph, her husband, since he did not want to shame Mary in public, decided to divorce her secretly.

Then an angel of the Lord came to him in a dream and said, "Joseph, son of David, don't be afraid to take your wife, Mary, home with you. The child within her is from the Holy Spirit. She will give birth to a boy, and you must name him Jesus, for he will save his people from their sins."*

_____

* *"Jesus" means "God saves."*

All this happened to complete God's word spoken through the prophet: "The virgin shall give birth to a boy, and they will name him Emmanuel," meaning, "God is with us."

Joseph woke up and did as the angel of the Lord had told him. He took Mary, his wife, home with him. She gave birth to a boy, and he named him Jesus.

## The Visit of the Wise Men

**Matthew 2**

After Jesus was born in Bethlehem of Judea at the time of King Herod, wise men from the

East came to Jerusalem and asked, "Where is the king of the Jews who has been born? We saw his star when it rose and have come to honor him."

When King Herod heard this, he was disturbed. He held a meeting with all the chief priests and law experts. He wanted to learn from them where the Messiah was to be born.

They said to him: "In Bethlehem of Judea. This is what was written by the prophet: 'You, Bethlehem, are not unimportant in the sight of the rulers of Judah, for out of you shall come a leader who will be a shepherd to my people, Israel.'"

When he heard this, Herod sent the wise men to Bethlehem. But, since he himself was the king of the Jewish people, he made plans to have this child-king killed.

Suddenly the star they had seen was there again—going ahead of them until it came to a stop over the place where the child was. When they saw the star, they were very happy.

They went into the house and saw the child with Mary, his mother. They bowed to the ground before him, and, opening their treasure chests, they offered him gifts of gold, frankincense and myrrh.

Then they went back to their own country by a different way, because they had been warned in a dream not to return to Herod.

Matthew's Gospel tells us that Joseph, too, was warned in a dream about King Herod and that he took Mary and the child and hurried away to Egypt. Meanwhile, Herod sent men to kill all the baby boys under two years old who were living in Bethlehem.

When Herod was dead, an angel of the Lord surprised Joseph in a dream in Egypt. The angel brought Joseph this message: "Get up, take the child and his mother and go to the land of Israel. Those who wanted to kill the child are dead."

Joseph got up, took the child and his mother and came to the land of Israel. When he arrived, he settled in a town called Nazareth.

## Jesus' Baptism

**Matthew 3**

At a certain time, John the Baptizer appeared in the wastelands of Judea, crying out this message: "Change your ways, for the kingdom of heaven is near!"

John wore clothes made of camel's hair. He had a leather belt around his waist. He lived on grasshoppers and wild honey.

People from Jerusalem and all Judea, as well as the whole region along the Jordan River, began going to him to be baptized in the river, while they admitted their sins.

Jesus came from Galilee to be baptized by John in the Jordan. But John tried to stop him, saying: "Are you coming to me, when instead I should be baptized by you?"

Jesus answered, "Let things be like this for now. It's best for us to do everything that is right." Then John gave in.

Jesus came up from the water as soon as he had been baptized. Suddenly the skies opened and he saw the Spirit of God coming down on him like a dove. All of a sudden a voice from heaven said, "This is my very dear Son, who makes my heart glad."

## Jesus Prepares for His Ministry

**Matthew 4**

*After his baptism—at which the Father and the Spirit had shown their support for him—Jesus went into the "wastelands."*

*Probably these wastelands were the rocky cliffs near Jericho. Jesus fasted, which means that he ate little or nothing and probably drank only water. The evangelist, or Gospel writer, says that the devil came to tempt Jesus to use his powers for his own sake, instead of only as his Father wished.*

The tempter came up to him and said, "If you are God's son, order these stones to turn into bread."

But Jesus answered, "This is what Scripture says: 'People shall not live only on bread, but on whatever words come from God's mouth.'"

Then the devil took him to the holy

city and set him on the highest part of the Temple. He said, "If you are God's son, throw yourself down, for Scripture says, 'He will give his angels orders about you, and they will support you in their hands, so you will not smash your foot against any stone.'"

Jesus told him, "Scripture also says, 'You shall not try to force God to give you proofs.'"

Then the devil took him to a very high mountain and showed him all the kingdoms of the world and how rich they were. He said, "I will give you all these things if you will throw yourself down and worship me."

This time Jesus said to him, "Away, Satan! Scripture says, 'You shall worship and serve only God.'"

Then the devil left him alone, and angels came and took care of his needs.

*The writer doesn't tell us what Jesus did next. In fact, experts say that we can't even be sure that these temptations happened at this time and in this way. The Gospels don't give us Jesus' whole life—only the parts that the first Christians liked to tell and retell. And the order in which things happened was not as important to those people as it might be to us.*

One day, King Herod (son of the first Herod) gave orders for John the Baptizer to be arrested. When Jesus learned that, he went back to Nazareth where he had grown up. Then he moved on again.

He went and settled in Capernaum, a town by the lake. From that time, Jesus began to announce this message: "Change your ways, because the kingdom of heaven is near."

When he was walking by the Sea of Galilee, Jesus saw two brothers, Simon, who was called Peter, and his brother Andrew. They were fishermen and were casting a net into the lake. He told them, "Come, follow me. I will make you fishers for people." Right away, they left their nets and followed him.

Moving on, he saw two other brothers—James, son of Zebedee, and his brother John. They were mending their nets in the boat with their father, Zebedee. Jesus called to them. And right away they left the boat and their father and followed him.

*From John's Gospel, we know that Andrew and Peter had already met Jesus by the Jordan River. Probably James and John had, too. They may have been thinking about following Jesus for some time, and when he called they were ready.*

Jesus went through Galilee, teaching in the synagogues—buildings for Scripture reading, prayer and religious instruction.

He announced the Good News of God's kingdom and cured all kinds of diseases and sicknesses. News about him spread and reached everyone in Syria, so they brought him all the sick people who were suffering from different kinds of diseases and pains. And he cured them. Also, large crowds walked along with him.

## The Sermon on the Mount

Matthew 5–8

Seeing the crowds, he went up a hill. When he sat down, his disciples came up to him. Then he began to teach them with these words:

"People who are poor in spirit are blessed, because the kingdom of heaven is for them.

"Sad people are blessed, because they will be comforted.

"Meek people are blessed, because they will inherit the land.

"People hungering and thirsting for goodness are blessed, because they will be filled.

"People who show mercy are blessed, because they will receive mercy.

"People with clean hearts are blessed, because they will see God.

"Peacemakers are blessed, because they will be called God's children.

"People who are persecuted for doing the right thing are blessed, because the kingdom of heaven is for them."

*Jesus had just turned the world upside down! He had offered people a whole new set of values.*

Then Jesus said that he wanted to improve the law that God had given through Moses. Here is an example.

"You've heard that this was said: 'Love your neighbor and hate your enemy.' But I'm telling you now: Love your enemies and pray for people who persecute you. This way you will prove that you are children of your Father in heaven, who makes his sun shine on people who commit sin and on people who live good lives. If you love people who love you, what kind of reward should you have? Be good to everyone, just as your Father is good to everyone.

"You must do for others whatever you would like them to do for you."

*In this section of Matthew, called the Sermon on the Mount, there are many other teachings of Jesus about how to live as his followers. Jesus probably said these things often, when he was teaching people in one place or another. The Our Father is in this section, too.*

## Some of Jesus' Miracles

**Matthew 8**

*Next, Matthew tells us about some of the wonderful things Jesus did to help people. Jesus worked miracles to show that he was from God and that God loves us.*

He came down the hill and large crowds went along with him. Suddenly a leper came up to him, bowed and said, "Lord, if you want to, you can cure me."

Jesus stretched his hand out and touched him, saying, "I want to. Be cured!" The man's leprosy was cured at once.

Jesus went to Peter's house and saw that his mother-in-law was in bed with a fever. So he touched her hand and the fever went away. She got up at once and began to wait on him.

When evening came, many people were brought to him because they were being bothered by the devil. He ordered the demons to go out of them. He also cured all the sick people. This brought completion to God's word that had been spoken through the prophet: "He took away our diseases and removed our illnesses."

*This is one way that Matthew relates Jesus to the Old Testament. Matthew often says that Jesus did things that the prophets had spoken about.*

## The Call of Matthew

**Matthew 9**

Jesus saw a man named Matthew sitting at the toll booth and said to him, "Follow me." He stood up and followed him.

*Tax and toll collectors usually kept more than their share of the money that they received. Because of this people hated them. How surprised the apostles and others must have been when Jesus called Matthew!*

*This story is also told in* Mark *and in* Luke, *but in* Luke *the tax collector is called* Levi. *Probably—like many other people in* Galilee at that time—Matthew had two names. "Levi" would have been used among Jewish people and "Matthew" among Greeks.*

Matthew was grateful for Jesus' call. He threw a party for Jesus and invited his own friends to it, as well as Jesus' disciples.

When Jesus was eating in Matthew's home, many tax collectors and sinners who had come were sitting with Jesus and his disciples.

Seeing this, the Pharisees asked his disciples, "Why does your master eat with those tax collectors and sinners?"

Jesus overheard this and said, "Sick people need a doctor; healthy people don't. I have come to call sinners."

## The Twelve Apostles

**Matthew 10**

Jesus called over his twelve disciples and gave them power to force devils out of people and to cure all sorts of diseases and illnesses. The names of the twelve apostles* are: first, Simon, known as Peter, and his brother Andrew; James the son of Zebedee and his brother John; Philip and Bartholomew; Thomas and Matthew the tax collector; James the son of Alpheus and Thaddeus; Simon the Zealot and Judas Iscariot, the man who would betray him.

When Jesus had finished instructing his twelve disciples, he went on his way, preaching and teaching in the towns.

## The Parable of the Sower

**Matthew 13**

*When Jesus taught, he used many comparisons called parables to explain how the Holy Spirit works in us as individuals or as a community. This is one of them:*

"A farmer went out to plant seeds. As he did, some seeds fell by the side of the path, and the birds came and ate them up. Other seeds fell on rocky ground, where they did not have much soil, so even though they shot up quickly, they were burned when the sun rose high, and they dried up because they had no roots. Still

other seeds fell among thistles, but the thistles grew up and choked them. And other seeds fell on good soil and produced good crops. Let anybody with ears listen to this."

Jesus' disciples asked him to explain the parable, and he did so.

"If anyone hears what is said about God's kingdom but does not understand, the devil comes and takes away what has been planted in his heart. This is the seed planted by the side of the path.

"The person who received the seed on rocky ground is someone who hears the word and is happy about it right away but holds on for only a little while. When trouble comes this person falls away at once. Someone who received the seed among thistles has heard the word, but worries and temptations about money choke it so it doesn't bring any results. The person who receives the word on good soil hears the word and understands it. For this person the word produces good results."

## Two Great Miracles

**Matthew 14**

At one point Jesus and the apostles were tired. Jesus suggested that they go away by themselves to rest. But a crowd followed. That was when Jesus multiplied the loaves. We will read about it in Mark's Gospel, because *Mark* has more details.

After Jesus multiplied the loaves, his disciples began to row across the Sea of Galilee while he stayed behind on the hillside.

---

*Persons who are sent out to represent someone else.*

When night came, Jesus was there alone, while the boat was already far from shore, being knocked about by the waves because the wind was against them. Toward sunrise, Jesus came walking toward them on the lake. When they saw him walking on the lake, the disciples were terrified and said, "It's a ghost!" And they screamed out in fear.

But Jesus called to them right away and said, "Courage! I'm here! Don't be afraid."

"Lord," Peter answered, "If that's really you, tell me to come to you over the water."

And Jesus said, "Come."

Peter got out of the boat and began to walk over the water toward Jesus. But when he felt the wind, he grew afraid and saw that he was beginning to sink. "Lord, save me!" he shouted.

Jesus reached out, grasped Peter and said, "You have such little faith! Why did you doubt?"

## Peter the Rock

**Matthew 16**

*Sometimes Jesus called himself the "Son of Man." That could mean an ordinary person. But in one of his visions, Daniel had seen "someone like a Son of Man" taking a seat next to God himself. So it was a name that could make people wonder.*

Jesus went to the region of Caesarea Philippi. While there, he asked his disciples this question: "Who do people say the Son of Man is?"

They answered, "Some say John the Baptizer; others, Elijah; and others, Jeremiah or another prophet."

He asked them, "But who do *you* say that I am?"

Then Simon Peter answered, "You are the Messiah, the Son of the living God."

Jesus said to him, "You are blessed, Simon, son of John, because no human being has told you this. My Father in heaven has told you. And in my turn, I tell you that you are the Rock, the rock on which I will build my Church. I will give you the keys of the kingdom of heaven." Then he warned his disciples not to tell anyone that he was the Messiah.

From that time on Jesus began to let his disciples know that he would have to go to Jerusalem and suffer much and be put to death—and be raised up on the third day.

Peter took him aside and tried to talk him out of it, saying, "God forbid, Lord! Such a thing must never happen to you!"

But Jesus turned and said to Peter, "Get out of my sight, Satan! You're in my way, because you have no feeling for how God does things."

*Jesus called Peter "Satan," because Peter was acting like the devil—tempting Jesus to take the easy way out instead of giving his life for the world.*

shone like the sun and his clothes were as bright as a light. All at once, Moses and Elijah appeared. They were talking with Jesus.

Then Peter said to Jesus, "Lord it is better for us to stay here. If you like, I will make three tents—one for you, one for Moses and one for Elijah."

## Surprising Events

**Matthew 17**

Six days later, Jesus took Peter, James and his brother John and brought them up a high mountain by themselves. And then his appearance changed. His face

While he was speaking, a shining cloud suddenly covered them, and a voice spoke from the cloud, saying, "This is my dear Son, who makes my heart glad."

When the disciples heard this, they fell to the ground face down and were very much afraid. So Jesus came over and touched them. "Get up and don't be afraid," he said. When they looked up, they didn't see anyone except Jesus.

They went back down the mountain and joined the other disciples.

On the way back to Galilee, Jesus repeated that he was going to be killed and that he would be "raised up" on the third day. The apostles tried to push the thought from their minds.

They entered Capernaum, and the officials who collected taxes for the Temple in Jerusalem came up to Peter and asked, "Isn't your master going to pay the tax?"

"Of course he is," said Peter.

As Peter went into the house, Jesus said to him, "What do you think, Peter? From whom do kings collect taxes—from their own sons or from strangers?"

"From strangers," Peter answered.

"So the sons don't have to pay," Jesus said. "Still, so that these people won't be shocked, go to the lake, catch a fish and open its mouth. There you will find a coin worth twice the Temple tax. Give it to them for both of us."

## Important Teachings

**Matthew 18**

The disciples came up to Jesus and asked, "Who is the most important in the kingdom of heaven?"

Jesus called over a little child, set him in front of them and said, "I tell you that if you don't change and become like children, you won't even enter the kingdom of heaven. This means that anyone who becomes little like this child is the most important in the kingdom of God. And anyone who welcomes a child like this in my name, welcomes me. Be careful not to neglect one of these little ones, because their angels in heaven see my Father all the time.

"I tell you that if two of you agree about anything at all to pray for, your prayer will be answered by my Father in heaven. For where two or three are gathered in my name, I am there in their midst."

Then Peter came up and asked, "Lord, how many times do I have to forgive a brother who keeps sinning against me? As many as seven times?"

Jesus said to him, "Not seven times, but as many as seventy times seven."*

## Jesus Sets Out for Jerusalem

**Matthew 20–21**

Jesus took the Twelve into a separate group, and as they were walking he told them, "We are going up to Jerusalem. There the Son of Man will be turned over to the chief priests and the law experts."

Jesus continued that he would be sentenced to death and turned over to the pagans, who would make fun of him, beat him and crucify him. But he would rise on the third day.

---

* *This means "always."*

The mother of Zebedee's sons came with them to ask for something, so he said, "What do you want?"

She replied, "Give orders that in your kingdom my two sons here will sit at your right and at your left."

Jesus answered, "Can you drink the cup I will have to drink?"

"We can," they said.

He replied, "Yes, you will drink from my cup, but as for sitting at my right or at my left, that isn't up to me. Those places are for the persons for whom my Father has saved them."

*Jesus was speaking about the "cup of suffering" that he would have to drink. Later, the apostles, too, would have to suffer and would even do it willingly, because of special strength from God.*

The prophet Zechariah had said that Jerusalem's king was to come into the city riding on a donkey. Jesus did just that. As he rode, his disciples and a large crowd walked along with him.

The crowd—both those ahead of him and those following—cried out, "Hosanna to the Son of David! The one who comes in God's name is blessed! Hosanna in the highest!"

*"Hosanna" meant "Save us," but these words were also used to give praise.*

## The Last Judgment

**Matthew 25**

*Matthew, Mark and Luke say that during the last days before Jesus suffered and died he often went to the Temple to teach the people. Here Matthew retells one of Jesus' most powerful parables:*

"When the Son of Man comes in his glory with all his angels, all the nations will be gathered. And, as a shepherd separates the sheep from the goats, he will separate people from one another, placing the sheep at his right and the goats at his left.

"Then he will say to those on his right, 'You people whom my Father blesses, come and enter the kingdom prepared for you from the beginning of the world. For I was hungry and you gave me food, thirsty and you gave me drink. I was a stranger and you took me into your home, in need of clothes and you gave them to me, sick and you looked after me, in prison and you went to see me.'

"Then those good people will say, 'Lord, when did we see you hungry and feed you, or thirsty and give you something to drink? Or when did we see you a stranger and take you into our home, or in need of clothes and clothe you? Or when did we see you sick or in prison and go to see you?'

"And he will answer them, 'I tell you, whatever you did for one of my least important brothers or sisters you did for me.' Then he will say to those on his left, 'Leave me and go to the lasting fire prepared for the devil and his followers, for I was hungry and you did not give me food, thirsty and you did not give me anything to drink, a stranger and you didn't take me in, in need of clothes and you didn't give me any, sick and in prison, and you didn't look after me. I tell you, whatever you did not do for one of my least important brothers or sisters you did not do for me.'"

## The Danger Grows

**Matthew 26**

*Jesus had enemies—people who for different reasons did not want him around—especially in Jerusalem. Among these people were some of the religious leaders and one of Jesus' own followers.*

The chief priests and elders of the nation held a meeting in the high priest's palace. They agreed to arrest Jesus secretly and put him to death.

One of the twelve, Judas Iscariot went to the chief priests and asked, "How much are you ready to give me if I turn him over to you?" They offered him thirty silver coins. From that moment, Judas was watching for his chance.

Jesus knew that Judas was going to tell the religious leaders where they could arrest him by night. At his last supper with the apostles, Jesus announced that one of them was going to turn him over to his enemies. All of them kept asking, "Who, Lord?" "Am I the one?"

And to Judas, Jesus answered, "You say so."

During the meal, Jesus took a loaf of bread, and after saying the blessing he broke it, gave it to his disciples and said,

"Take it and eat. This is my body." Then he took a cup and, after giving thanks, handed it to them, while he said, "Drink from this, all of you, for this is my blood. It is the blood of the covenant, which is to be poured out for many, so that sins may be forgiven."

After they had sung a hymn, they went out to the Mount of Olives. Jesus told them, "Tonight the faith of all of you will be shaken on my account. For Scripture says, 'I will strike down the shepherd, and the sheep will scatter.' But after I rise, I will go to Galilee ahead of you."

Then Peter said, "Everybody else's faith might be shaken, but not mine."

Jesus replied, "I tell you that this very night, before a rooster crows, you will disown me three times."

Peter and the others protested that none of them would disown or leave Jesus. Then they set out into the night.

When they reached a garden where Jesus often liked to pray, he left most of the apostles near the entrance.

Jesus took along Peter and the two sons of Zebedee. Then he began to feel sadness and fear. He said, "I'm sad enough to die. Wait here and keep me company by staying awake."

He walked a little further and fell on his face, praying, "My Father, let me not have to drink this cup if possible. Still, let it not be what I want but what you want."

He went back to the disciples and found them sleeping. He said to Peter, "So you weren't able to stay awake even one moment to keep me company! Stay awake and pray, so you won't give in to temptation. Of course, your spirit is willing, but your flesh is weak."

Jesus left them again and prayed the same way as before. Then he returned to his disciples and found them sleeping. A third time he left them and repeated his prayer.

He went back to the disciples and told them, "You're still sleeping and resting! Already the time has come for the Son of Man to be turned over to sinners. Stand up and let's go. The man who is betraying me is here."

He was still speaking when Judas appeared. A large crowd carrying swords and clubs was with him. They had been sent out by the chief priests and the elders. Judas had given them this signal: "The man I will kiss is the one. Arrest him." So he went straight to Jesus and said, "Hello, Master," and kissed him.

They came forward, grabbed Jesus and began to lead him away. But someone who was with Jesus took out a sword and struck at the high priest's servant, cutting his ear off. At this, Jesus told him, "Put your sword back where it belongs. Everybody who uses the sword will die by the sword. Don't you think that I can call on my Father, who would send more than twelve legions of angels to help me right away? But in that case, how would the Scriptures be brought to completion? It has to be this way."

They brought Jesus to the high priest, who sent for other leaders so they could hold a trial. They wanted to find Jesus guilty of some fault that could be punished with death. But even though their witnesses were lying, they did not say the same thing.*

So the high priest stood up and asked him, "Don't you have any answer? Jesus kept silent. So the high priest said to him, "I command you to tell us whether you are the Messiah, the Son of God."

Jesus replied, "You have said so. I tell you this: you will see the Son of Man seated at the right hand of the Power and coming on the clouds of heaven." **

In response, the members of the council cried out that Jesus deserved death.

Then they spat in his face and struck him with their fists and beat him.

Peter was sitting outside in the courtyard. A maid came over and said, "You were with Jesus the Galilean, too."

But Peter denied it in front of everybody. He said, "I don't know what you're talking about!"

Then he went out to the gateway and another maid saw him and said to the

------

*The agreement of two witnesses was necessary.*
**This refers to a vision in the* Book of Daniel.

people there, "This man was with Jesus of Nazareth."

And again Peter denied it, adding, "I don't even know that man!"

After a while, someone standing there came up and said to Peter, "It's true! You're one of them, too, because even the way you talk gives you away."

At this point Peter burst out, cursing and swearing, "I don't even *know* that man!"

And right away a rooster crowed. Then Peter remembered what Jesus had said: "This very night, before a rooster crows, you will disown me three times." So he went outside and began to sob.

## The Crucifixion and Death of Jesus

**Matthew 27**

When it was morning, all the chief priests and the leaders of the nation held a meeting against Jesus to sentence him to death. Then they led him to Pilate, the governor.

Judas saw that Jesus had been declared deserving of death. He brought the thirty coins back to the chief priests and elders and said, "I committed a sin when I betrayed an innocent man."

But they answered, "What do we care? Straighten it out yourself."

Then Judas threw the coins down in the Temple and left. He went out and hanged himself.

*The chief priests and others wanted Jesus to be crucified by the Romans. They brought him to Pontius Pilate, the Roman governor.*

When the chief priests and leaders accused him, Jesus did not answer. Then

Pilate asked him, "Don't you hear how many things they're saying against you?" Jesus didn't answer even a word, which made the governor really wonder.

Every year at Passover, the Romans used to set one Jewish prisoner free. Pilate offered to free Jesus. But Jesus' enemies

stirred up the crowd that had gathered, urging them to ask for a murderer named Barabbas instead of Jesus. Even though Pilate's wife had begged him not to get involved, the governor gave orders for Jesus to be whipped and crucified.

After the soldiers had whipped Jesus they added their own cruel torture. They made a crown of thorns and pressed it down on his head.

When they had stopped making fun of him, they led him away for crucifixion. As they went out of the city, they met a man from Cyrene who was named Simon and forced him to carry Jesus' cross.

When they came to a place known as Golgotha, which means "Place of a Skull," they gave him wine mixed with gall to drink, but when he had tasted it he wouldn't drink it. *

After they crucified him, they sat there, keeping watch. The charge against him was posted over his head: "This is Jesus, the King of the Jews."

From twelve noon till three in the afternoon it was dark all over the land. Then at about three o'clock, Jesus cried out in a strong voice, "My God, my God, why have you left me alone?"**

Crying out again in a powerful voice, Jesus gave up his spirit.

Suddenly, the earth was shaken and rocks split apart. Seeing the earthquake, the officer and his men exclaimed, "This man really must have been God's Son."

Joseph, a wealthy man from Arimathea, who had become a disciple of Jesus, went to Pilate and asked for Jesus' body. Pilate ordered it to be given to Joseph. So Joseph took it, wrapped it in a clean linen cloth and laid it in his own new tomb that had been cut out of the rock. Then he rolled a big stone against the opening and went away.

Because Jesus' enemies were afraid the disciples would steal his body, they made an agreement with Pilate to have guards watch at the tomb.

---

*This contained a drug to deaden the pain.*

**Those words are the beginning of a sorrowful psalm that ends in joy.*

## The Resurrection of Jesus

**Matthew 28**

As the sun rose on the first day of the week, Mary Magdalen and another Mary went to see the tomb. Suddenly there was a strong earthquake. An angel of the Lord came down from heaven, rolled away the stone and sat on it. His face was like lightning and his clothes as white as snow. The guards were shaking with fear and lay still.

Then the angel said to the women, "You mustn't be afraid. I know you're looking for Jesus, who was crucified. He isn't here, because he has risen as he said he would. Come and see where he lay, and then go quickly and tell his disciples, 'He has risen from the dead and will arrive in Galilee ahead of you; you will see him there.'"

They left the tomb quickly in fear and great joy and ran to tell the disciples. Suddenly Jesus met them and greeted them. They bowed down before him and grasped his feet. Then Jesus said to them, "Don't be afraid. Go and tell my brothers to go to Galilee. They will see me there."

The eleven disciples went to Galilee, to the mountain where Jesus had told them to meet him.

Jesus came closer and told them, "Complete authority has been given to me in heaven and on earth. So go and make all nations my disciples, baptizing them in the name of the Father and of the Son and of the Holy Spirit, teaching them to do everything I have commanded. And know that I am with you every day—until the end of the world."

# THE GOSPEL AS TOLD BY MARK

This is the shortest of the four Gospels, and it was probably the first to be finished. The Gospels as told by Matthew and Luke contain many of the same events and teachings that Mark's does. Parts of these three Gospels are in the same order. (This does not mean that it was the real order in which things happened. People in those times weren't as concerned about time order as people may be today.)

*Mark* was written for gentiles—a general name for persons who were/are not Jewish. This may be why this Gospel says very little about the Hebrew Scriptures. Instead, it concentrates on what Jesus did and how Jesus' actions showed God's power. Experts are not sure who its author was.

(Notice that the *Gospel As told by Mark* begins with John the Baptizer and does not tell us about Jesus' birth, as *Matthew* and *Luke* do.)

**Mark 1**

The beginning of the Good News about Jesus Christ the Son of God. The prophet Isaiah had written, "I hear someone shouting in the wasteland, 'Prepare the way for the Lord—make the path straight for him.'"

John the Baptizer was seen in the desert. He was announcing a baptism of change of heart, so that people's sins could be forgiven.

John announced this message: "Someone with greater powers than mine is coming. I am not good enough to bend down and untie his sandal straps. He will baptize you with the Holy Spirit."

In a very few words, *Mark* tells about Jesus' baptism and temptations. Then he states that after John was put in prison Jesus began to announce the Good News in Galilee and invited Peter, Andrew, James and John to follow him.

This is one of the events that took place in the synagogue* at Capernaum.

On the Sabbath he went to the synagogue and explained the Scripture reading of the day. His listeners were greatly impressed by what he said, because he gave the impression that he had a *right* to teach them.

There in the synagogue was a man whom the devil was holding in his power. He screamed out, "What problem is there between you and us, Jesus of Nazareth? You have come to destroy us. I know who you are—the Holy One of God!"

Jesus scolded the devil, saying, "Be quiet and come out of him!"

And the devil went out of him with a loud scream.

Everybody was amazed. They began asking each other: "What is this all about? He gives orders to the devils and they obey him." Right away the news spread through the whole region of Galilee.

---

*A building where Jewish people meet to read the Scriptures, study and pray.

## Jesus Forgives Sins

**Mark 2**

After describing some of the miracles that we also found in *Matthew*, *Mark* tells about the healing of a paralyzed man in Capernaum—perhaps in Peter's house.

Such a large crowd gathered that there wasn't any space left, even around the door. He was announcing God's word to them when four men came along carrying a paralyzed man. Because of the crowd, they couldn't bring him near enough, so they took off part of the roof above where Jesus was and lowered down the mat on which the paralyzed man was lying.

Jesus saw that they had much faith, so he said to the sick man, "My son, your sins are forgiven."

But some religious experts were there. In their own minds they thought, "Why is he saying such a thing? Who except God himself can forgive sins?"

Right away Jesus knew what they were thinking. "Why are you thinking that?" he asked. "Really, which of these two things is easier: to say to the paralyzed man, 'Your sins are forgiven,' or to say, 'Stand up, pick up your mat and walk?' So you will know that the Son of Man has power to forgive sins"—he said to the paralyzed man—"I tell you, get up, pick up your mat and go home."

Right away, the man stood up, picked up his mat and walked out. Everybody was amazed and praised God. People were saying, "We've never seen anything like this!"

But, while some people were pleased with what Jesus taught and did, others were not. Some of the Pharisees and law experts began to watch him. They wanted to catch him doing something wrong.

## More Miracles

**Mark 3–4**

Another time, when Jesus went into a synagogue, he saw a man whose hand was shrunken and thin. Some people were watching Jesus carefully to see whether he would cure the man on the Sabbath.

Jesus said to the man with the shrunken hand, "Come up here." Then he asked the men who were watching him, "Does the law let people do good or evil, save lives or destroy them, on the Sabbath day?"

But they did not answer.

Jesus was upset as he looked at them. He was disturbed by how hard their hearts were becoming. Then he said to the man, "Stretch your hand out." The man did so, and his problem was cured.

Right away the Pharisees went out and held a meeting with King Herod's followers. They began to make plans to kill Jesus.

Jesus walked toward the lake with his disciples. A large crowd from Galilee went along. He had told his disciples to always have a boat ready, because of the crowd, so people wouldn't press too tightly around him. Since he had cured so many people, everyone with health problems came crowding around him in the hope of touching him. When the devils saw him, they said loudly, "You are the Son of God," but he ordered them not to say it.

*Mark* tells some of Jesus' parables and says that Jesus explained their meaning to the disciples when they were alone.

That evening, he said to them, "Let's cross over to the other side of the lake." So they left the crowd on the shore. Soon a strong wind came up, and the waves began to beat against the boat, to the point that it was getting filled with water. Meanwhile, Jesus was in the back, sleeping on a cushion. They woke him up and said, "Master, doesn't it matter to you that we're going to die?"

He looked around, then scolded the wind and said to the sea, "Be quiet." The wind stopped blowing and everything became very calm. Then he asked them, "Why are you so frightened? Why do you have so little faith?" They were filled with wonder and asked each other, "Who is this, whom even the winds and the sea obey?"

## The Girl Who Had Died

**Mark 5**

When Jesus was at the lakeside, a leader from the synagogue came up. His name was Jairus. He threw himself down at Jesus' feet and begged, "My little daughter is going to die any minute. Please come

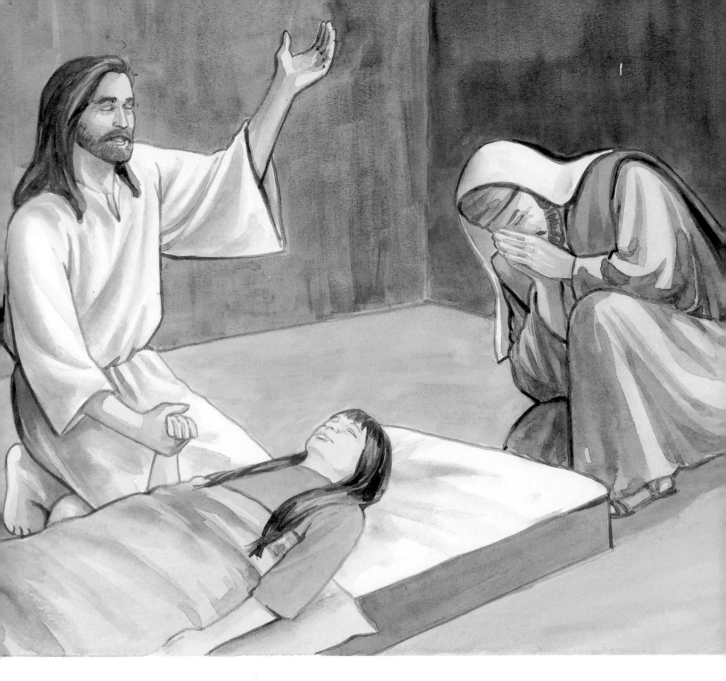

and lay your hands on her, so she may be saved and live." Jesus left with him, and a large crowd went along.

As they were walking, a woman who had had a long illness reached out and touched Jesus' robe. Right away she knew that her illness had been cured. Meanwhile, some people came hurrying up to Jairus. They had come from his house.

They said, "Your daughter is dead. Why should you bother the Master any longer?"

But Jesus overheard their message and said to Jairus, "Don't worry. Just have faith." He let no one go with him except Peter, James and James' brother John.

When they came to Jairus' house, Jesus heard people crying loudly. Taking the child's father and mother with his own companions, he went in where the child was. He held her hand and said to her, "Little girl, I tell you to get up." She stood up, and everybody was astonished. Then he ordered them not to let anyone know about this. He also told them to give her something to eat.

## Jesus Travels through Galilee

**Mark 6**

*Mark is the Gospel that tells us what Jesus' relatives and neighbors thought about his teachings and miracles. His "brothers" (cousins) didn't believe that Jesus had a special mission. At one point they had even taken Mary with them to try to get Jesus to leave Capernaum and go back to Nazareth. When Jesus did go back to Nazareth and spoke in the synagogue, the people of his village did not accept him as someone speaking for God.*

Most of his hearers were surprised and said, "Where did this man get this from? Isn't this man the carpenter, the son of Mary and brother of James and Joses and Jude and Simon? And aren't his sisters here with us?" So they found it hard to believe in him.

Jesus said to them, "A prophet isn't looked down on anywhere except in his own hometown, among his relatives and in his own family."

He wasn't able to perform miracles there, except for curing a few sick people by laying his hands on them. He was amazed at their lack of faith.

*This shows how important faith is. Many times in the Gospels we see that Jesus praised people for believing in his power to work miracles.*

Jesus went through the villages teaching. At one point he called the Twelve together and sent them away two by two, giving them power over the devils. So they went out and urged people to have a change of heart. They threw out devils and anointed many sick people with oil and cured them.

When the apostles came back, they told Jesus everything they had done and taught. And he said, "Come by yourselves to a lonely place and rest a little." So they left by boat for a lonely place to be by themselves. But people saw them leaving, and many found out where they were heading. So they went hurrying out from all the villages and gathered there ahead of them.

When he got out, he saw a large crowd and felt sorry for them because they were like sheep without a shepherd. He began to teach them and continued for several hours.

When it was late, his disciples went up to him and said, "Send the people away, so they may go to the farms and villages nearby and buy themselves something to eat."

But Jesus answered, "Give them food yourselves."

They said, "Are we supposed to go and buy bread at the cost of two hundred days' pay and give them food?"

"How many loaves of bread do you have?" Jesus asked. "Go check."

They checked and said, "Five. And two fish."

Then he told them to have everyone sit down in groups on the grass.

So the crowd relaxed in rows, grouped by hundreds and fifties. Then Jesus took

the five loaves and the two fish, looked up towards heaven and said a blessing. He broke the loaves into pieces and gave them to his disciples to give to the people. He also passed out the two fish. All ate as much as they wanted. Then, they picked up enough leftovers to fill twelve baskets. Five thousand people had eaten the loaves.

Then *Mark* tells about Jesus' walking on the water. We have already read about this in *Matthew*.

They crossed the lake and reached the shore at Gennesaret, where they came into harbor. When they got out of the boat, people recognized Jesus right away. They ran through the area and began to bring the sick on their mats anywhere they heard he was—villages, towns or farms. They set down the sick and begged Jesus to let them touch even the edge of his robe. Everybody who did so was cured.

## Healing the Deaf and the Blind

**Mark 7–8**

*The two miracles that follow are told only in* Mark.

Jesus came again to the Sea of Galilee through the land of the Ten Cities. Some people brought him a man who was deaf and had a speech problem and asked him to touch him. Jesus took the man away from the crowd and put his fingers into the man's ears. He also touched his tongue with his own saliva. Then he looked upward, sighed and said, "Ephphatha," which means, "Be opened."

The man's ears were opened, and he began to talk normally. Jesus ordered them not to tell anybody about it, but

the more he insisted on this, the more they said. People were amazed and exclaimed, "He does everything so well! He even makes deaf people hear and mute people speak."

Jesus and his disciples came to Bethsaida. People brought a blind man to him and begged him to touch him. He took the blind man by the hand and brought him outside the village. When Jesus had placed saliva on his eyes and laid his hands on him, he asked, "Do you see anything?"

The man looked up and said, "I see people. I mean that I see something like trees, but they're walking around."

Jesus laid his hands on the man's eyes again and he opened his eyes wide. He was cured and could see everything clearly.

Jesus knew that his life was in danger. The more the crowds talked about his miracles, the more disturbed his enemies became.

## Jesus Sets Out for Jerusalem

**Mark 10**

*Mark* repeats what we already saw in *Matthew:* Jesus began to tell his disciples that he was going to suffer and die. He showed himself to them in glory on the mountain top, so that after he was crucified, they would remember his glory and realize that God was with him even when he died.

After that, he predicted his sufferings again.

They were on the road that goes up to Jerusalem. Jesus was walking ahead of them, and they were confused and afraid. So again he took the Twelve aside and began to tell them what would happen to him. "You see," he said, "we're going up to Jerusalem, and the Son of Man will be turned over to some religious leaders. They will sentence him to death and turn him over to the pagans. The pagans will insult him, spit on him, whip him and kill him. And after three days he will rise."

James and John still thought that Jesus was going to have a kingdom of wealth and power and they asked to have a good share in it. So Jesus explained how his kingdom was to be.

"You know that the people who rule over the pagans show off their power. But not so with you. Instead, if somebody

among you wants to become great, he has to be a servant to everybody. Even the Son of Man came not to be served but to serve—and to give his life to save many people."

## Jesus Dies and Rises

**Mark 11–16**

All four Gospels tell us that a few days before he suffered, Jesus entered Jerusalem riding on a donkey while people shouted for joy. The four Gospels also tell us that Jesus was arrested and put on trial. We learn different details from each Gospel. Here is Mark's description of Jesus' death and resurrection.

It was twelve noon, and darkness came over the whole land until three in the afternoon. And at three o'clock Jesus cried out in a powerful voice, "My God, my God, why have you left me alone?"

When some people heard this, they said, "Listen! He's calling for Elijah!"

*The name for God that Jesus had prayed sounded like the name "Elijah." The prophet Elijah was the patron of hopeless cases.*

Someone hurried to fill a sponge with wine vinegar and stick it on a reed so Jesus could drink. Then Jesus gave a loud cry and died.

Jesus' body was taken down from the cross and placed in the tomb of Joseph of Arimathea.

When the Sabbath had ended, Mary of Magdala, Mary the mother of James, and Salome bought perfumed oils so they could anoint his body. On the first day of the week they arrived at the tomb very early, when the sun was just beginning to rise.

They were wondering, "Who will roll away the stone from the opening of the tomb for us?" But then they saw that the stone had already been rolled aside.

They went into the tomb and were startled to see a young man in a white robe sitting at the right-hand side. He told them, "Don't be afraid. You are looking for Jesus of Nazareth, the man who was crucified. He isn't here. This is where they laid him. Go and tell his disciples—especially Peter—'He will go to Galilee ahead of you.'"

But the disciples were very slow to believe the women.

Jesus appeared to the Eleven* when they were eating and scolded them for their lack of faith and stubbornness, since they had not believed those who had seen him after he had risen. Then he said, "Go out into the whole world and announce the Good News everywhere."

Then the Lord Jesus was taken up into heaven, where he was seated at the right hand of God. And they went out and announced the Good News everywhere, while the Lord helped them with miracles.

---

*\* There were only eleven apostles now, because Judas had left them and killed himself.*

# THE GOSPEL AS TOLD BY LUKE

It is believed that Luke had been a pagan, rather than a Jew, before he became Christian.

Luke wrote his Gospel for Christians who had once been pagans, and he planned it as part of a two-volume set. The other volume is the *Acts of the Apostles.* His Gospel contains many of the stories and teachings found in *Matthew* and *Mark,* plus several others. At the beginning of Luke's Gospel there are stories about the birth of John the Baptizer and the birth and childhood of Jesus. Other teachings and events found only in *Luke* form part of a long section called the "journey to Jerusalem."

When we read *Luke,* we can see that the Gospel-writer wanted to stress several truths: the role of the Holy Spirit in the lives of people who live close to God; God's forgiveness for people who do wrong; the importance of prayer; the importance of women in God's people; God's love for the poor.

Luke *begins by addressing a reader, someone called Theophilus. This name means "lover of God." We can think of each one of us as Theophilus.*

**Luke 1**

Many persons have written accounts of the things that have been done in our midst—things that were told to us by eyewitnesses. I, too, have checked into everything carefully, Theophilus, and I think it is right for me to write it all down in an orderly way for you. This way you will know that what you have been taught is true.

At the time of King Herod of Judea, there was a priest named Zechariah, who had a wife named Elizabeth. They had no children and they were both growing old.

One day something happened. It was the turn of Zechariah's group to serve in the Lord's presence, and he was chosen to burn incense. So he entered the holy place of the Lord. A large group of people stood praying outside.

An angel of God appeared to him—standing at the right side of the altar of incense.

Zechariah was startled and became frightened. But the angel told him, "Don't be afraid, Zechariah. Your prayer has been heard. Your wife Elizabeth will give you a son, and you will name him John. He will be a joy to you, and his birth will make many people happy. He will be great in the sight of the Lord. He will not drink any strong drink and will be filled with the Holy Spirit. He will bring many people back to the Lord."

Zechariah asked, "How can I be sure of this? You see, I'm an old man and my wife is along in years."

The angel answered, "I am Gabriel. I stand in God's presence and I have been sent to bring you this good news. But until

the day that this happens, you won't be able to speak, since you didn't believe what I said. It will come true at the right time."

The people who were waiting for Zechariah were surprised that he had stayed so long in the holy place. When he came out, he couldn't speak. They began to realize that he had had a vision. He kept nodding to them, without saying a word.

When the time of his service in the Temple was over, he went home. Afterwards, his wife Elizabeth conceived a child.

Six months later, the angel Gabriel was sent by God to a town of Galilee called Nazareth, to a virgin engaged to a man named Joseph, from David's family. The virgin's name was Mary. The angel went in and said to her, "Favored one, be glad! The Lord is with you."

She was greatly puzzled by these words and began to ask herself what this greeting could mean.

So the angel told her, "Don't be afraid, Mary. You have won God's favor. You will conceive and give birth to a boy, whom you are to call Jesus. He will be great and will be named Son of the Most High God.

The Lord God will give him the throne of David, his father. He will be king over the house of Jacob forever."

But Mary replied to the angel, "How will this happen, since I am a virgin?"

The angel answered, "The Holy Spirit will come down on you and the power of the Most High God will cover you with its shadow. That is why the holy one to be born will be called the Son of God. And, think of this: even your relative Elizabeth has conceived a son in her old age. This is her sixth month. You see, nothing is impossible as far as God is concerned."

In turn, Mary said, "I am the servant of the Lord. May what you have said happen to me." And the angel left her.

*We can see that Mary was free to answer "yes" or "no" to what the angel said. By saying "yes," she entered into the greatest events in human history.*

Eagerly Mary set out for a town in the hill country of Judea, where she entered Zechariah's house and greeted Elizabeth.

When Elizabeth heard Mary's greeting, the child within her leaped and Elizabeth was filled with the Holy Spirit.

Elizabeth cried out, "You are blessed among women, and your child is blessed! How have I deserved this—that the mother of my Lord should come to see me? When I heard your voice and your greeting, the child within me jumped for joy. Blessed is the woman who believes, because what she has been told by the Lord will truly happen."

Then Mary said, "My soul praises the greatness of the Lord! My spirit rejoices in my saving God, because he has looked kindly on his servant's littleness. From this very moment all generations will call me blessed, since the Almighty has done great things for me. His name is holy and his mercy reaches out through one generation after another to everyone who honors him.

"He has shown the power of his arm; he has scattered people whose minds and hearts are proud. He has taken kings down from their thrones, and at the same time he has raised up people who are unimportant. He has given many good things to the hungry but has sent the rich away empty-handed.

"He has stood by Israel his servant, as he remembered his mercy—everlasting mercy promised to Abraham and his descendants."

About three months later Elizabeth gave birth to a son. Her neighbors and relatives heard about the Lord's great kindness to her and came to celebrate with her.

They were going to call the child "Zechariah" after his father, but his mother spoke out and said, "Not at all! His name will be John."*

"Nobody in your family has that name," they protested. So they made signs to his father, asking what he would like him to be called. He motioned for a writing tablet and wrote, "His name is John."

Then suddenly Zechariah's lips and tongue were set free and he began to speak, praising God.

---

* *John means "gift of God."*

# The Birth of Jesus

An order was given by the Emperor Augustus for the names of everyone in the empire to be listed. Each person went to his family's hometown. So, since Joseph was from the family of David, he went from Galilee, from the town of Nazareth, to Judea, to David's town, Bethlehem, to register with Mary, his wife, who was going to have a child.

While they were there, the time came for her child to be born. She gave birth to a son and wrapped him in swaddling clothes. She put him to bed in a manger, because there was no space for them in the inn.

In the countryside shepherds were living in the open guarding their flocks at night. An angel of the Lord appeared to them and God's brightness shone around them. They were filled with fear, but the angel said, "Don't be afraid. I am bringing good news of great joy for the whole nation. Today in the city of David, the Savior—the Messiah-Lord—has been born from among your people. This is how you will recognize him: you will find a baby wrapped in swaddling clothes and placed in a manger."

Then suddenly a great crowd of angels appeared. They praised God, singing, "Glory to God in the heights of heaven, and peace on earth to the people with whom he is pleased."

The angels left them and went back to heaven. So the shepherds said to each other, "Let's go over to Bethlehem and see what the Lord has told us about."

They went eagerly and managed to find Mary and Joseph, and the baby lying in the manger. When they saw them, they repeated what they had been told about this child. Everyone who heard the shepherds was surprised at what they said, but Mary kept all these things in her heart and thought about them.

*A week later, the child was given the name "Jesus." Both Mary and Joseph had been told to call the child Jesus. It was a common name that meant "God saves."*

Forty days after Jesus was born, Mary and Joseph took him to the Temple. An old man named Simeon came up to them there. For years he had been waiting to see the Messiah, and the Holy Spirit helped Simeon to recognize him. He took Jesus in his arms and praised God.

They went back to Galilee, to their own town of Nazareth. The child grew into a tall and strong boy. He was wise and pleasing to God.

His parents went to Jerusalem every year for the Passover. So when Jesus was twelve they went for the celebration as usual.

*Pilgrims going to and from Jerusalem would travel in large groups. The men would walk together and the women in a separate group. Children walked with a parent, relatives or friends.*

As they started home after the days of celebration, the boy Jesus stayed behind in Jerusalem without his parents' knowing it. They traveled a day's journey, thinking he was in the group and looking for him among their relatives and friends.

When they couldn't find him, they went back to Jerusalem to look for him. On the third day they found him in the area of the Temple, sitting with the religious experts, listening to them and asking questions. Everyone who heard him was amazed. He was very bright and gave good answers.

Mary and Joseph were surprised when they saw Jesus, and Mary asked, "Son, why have you acted this way? Your father and I have been looking for you frantically."

He answered, "Why were you looking for me? Didn't you know that I have to be in my Father's house?" But they didn't understand what he was saying.

Then Jesus went back to Nazareth and lived a life of obedience to them. His mother kept all this in her heart and thought about it. And Jesus grew in wisdom as he grew in age. He was pleasing to God and to people as well.

## The Sermon on the Plain

**Luke 6**

*Next,* Luke *tells about John the Baptizer and Jesus' baptism. He gives a list of Jesus' ancestors and describes the beginning of Jesus' preaching in Galilee.*

Luke *says that after spending a night on a mountain top in prayer, Jesus chose his apostles, came down the mountainside and stopped at a level place to heal the sick people who were brought to him. He began to teach.*

*This section of Luke's Gospel is called "the sermon on the plain." It's very much like the "sermon on the mount." Here are some of the teachings:*

"Love your enemies. Do good to those who hate you. Bless those who curse you and pray for those who treat you badly. To anyone who hits you on one cheek, offer your other cheek too."

## Two Women in Need

**Luke 7–8**

Jesus went to a town called Naim, and his disciples and a large crowd went along with him. He was coming near the gate of the town when he saw a dead man being carried out. This man was the only son of his mother, who was a widow. Many people were keeping her company.

When he saw her, the Lord felt sad and said, "Don't cry." Then he went over to the stretcher and the men carrying it stood still. And he said, "Young man, I tell you to get up."

The dead man sat up and began to talk. Jesus gave him back to his mother.

Amazement came over all the people. They praised God and said, "A great

prophet has appeared among us," and "God has visited his people."

This talk about him spread through the whole of Judea and the areas around it.

A Pharisee invited Jesus to dinner at his home. So he went into the Pharisee's house and sat down to eat.

*It was the custom to greet guests with a kiss. It was also a custom to provide water so a guest could wash his feet, since people wore sandals and the streets were not paved. But Simon the Pharisee did not do these things.*

A woman whom people called a sinner learned that Jesus was eating at the Pharisee's house. She came there, carrying a jar of perfume. She was crying, and her tears wet his feet, but she wiped them dry with her hair. She kept kissing his feet and then rubbed perfume on them.

Seeing this, the Pharisee who had invited him thought, "If this man were really a prophet, he would know what kind of woman is touching him; he would know that she is a sinner."

Jesus said to him, "Simon, I have to tell you something."

And Simon said, "Speak, Master."

"A money-lender had two people who owed him money. One owed him five hundred days' wages and the other fifty. Since neither one of them could pay their debt, he released both. So, which of them will love him more?"

Simon answered, "I suppose, the one to whom he forgave more."

"Your judgment is correct," Jesus said to him. Then he turned toward the woman and said to Simon, "Do you see this woman? When I came to your house, you didn't provide any water for my feet, but she wet my feet with her tears and wiped them with her hair. You didn't give me any kiss, but she hasn't stopped kissing my feet since I came in. You didn't anoint my head with oil, but she has anointed my feet with perfume. I tell you that, even though she has committed many sins, they have been forgiven, as you can see by her great love. Instead, someone who has had less forgiven shows little love."

Then he said to her, "Your sins have been forgiven."

The guests began to say among themselves, "Who is this who even forgives sins?"

Jesus said to the woman, "Your faith has saved you. Go in peace."

Afterwards he went from town to town announcing the Good News of God's kingdom. With him went the Twelve and some women who had been cured from evil spirits and diseases.

## What Is Most Important?

**Luke 10**

*After repeating some of the events and teachings that are found in* Matthew *and* Mark, Luke *tells us that Jesus chose seventy-two disciples and sent them out to the towns he was planning to visit.*

*Next* Luke *gives us the famous "great commandment" (which is also found in* Matthew *and* Mark*). Luke adds Jesus' parable of the good Samaritan to show us that our neighbor is everybody.*

A religious expert stood up and asked this question to test him: "Teacher, what should I do to have everlasting life?"

And Jesus asked him, "What is written in the law? How do you understand it?"

He answered, "You must love your God with your whole heart, your whole soul, your whole strength, and your whole mind, and your neighbor as yourself."

And Jesus told him, "Your answer is right. Do this and you will live."

But the man felt that he was already doing this, so he asked, "Who is my neighbor?"

Jesus said, "A man who was going from Jerusalem down to Jericho was attacked by robbers. They stripped him, gave him a beating and went away, leaving him nearly dead. A priest happened to be traveling that way. He saw the man but passed by. A priest's helper also came by that place. He saw the man, too, but passed by.

"But a Samaritan came along on a journey, and when he saw the man he was filled with pity. He went and poured oil and wine on his wounds and wrapped them up. He put him on his own donkey, took him to an inn and looked after him. The next day he took out two days' wages and gave it to the manager, saying, 'Take care of him. If you have any more expenses, I'll repay you on my way back.'

"Which of these three persons do you think became a neighbor to the man who had been attacked by robbers?"

And he said, "The one who was kind to him."

So Jesus told him, "Go and do the same yourself."

On their journey they came to a village, and a woman named Martha invited him for dinner. She had a sister called Mary, who sat down at the Lord's feet and listened to what he was saying. Instead, Martha was busy preparing the meal, so she came over and said, "Lord, doesn't it bother you that my sister has left me to do the serving alone? Tell her to help me."

The Lord replied, "Martha, Martha! You are worried and bothered about so many things, but only a few things are necessary—only one, in fact. Mary has chosen what is better, and it shouldn't be taken away from her."

*In the story of the good Samaritan, Jesus taught the importance of helping others. In his conversation with Martha, he taught that while it is important to help others it is also important to spend time with God.*

## Teachings about Prayer

**Luke 11**

*Here* Luke *gives us a form of the Lord's Prayer, or Our Father, that is different from the familiar form in* Matthew. *He also gives us some of Jesus' parables about prayer.*

Jesus was in a certain place praying, and when he had finished, one of his disciples said to him, "Lord, teach us to pray, just as John taught his disciples."

So he told them, "When you pray, say, 'Father, hallowed be your name. Your kingdom come. Continue to give us our bread every day. And forgive us our sins, for we ourselves forgive everyone who owes anything to us. And lead us not into temptation.'"

Then he said to them, "Suppose someone has a friend who comes to him at midnight and says, 'Lend me three loaves of bread, because a friend of mine is here from a journey and I don't have any food for him,' and from inside he answers,

'Don't bother me. The door is already locked. The children are in bed and so am I. I can't get up to give you anything.' I tell you that even though he won't get up and give him something because he is his friend, at least because he keeps pestering him he will get up and give him everything he needs.

"I tell you, ask and you will receive; search and you will find; knock and the door will be opened. Yes, everyone who asks, receives; and everyone who searches, finds; and to everyone who knocks the door will be opened."

## Three Parables about God's Mercy

**Luke 15**

Jesus told the following parable: "If any of you has a hundred sheep and loses one of them, won't he leave the other ninety-nine behind in the countryside and go look for the lost one till he finds it? And when he has found it, he happily puts it on his shoulders and goes back home. He calls over his friends and neighbors and says, 'Celebrate with me, for I have found my lost sheep.'

"Or, again, if a woman has ten coins and loses one, doesn't she light a lamp, sweep the house and search carefully till she finds it? And when she has found it, she calls her friends and neighbors and tells them, 'Celebrate with me, for I have found the coin I had lost.' When one sinner comes back, the joy of God's angels is as great as this."

Then he said, "A man had two sons. The younger said to his father, 'Father, give me the part of the property that I'm supposed to inherit from you.' So he divided the property between them.

"Soon after that, the younger son collected all his things and set out for a distant country, where he spent all his money wildly and wastefully. When he had finished everything he had, a severe crop failure struck that country and he needed food. So he hired himself out to a local farmer, who sent him to take care of his pigs. He wanted to have his fill of the pods that the pigs ate, but no one gave him anything.

"Then he came to his senses and said, 'How many of my father's hired men have more than enough to eat, while I'm here dying of hunger! I'm going to go to my father and tell him: "Father, I have sinned against heaven and you. I don't deserve to be called your son anymore. Treat me like one of your hired men."'

"So, after deciding this, he went back to his father. While he was still quite far away, his father saw him and was deeply moved. He rushed to him, and hugged and kissed him again and again. Then the son said to him, 'Father, I have sinned against heaven and you. I don't deserve to be called your son anymore.'

"But the father told his servants, 'Quick! Take out a robe—the best one—and put it on him. Put a ring on his finger and shoes on his feet. Get the calf that has been fattened up and kill it. Let's eat and be happy, because this son of mine was dead and is alive again—he was lost and has been found.' And they began to celebrate.

"His older son had been in the fields. As he came near the house, he heard music and dancing. So he called one of the servants and asked what this was all about. And the servant told him, 'Your brother is here, and your father has killed the calf that had been fattened, because he has him back alive and well.'

"But the son became angry and wouldn't go in. His father came out and pleaded with him. But he said to his father, 'Look, I've worked for you for years without ever disobeying any of your commands, yet you never gave me a kid goat so I could have a good time with my friends. But when this son of yours comes—who has wasted your money on bad-living women—for him you killed the calf we had been fattening.'

"The father answered, 'My son, you are with me all the time, and everything I have belongs to you, too. But it was only right to have a good time and be happy, because this brother of yours was dead and is alive again. He was lost and has been found.'"

*This well-known story shows us that God loves and forgives people who admit they have done wrong and even people who think they are better than others—if they let God reach out to them.*

# The Rich Man and the Beggar

Luke 16, 18

*Here are two more famous parables of Jesus that are found only in the* Gospel As Told by Luke:

"There was a rich man who wore fine purple and linen clothing and had a banquet every day. But in front of his door lay a poor man named Lazarus who was all covered with sores. Lazarus wished he could eat the scraps that were dropped from the rich man's table.

"The beggar died and angels took him away to rest in the arms of Abraham. Then the rich man died, too. And from hell, where he was suffering, he looked up and saw Abraham far away with Lazarus in his arms. So he called out, 'Father Abraham, take pity on me and send Lazarus to dip his finger in water and refresh my tongue with a drop. I am suffering terribly in these flames.'

"But Abraham said, 'My son, remember that you had happy times during your life, while Lazarus had sorrows. Now he is being comforted here while you instead are suffering. Besides, there is a huge canyon between us and you, so those who might want to cross over to you from here cannot do it, nor can anyone cross from you to us.'

"Then the rich man said, 'Please send him to my father's house, for I have five brothers. He can warn them and keep them from coming to this place of suffering.'

"But Abraham answered, 'They have Moses and the prophets. They should listen to them.'

"And he replied, 'That isn't the point, Father Abraham. If someone goes to them from the dead, they will change their ways.'

"But Abraham said, 'If they don't listen to Moses and the prophets, they won't change their minds even if someone rises from the dead.'"

He also told this parable. It was aimed at people who were sure they were living right and looked down on others: "Two men went to pray in the Temple. One was a Pharisee and the other a tax collector. The Pharisee stood up straight and said this prayer: 'God, I thank you that I am not like the rest of men—who cheat and commit adultery—or like this tax collector here. I fast twice a week and pay a tenth of my whole income to the Temple.'

"Instead, the tax collector stood quite far away and would not even look up. He kept striking his breast and saying, 'O God, have mercy on me, for I am a sinner.'

"I tell you, the second man went to his home with God's favor but the first one did not. Anyone who tries to make himself great will be lowered down, while anyone who tries to lower himself will be made great."

# Jesus Visits Zacchaeus

Luke 19

*Now* Luke *returns to the events of Jesus' life, described as happening during a long journey to Jerusalem.*

He had reached Jericho and was walking through it when a man named Zacchaeus came along. He was one of the leading tax collectors and quite rich. He was trying to get a look at Jesus but couldn't do so because of the crowd, since

Zacchaeus was short. So he ran ahead and climbed a sycamore tree to see Jesus, since Jesus was going to pass by that spot.

When Jesus reached the place, he looked up and said, "Zacchaeus, hurry down. Today I have to stay at your house."

Zacchaeus climbed down quickly and welcomed him happily. Seeing this, everybody began to complain, "He went to stay with a sinner."

But Zacchaeus held his ground and said to the Lord, "See, Lord, I am going to take half my property and give it to the poor. And if I have cheated anyone, I'll repay him four times the amount."

And Jesus said, "This household has been saved today. The Son of Man came to search out and save what was lost."

*Like Matthew, Mark and John, Luke tells us about Jesus' entry into Jerusalem a few days before his death. Then, like Matthew and Mark, Luke continues with various events and teachings.*

*People were doing business in the Temple's outer courts—selling animals to be used for sacrifices. There was much noise and confusion.*

When he entered the Temple area, he began to drive out the sellers, telling them, "Scripture says, 'my house will be a house of prayer,' but you have turned it into a den of thieves."

## Jesus' Lasts Days in the Temple

**Luke 21**

Jesus looked up and saw rich people tossing their donations into the contribution box. Then he noticed a poor widow dropping in two tiny coins. He said, "I tell you that even though this widow is poor, she has dropped in more than all of them. All the others have put in something extra, but she's so poor that she put in what she had to live on."

Someone mentioned that the Temple was decorated with beautiful stones. Jesus said, "As for these things you are looking at—a time will come when not even one stone will be left on top of another.

They will all be thrown down. When you see Jerusalem surrounded by armies, you must realize that the city will be destroyed. There will be great sorrow in the land and great cruelty against the people."

*These sad events took place about forty years later. Some of the Jewish people, called Zealots, rebelled against Rome and their revolt was crushed.*

*Next, Jesus spoke about the end of the world:*

"In the sun, moon and stars there will be frightening signs. Nations will suffer. And then they will see the Son of Man coming in a cloud with power and bright light."

## Jesus' Sufferings and Death

**Luke 22–23**

*All four Gospels tell us about the Last Supper and Jesus' sufferings and death. Here are some details that Luke gives us which are not found in the others:*

An argument began among the apostles as to which of them should be considered the most important. Jesus said to them, "The kings of the pagans lord it over them. But it isn't that way with you. Instead the greatest among you must act as if he were the youngest and the leader as a servant.

"Simon, Simon! Certainly, Satan has asked to sift all of you like wheat. But I have prayed for you, that your faith may not fail. And in your turn, once you have come back again, you must give strength to your brothers."

Jesus said this to Simon Peter. That

night Peter would say he did not know Jesus; afterwards, he would be sorry.

Then he went out to the Mount of Olives as he usually did. And an angel from heaven appeared to him and encouraged him. His sorrow became terribly painful. He prayed even harder, and his sweat became like drops of blood flowing down to the ground.

After the high priest and the council had sent Jesus to Pilate, the governor, Pilate sent Jesus to King Herod. Herod made fun of Jesus and sent him back to Pilate. After that, Jesus was sentenced to death and led to Calvary.

Jesus was followed by a large crowd, especially of women, who were crying for his sake. He said to them, "Daughters of Jerusalem, don't cry for me. Cry for yourselves instead, and for your children."

*Jesus was speaking of the time when Jerusalem and its people would be destroyed by the Romans.*

Besides Jesus, two other men—criminals—were led along to be crucified. When they reached the place called the Skull, they crucified him there with the criminals. Then Jesus said, "Father, forgive them, because they don't know what they're doing."

One of the criminals hanging there insulted him, saying. "Aren't you the Messiah? Save yourself and us."

But the other one answered him sharply. "Don't you have any fear of God?" he asked. "You're under the same sentence, and it's right as far as we're concerned, because we're getting what our actions deserve. But this man hasn't done any harm." And then he continued,

"Jesus, remember me when you enter into your kingdom."

Jesus replied, "I tell you that today you will be with me in heaven."

Between them, the four evangelists tell us what Jesus said during those painful hours on the cross. We have seen some of them already. *Luke* gives us a beautiful expression that Jesus quoted from a psalm: "Father, I put my spirit into your hands." After Jesus said this, he died.

## The Disciples of Emmaus

**Luke 24**

*The last chapter of Luke gives us detailed accounts of Jesus' appearances to his followers after his resurrection.*

Two disciples were on their way to a village called Emmaus, about seven miles from Jerusalem. They were talking about all the things that had happened. As they talked and argued, Jesus himself joined them and walked along with them, but somehow they couldn't recognize him. So he asked them: "What are you talking about as you walk along?"

With sad faces, they stopped, and one of them, named Cleopas, answered him: "Are you the only person who is so new in Jerusalem that you don't know what's been happening there in these past days?"

"What's been happening?" he asked.

They replied, "Jesus of Nazareth had been a powerful prophet by his deeds and words in the eyes of God and of all the people. Our chief priests and leaders handed him over to be condemned to death and crucified. But we had been hoping that he would have been the one

who was supposed to set Israel free. And this is the third day since these things happened. Besides, some of our women have startled us: they went to the tomb early in the morning and did not find his body. They came back saying that they had seen a vision of angels who said he is alive.

"So some of our companions left for the tomb and found everything the way the women had said, but they did not see him."

And he said to them, "How foolish you are, and too dull to believe everything the prophets said! Wasn't the Messiah supposed to suffer such things and then enter his glory?"

Then, starting from Moses and all the prophets, he explained everything in every passage of Scripture that referred to him.

They were coming to the village for which they had set out, but he acted as if he were going farther. So they begged him, "Stay with us, because it's getting late. The day is almost over." So he went in to stay with them.

And when he was eating with them he took the bread, said a blessing, broke it and handed it to them. Then they recognized him, but he disappeared.

They said to each other, "Weren't our hearts on fire within us, while he was talking to us on the road, explaining the Scriptures?"

They jumped up from the table and went back to Jerusalem, where they found the Eleven gathered together with other disciples. And they told about what had happened on the road and how Jesus had shown himself to them at the breaking of the bread.

They were still talking about it when Jesus himself stood in front of them and said, "Peace to you."

They were startled and filled with fear, because they thought they were seeing a ghost. But he said to them, "Why are you upset? Why do you have doubts? Look at my hands and feet. I'm here in person. Touch me. Look at me. A ghost doesn't have flesh and bones, yet you see that I have them." While he was saying this, he showed them his hands and feet.

But in their joy they still couldn't believe it and kept wondering. So he asked, "Do you have anything here to eat?" They gave him a piece of cooked fish, which he took and ate in front of them.

Then he said to them: "While I was with you, I told you that everything written about me in the law of Moses, in the prophets and in the psalms had to happen." Then he opened their minds to understand the Scriptures.

He said, "It is written that the Messiah was to suffer and rise from the dead on the third day and that in his name forgiveness of sins would be announced to all the nations, starting from Jerusalem. You must be my witnesses about this. I'll send you what the Father has promised. Stay in the city till you receive power from above."

Then he led them out near Bethany. He raised his hands and blessed them, and as he was blessing them he was lifted up into heaven. They worshiped him and returned to Jerusalem full of joy. They spent their time in the Temple, praising God.

# THE GOSPEL AS TOLD BY JOHN

This Gospel is different from the Synoptics (*Matthew, Mark* and *Luke*). It repeats only a few of the events and teachings that we find in the Synoptics. Instead, John's Gospel tells us about other events and teachings from the life of Jesus.

In *John,* Jesus' miracles are called "signs"—signs of who Jesus is, of what God is like, of what Jesus would later do for his followers through the sacraments. Jesus used symbols, such as light and water, to help us understand his message.

At least two persons were involved in putting this Gospel together. They are thought to have belonged to a group of disciples of John the apostle.

*John's Gospel begins with a piece of poetry that may have been an early Christian hymn. But mixed in with the hymn are references to John the Baptizer. If you skip the paragraphs about John, it will be easier to follow the hymn. Then you can go back and read everything together.*

---

### John 1

The Word* was in the beginning, and the Word was with God, and the Word *was* God. He himself was with God in the beginning. Everything began to be because of what he did, and nothing at all came into being without him. There was life in him, and this life was light for people. This light shone in the dark, and the darkness could not put it out.

A man came, sent from God. His name was John. He came to be a witness about the light, so that everyone could believe through him. He was not the light himself, but was only a witness to the light.

The true light that shines on all people was coming into the world. He was in the world—in fact, the world began to exist because of him—but the world did not know him. He came to those who belonged to him, but they did not accept him. But to everyone who did accept him—who believe in him—he gave the power to become children of God.

And the Word became human and lived in our midst. And we saw his glory, a glory coming from the Father and belonging to an only Son, in his loving-kindness and faithfulness.

John was a witness about Jesus. He announced, "The person who is coming after me is more important than I am, because he was alive before I was."

From his riches we have all received one favor after another. For even though the law was given through Moses, loving-kindness and faithfulness came through Jesus Christ. No one has ever seen God. God's only Son, who is in the Father's heart, has told us about him.

---

*The "Word" means the Wisdom of God. The Word is another name for the second Person of the Trinity.

*The words "loving-kindness" and "faithfulness" are found in the Old Testament, especially in the* Book of Psalms. *They show God's closeness to his people and his loyalty to them. Now, says* John, *Jesus lets people see this loving-kindness and faithfulness in person. This is how he shows God's glory.* \*\*

---

\*\**Glory means "light"; it can also mean God's presence.*

This was the witness that John gave: When priests and their helpers were sent from Jerusalem to ask him, "Who are you?" he gave a straightforward answer. He said, "I am not the Messiah."

So they asked him, "Then who are you? Elijah?"

He said, "I am not."

"Are you the prophet?"

*People thought Elijah would come back*

before the Messiah came. They were also expecting a great prophet.

And he answered, "No."

So they asked him, "Who are you? Tell us, so we can bring an answer to the people who sent us. What can you say about yourself?"

He said, "I am a voice crying out in the wasteland: 'make the road straight for the Lord,' as the prophet Isaiah said."

*From John's Gospel we learn that Jesus first met some of his disciples by the Jordan River, where John the Baptizer had gathered a group of followers.*

John saw Jesus coming toward him and said, "There is the lamb of God who takes the sins of the world away. The reason why I came baptizing with water was for Israel to know about him."

John also said, "I have seen the Spirit coming down from heaven like a dove and resting on him. I didn't recognize him, but he who sent me to baptize with water told me, 'The man who baptizes with the

Holy Spirit is the one on whom you see the Spirit come down and rest.' I have seen and give witness that this is the Chosen One."

The next day, John and two of his disciples were standing there again. As John watched Jesus walking by, he said, "There is the lamb of God." The two disciples heard him say this and followed Jesus.

Jesus turned around and saw them. "What are you looking for?" he asked.

They answered, "Rabbi (which means 'teacher'), where are you staying?"

He said, "Come and see for yourselves." So they went and saw where he was staying and spent the rest of the day with him. It was about four in the afternoon.

One of these two who had followed Jesus was Andrew, Simon Peter's brother. He first looked for his brother Simon and told him, "We have met the Messiah." He

took him to Jesus. Jesus looked straight at him and said, "Simon, son of John, you will be called Peter."

The next day, when Jesus had decided to leave for Galilee, he met Philip. Jesus said, "Follow me."

Philip met Nathanael and told him, "We have met the man whom Moses wrote about. He is Jesus, the son of Joseph, from Nazareth."

Nathanael (probably the same person as the apostle Bartholomew) had a hard time believing that the Messiah could come from a town like Nazareth. He quoted a proverb: "Can anything good come from Nazareth?" Philip simply replied, "Come and see for yourself."

Jesus saw Nathanael coming towards him and said, "Here's a real Israelite. There's nothing dishonest about him."

"How do you know me?" Nathanael asked.

"I saw you under the fig tree before Philip called you."

*We don't know what that meant to Nathanael, but it certainly convinced him that Jesus had been sent by God.*

"Rabbi," Nathanael answered, "you are the Son of God, you are the king of Israel."

## The Wedding at Cana

John 2

On the third day there was a wedding at Cana in Galilee, and Jesus' mother was there. Jesus and his disciples had also been invited to the wedding. Suddenly, the wine ran out. Jesus' mother said, "They don't have any more wine."

Jesus answered, "Woman, what does that matter to us? My time hasn't come yet."

*There is a mystery here. Jesus seemed to be saying, "No" to Mary, yet we can see that it wasn't really a refusal.*

His mother said to the waiters, "Do whatever he tells you."

Six stone water jars had been placed there to use for washing. Each was large enough to hold from twenty to thirty gallons. Jesus told them, "Fill the jars with water." They filled them to the brim. Then he told them, "Dip some out and bring it to the head waiter." They did so.

When the head waiter tasted the water that had become wine, he didn't know where it had come from. (But the waiters who had poured the water knew.) So the head waiter called the bridegroom over and said, "Everyone serves the good wine first, and then a poorer quality after people have been drinking for a while. But you've kept the good wine till now!"

This event in Cana of Galilee was the beginning of the signs that Jesus did. He showed his glory and his disciples believed in him.

## God So Loved the World....

John 3

John next tells us about a visit of Jesus to Jerusalem for the feast of Passover. He says that Jesus went to the Temple and chased out the people who were selling birds and animals to be sacrificed. He also worked "signs" (miracles).

A Pharisee named Nicodemus was impressed by the signs and went to speak

with Jesus. Jesus spoke about the Holy Spirit, Baptism and everlasting life. He also hinted about his own death. All this was hard for Nicodemus to understand, but later he became Jesus' disciple.

*This section of John's Gospel contains a very famous sentence:*

"God loved the world so much that he gave [sacrificed] his own dear Son, so that everyone who believes in him may not be lost but instead may have everlasting life."

## The Samaritan Woman

**John 4**

Jesus and his disciples went back to Galilee by way of Samaria.

Jesus came to a Samaritan town called Sychar, close to the field that Jacob once gave to his son Joseph. There was a well there—Jacob's well. Tired from the journey, Jesus sat down by the well. It was around noon.

A Samaritan woman came to take some

water. Jesus said to her, "Let me have a drink." His disciples had gone into the town to buy food.

The woman said to him, "Why are you asking me for a drink when I am a Samaritan and you are a Jew?" (Remember that Jews had no dealings with Samaritans.)

Jesus answered, "If you only knew God's gift and who is asking, 'Let me have a drink,' you would have asked him and he would have given you living water."

The woman answered, "Sir, you don't even have a bucket and the well is deep. Where, then, can you get living water? Do you happen to be greater than our father Jacob, who gave us the well?"

*Jesus was talking about the Holy Spirit and the life of God within us—grace—but the woman was thinking only about the kind of water we can see and touch. In John's Gospel we find many of these "misunderstandings."*

Jesus answered, "Everyone who drinks *this* water will grow thirsty again. But anyone who drinks the water that I will give, will never grow thirsty. Instead, the water that I will give will become a fountain within the person, leaping up into everlasting life."

The woman said, "Sir, give me this kind of water, so I may not grow thirsty or have to come all the way here to get water."

Jesus answered, "Go and call your husband and come back."

The woman answered, "I don't have any husband."

Jesus said to her, "You're right in saying, 'I don't have any husband.' You've had five, and the one you have now isn't your husband."

The woman said, "I know that the Messiah is coming. When he comes he'll tell us everything."

Jesus answered, "The Messiah is the man speaking to you. I'm the Messiah."

The woman left her water jar, went into the town and said to the people, "Come and see a man who told me everything I've done. Couldn't this be the Messiah?"

The people left the town and went out toward where he was.

When the Samaritans came to him, they asked him to stay with them. He stayed there for two days, and many believed because of what he told them. Then they said to the woman, "It's no longer because of what you told us that we believe. Now we've heard for ourselves and are sure that he is the savior of the world."

## The Sick Man at the Pool

John 5

After this a feast day took place, and Jesus went up to Jerusalem. In Jerusalem near the Sheep-Pool there is another pool, which has five porches. Many sick people were lying there—blind, lame and paralyzed. They were waiting for a movement in the water.

*People believed that when a movement could be seen in the water the next sick person to go into the pool would be healed.*

A man was lying there whose illness had lasted thirty-eight years. When Jesus saw him, knowing that he had been there for a long time, he asked him, "Do you want to get well?"

The sick man answered him, "Sir, I don't have anyone to take me into the pool when the water is stirred up. While I am going there someone else goes down ahead of me."

Jesus said to him, "Stand up, pick up your mat and walk."

The man got well right away. He picked up his mat and began walking around.

But the Pharisees had rules about carrying things on the Sabbath, the day of rest. So someone scolded the man for carrying his mat. He explained that he had just been healed. When some of the religious leaders found out that Jesus was healing people ("working") on the day of rest, they complained to him.

Jesus answered, "My Father works on this day and so do I."

For this reason they wanted more than ever to kill him—not only because he was breaking the Sabbath but also because he called God his own Father, meaning that he was equal to God.

*John's Gospel contains several discussions between Jesus and the religious leaders of the Jewish people. In these discussions Jesus says indirectly but clearly that he is God. This helps us to understand why Jesus was put to death. It seemed to the religious leaders that, by saying this, Jesus was committing a horrible sin.*

## The Bread from Heaven

**John 6**

*Two of the events that John's Gospel shares with the Synoptics are the multiplication of the loaves and the walking on the water. But* John *adds something that happened after these two events.*

Some of the people who had been filled by the loaves came looking for Jesus in the hope that he would repeat the miracle. When Jesus started to speak to them about the "real bread from heaven," they asked, "Give us this bread constantly."

Jesus said to them, "I myself am the bread of life. Anyone who comes to me will surely not get hungry, and anyone who believes in me will surely never be thirsty.

"Your ancestors were fed on manna in the desert—and died. The bread coming down from heaven is of this kind: a person eats it and does not die. I am the living bread, the bread coming down from heaven. Someone who eats this bread will live forever."

*Up to this point, Jesus emphasized believing, and his words could be understood as referring to the bread of God's Word. The Old Testament speaks about the banquet of divine wisdom. But now Jesus went further:*

"The bread that I will give is my flesh, given [sacrificed] for the life of the world. Anyone who eats my flesh and drinks my blood has everlasting life and I will raise that person up on the last day—because my flesh is real food and my blood is real drink. Anyone who eats my flesh and drinks my blood lives in me and I live in that person."

*This was the first time anyone had heard anything like this. No one could understand how this was possible.*

As a result, many of his disciples said, "This kind of teaching is difficult. Who can accept it?"

Jesus knew that his disciples were murmuring about it and asked, "Does this shake up your faith? The words I've spoken to you are spirit and life. But some of you don't believe."

Because of this, many of his disciples stopped traveling with him.

Jesus said to the Twelve, "Do you want to go, too?"

Simon Peter answered him, "Go to whom, Lord? You are the one who has the words of everlasting life. We have come to believe and to be sure that you are the holy One from God."

Next, *John* tells us about discussions Jesus had with the religious leaders in Jerusalem during the feast of Booths. One of his amazing and clear statements was: "Before Abraham ever was, I AM." The very name that God had used when he called Moses was "I AM." Jesus was trying to lead the religious leaders to a new understanding of God—a God not only above and beyond everything but also close to us in the Person of his Son.

## A Woman Caught in Sin

**John 8**

This section of John's Gospel contains some interesting events. Temple guards were sent to arrest Jesus but did not do it because they were so impressed by the way he spoke. Then, one morning as Jesus was sitting in one of the Temple courts teaching the people, the leaders tried to trap him.

The religious experts and Pharisees brought a woman caught in adultery, made her stand in front of him and said, "Master, this woman has been caught committing adultery. In the law, Moses told us to stone women like this. So, what do you say?"

*If Jesus had said, "Yes, kill her by stoning," he wouldn't have followed his own teachings of love and forgiveness. If he had said, "Don't stone her," he would have disobeyed the law. But Jesus knew what they were trying to do.*

Jesus bent down and started writing on the ground with his finger. Then he sat upright and said, "Let whoever is free from sin throw the first stone at her." He bent down and again wrote on the ground.

They began to move away, beginning with those who were older. Jesus was soon left alone, with the woman standing in front of him. He sat upright again and asked, "Woman, where are they? Hasn't anyone sentenced you to death?"

"No one, sir," the woman answered.

So Jesus said, "I don't either. Go away, but don't sin anymore."

## The Man Blind from Birth

**John 9**

As Jesus was walking along, he saw a man who had been born blind.

His disciples asked him, "Rabbi, who committed a sin—this man or his parents—that he was born blind?"

*People at that time thought that handicaps were punishments for sin. But Jesus corrected his disciples' wrong ideas:*

"Neither he nor his parents sinned. He was born blind so God's actions could be shown in him. We must do the work of the One who sent me while it is day. The

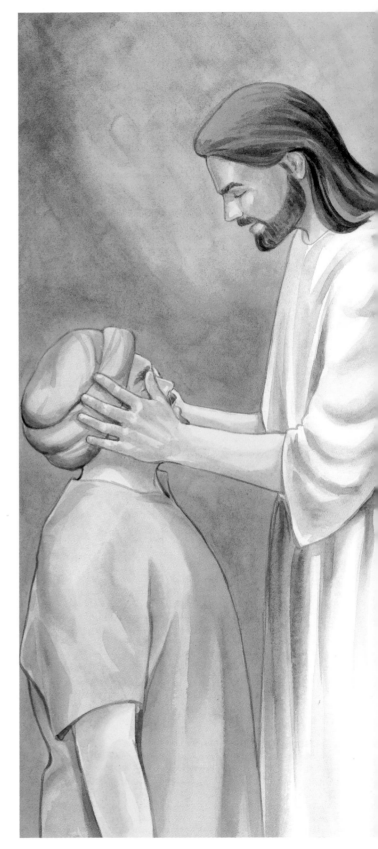

night is coming, when no one can work. While I am in the world, I am the light of the world."

Jesus made mud from dust and saliva, put the mud on the man's eyes and told him, "Go and wash in the pool of Siloam."

So he went and washed and came back able to see.

Because this happened on a Sabbath day, some of the Pharisees were disturbed, although others felt that a person who worked such a miracle really must have come from God.

*Christians see this miracle as a "sign" of Baptism: "I washed and I saw." With Baptism we received the gift of faith, by which we can "see" the things of God.*

## The Good Shepherd

**John 10**

Jesus taught: "I am the good shepherd. A good shepherd gives up his life for his sheep. When a hired helper sees a wolf coming, he leaves the sheep and runs away, so the wolf snatches and scatters them.

"I am the good shepherd, and I know my own and my own know me—just as the Father knows me and I know the Father—and I give up my life for the sheep.

"I still have other sheep which do not come from this corral. I have to lead those, too, and they will listen to my voice. Then there will be just one flock, just one shepherd.

"This is why the Father loves me—because I give up my life, and afterwards will take it back again. No one will take it from me. I will give it up by my own choice."

Jesus went back to the place across the Jordan where John had been baptizing earlier, and he stayed there. Many people came to him.

## The Raising of Lazarus

**John 11**

Then Martha and Mary of Bethany sent word that their brother Lazarus was sick. Two days later, Jesus told his disciples that he wanted to go back to Judea.

"Lazarus, our friend, has fallen asleep, but I'm going to wake him."

The disciples said, "Lord, if he has fallen asleep he will get well."

Jesus meant that Lazarus had died, but they thought he was speaking about sleep as slumber.

Then Jesus said to them openly, "Lazarus is dead. For your sakes I am glad that I wasn't there, so you will believe. Anyway, let's go to him."

When Jesus arrived, he found that Lazarus had been lying in the tomb for four days. Many people had come out from Jerusalem to express their sympathy to Martha and Mary.

Martha learned that Jesus was arriving, and she went to meet him. Martha said to Jesus, "Lord if you had been here, my brother wouldn't have died. But I'm sure that even now God will grant you anything you ask of him."

Jesus told her, "Your brother will rise."

Martha answered, "I know that he will rise at the resurrection on the last day."

"Do you believe this?" he asked.

She answered, "I do, Lord. I believe that you are the Messiah, the Son of God."

When Mary heard this, she stood up right away and went to him. Jesus still hadn't entered the village.

The people who were keeping Mary company and comforting her saw her jump up and go out, so they followed her, thinking that she was going to cry at the tomb. Mary arrived where Jesus was, and when she saw him she dropped down at his feet and said, "Lord if you had been here, my brother wouldn't have died."

When Jesus saw her crying and the

Jesus said to her, "I myself am the resurrection and the life. Anyone who believes in me will live even after death."

*Jesus was speaking about everlasting life with God, which will be given to people who believe and try to live right.*

Martha went and quietly called Mary her sister, saying, "The Master is here and is asking to see you."

people with her crying too, his soul was deeply shaken. He asked, "Where have you laid him?"

"Come and see," they said. Jesus burst into tears. So some of the people said, "See how much he loved him!" But others said, "This man who opened the blind man's eyes couldn't keep this man from dying."

Once again shaken in spirit, Jesus came to the tomb, which was a cave with a stone lying against it. Jesus said, "Take away the stone."

Martha, the dead man's sister, said, "Lord, there must be an odor. He died four days ago."

Jesus said to her, "Haven't I told you that if you believe you will see God's goodness?" So they took away the stone.

Then Jesus looked upwards and said, "Father, thank you for listening to me. For my part, I know that you always listen to me, but I said this because of the people standing here, so they may believe that you sent me."

Then Jesus called in a loud voice, "Lazarus, come out!" The dead man came out, tied up in strips of cloth from head to foot. Jesus said to them, "Untie him and set him free."

*John* tells us that this miracle disturbed the religious leaders in Jerusalem. Jesus was becoming more and more popular. The leaders were afraid that people would try to make Jesus a king. If that happened, they said, the Romans would march in and destroy the Jewish nation. So they decided that one man would have to die for the sake of the nation.

*They didn't realize that this man would die for the sake of the whole world.*

## The End of Jesus' Ministry

**John 12–16**

*At this point,* John *tells us some things that Jesus said about himself and his mission:*

"The hour has come for the Son of Man to be glorified. I tell you truly that unless the grain of wheat falls into the ground and dies, it will simply be one lonely grain. But if it dies, it will produce much fruit.

"I have come into the world as light, so that everyone who believes in me may not stay in the darkness. I have come, not to judge the world, but to save it."

Jesus had always shown his love for his disciples. But now, knowing that the hour had come for him to leave this world and go to the Father, he showed his love for them to the end.

During a supper, Jesus got up from the table and took off his robe. He reached for a towel and tied it around himself. Then he poured water into a basin and began to wash his disciples' feet and to wipe them with the towel he was wearing. Then he asked, "Do you realize what I've done? You call me 'Master' and 'Lord,' and you're right. So I am. If I, the Lord and Master, have washed your feet, you, too, must wash each other's feet. I've given you an example, so that you yourselves may do what I've done for you."

*John* tells us many other things that Jesus said as he was preparing his disciples for the great change in their lives. Soon, they would have to go ahead without him.

"You must love one another the way I've loved you. They will all recognize that you are my disciples if you love one another.

"If you love me, you will keep my commandments. And I will ask the Father, and he will give you the Sprit of Truth. He is at your side; in fact, he is in you. He will teach you everything and help you remember everything I've told you.

"You are going to have pain now, but I will see you again and your hearts will be glad, and no one will take your joy away from you."

## Jesus' Crucifixion

**John 18–19**

John *gives us some information about Jesus' meeting with Pontius Pilate.*

Pilate called Jesus to him and asked, "Are you the king of the Jews?"

Jesus answered, "You say so yourself. I was born for this—to be a witness to the truth."

Pilate asked, "What does 'truth' mean?"

Pilate ordered his soldiers to whip Jesus. Then he brought him out to the crowd and said, "I don't find any case against him. Look at him." But some of their leaders kept urging some of the people to ask for his death.

"We have a law," they cried out, "and according to that law he has to die, because he called himself God's Son."

When he heard this, Pilate was afraid. He said to Jesus, "Where are you from?" But Jesus did not answer. So Pilate said to him, "Don't you know that I have power to free you and also power to crucify you?"

Jesus answered, "You would not have any power over me if it hadn't been given to you from above."

Pilate still wanted to free him. But the people shouted, "If you free this man you aren't any friend of the emperor's. Anyone who calls himself a king is against the emperor."

Pilate's career depended on the emperor, so he ordered his soldiers to crucify Jesus.

John *tells us more of Jesus' last words on the cross:*

Standing there by Jesus' cross were his mother, his mother's sister, Mary the wife of Clopas, and Mary Magdalen. Seeing his mother and the disciple dear to him [probably John himself], who was also there, Jesus said to his mother, "Woman, here is your son." Then he said to his disciple, "Here is your mother." And from then on, the disciple took her into his own home.

After this Jesus said, "I am thirsty." They took a sponge that had been soaked in vinegar and held it to his lips. When he had taken the vinegar, Jesus said, "It is finished." Then he bowed his head and gave up his spirit.

## Jesus' Resurrection

**John 20**

*John* tells us that one of the first women to go to the tomb on Easter morning was Mary Magdalen. When she found it empty, she thought Jesus' body had been stolen and ran to tell the apostles. Peter and the disciple whom Jesus loved* went to look at the empty tomb and left, puzzled.

Mary came back and stood crying at the tomb. Then she turned around and saw Jesus standing there, but she did not recognize him.

Jesus asked her, "Why are you crying, woman? Whom are you looking for?"

She thought he was the gardener and said, "Sir, if you have carried him away, let me know where you have laid him and I will come to take him."

Jesus said to her, "Mary!"

She turned to him and exclaimed, "Master!"

Jesus asked Mary Magdalen to tell his disciples that he had risen.

That evening, when the doors of the place where the disciples were staying had been locked out of fear, Jesus came and stood in front of them and said, "Peace be with you." He showed them his hands and side. How happy they were to see him!

---

*Perhaps John?*

Then he said, "Just as the Father has sent me, so I am sending you." He breathed on them and said, "Receive the Holy Spirit. If you forgive anyone's sins they will be forgiven. If you leave anyone's sins unforgiven, they will be left that way."

Thomas, called the Twin, was not with them when Jesus came. The other disciples told him, "We have seen the Lord."

But he answered, "I'll never believe it unless I see the mark of the nails in his hands and put my finger into it and my hand into his side."

Eight days later, the disciples were again inside and Thomas was with them. Although the doors were locked, Jesus came, stood in front of them and said, "Peace be with you." Then he told Thomas, "Reach out your finger and feel my hands. Reach out your hand and put it into my side. And don't doubt but believe."

Thomas answered, "My Lord and my God!"

Jesus said, "You have believed because you've seen me. Blessed are those who have not seen, yet have believed."

## Peter, the Shepherd

**John 21**

Jesus showed himself to some of his disciples again by the Sea of Tiberias (the Sea of Galilee). They had been fishing all night without catching anything.

Toward sunrise, Jesus was standing on the shore, even though the disciples did not realize it was Jesus.

Jesus called to them, "Have you caught anything?"

They answered, "No."

He said, "Throw the net to the right and you'll find something." They threw out the net and couldn't pull it in because there were so many fish in it.

The disciple whom Jesus loved cried out that the man was Jesus, so Peter dove in and swam to the shore. Meanwhile, the others brought the boat to the land, towing the full net. Jesus had built a fire on the beach and was already cooking a fish on it for breakfast.

When they had finished their meal, Jesus asked Simon Peter, "Simon, son of John, do you love me more than these others do?"

He answered, "Yes, Lord, you know I love you."

Jesus said to him, "Take care of my lambs." Again, he asked him a second time, "Simon, son of John, do you love me?"

Jesus answered, "Yes, Lord, you know I love you."

Jesus said to him, "Shepherd my young sheep." For the third time he asked him, "Simon, son of John, do you love me?"

Peter was sad because for the third time Jesus had asked, "Do you love me?" He answered, "Lord, you know everything—you know that I love you."

Jesus said to him, "Shepherd my sheep."

*Did Peter realize that he had just made three declarations of love—in place of his three denials?*

Jesus also did many other things. If all of them were written down, I don't think the whole world would have enough space to hold all the books they would fill.

# THE ACTS OF THE APOSTLES

The "acts" of the apostles were the deeds the apostles did. This book tells about two apostles in particular: Peter, leader of the Twelve, and Paul, who was chosen later by Jesus after the Church began to spread. A few other early Christians are also mentioned in the *Acts of the Apostles*—for example, the deacons Stephen and Philip and another Christian leader named Barnabas.

This book was written by St. Luke and continues the account found in Luke's Gospel. But it seems that Luke did not intend to write a complete history of the early Church. Rather, he wanted to tell about some of the main events in the growth of the Church and give some explanations, which are found in the apostles' speeches.

The book opens in Jerusalem, where all the first Christians were Jewish. Later, in Antioch, Syria, the Christian community had many gentile members. From Antioch the Church spread to many gentile cities and towns, chiefly because of the missionary journeys of Paul. At the end of the book, Paul reaches the capital of the Roman Empire, where a community of Christians welcomes him.

So *Acts* shows us that in its first years the Church spread very quickly. What was the reason for this rapid growth? Throughout the book, Luke tells us that the Holy Spirit was working through the first Christian missionaries and in the hearts of people everywhere. The *Acts of the Apostles* is sometimes called "the gospel of the Holy Spirit."

*Acts begins with a longer account of Jesus' ascension than the one with which Luke ends his Gospel. But before that, Luke greets "Theophilus," as he did at the beginning of his Gospel:*

**Acts 1**

Theophilus, my first report was about everything that Jesus did and taught until the day he was taken up into heaven. This happened after he taught the apostles whom he had chosen through the Holy Spirit.

After his sufferings he gave them many clear proofs that he was alive by showing himself to them for forty days and speaking to them about the kingdom of God. During this time, he told them not to leave Jerusalem but to wait for the Father's promise. He said, "John baptized with water, but in a few days you will be baptized with the Holy Spirit. You will be my witnesses in Jerusalem, in all Judea and Samaria, and even to the farthest parts of the world."

After he said this, he was taken up while they watched. Then a cloud carried him out of their sight.

They kept looking up until two men wearing white suddenly stood beside them. They asked, "Men from Galilee, why are you looking at the sky? This Jesus who was taken up from you will come back in the same way that you have seen him go."

Then they went back to Jerusalem from the Mount of Olives, which is a short walk away. They went to the upper floor where they had been staying. Peter was there, and John, James, Andrew, Philip, Thomas, Bartholomew, Matthew, James son of Alpheus, Simon the Zealot and Jude, son of James. All of them spent the time in prayer. The group included Jesus' mother Mary and some other women, as well as Jesus' brothers.*

At one point, Peter stood up in front of the brothers and sisters (there were about one hundred twenty people there). He said, "My brothers, the piece of Scripture had to reach completion in which the Holy Spirit, speaking through David, told beforehand about Judas, the man who guided the people who arrested Jesus. In the *Book of Psalms* it is written: 'Let his land be left alone, with no one living on it,' and also, 'Let someone else take his place.'

"So from among the men who were with us all the time that the Lord Jesus walked among us, from his baptism by John till the day he was taken up from us, someone must become a witness to his resurrection along with us."

They suggested two men—Joseph Justus, who was called Barsabbas, and Matthias. Then they prayed, "Lord, since you know the hearts of everyone, you are

*Jesus' cousins.

the one who must show us which of these two men you have chosen to take over this ministry from which Judas turned away."

They drew lots, and the lot fell to Matthias, so he joined the eleven apostles.

## The Coming of the Holy Spirit

### Acts 2

The tiny Church began to grow on Pentecost, the feast of the spring harvest. Jerusalem was full of pilgrims who had come for the celebration.

On the day of Pentecost they were all together in one place, when suddenly a noise came from above them. It sounded like a strong, rushing wind. It filled the whole house where they were staying. Then they saw what looked like tongues of fire breaking away from each other. The flames went to rest on each one of them. All of them were filled with the Holy Spirit and began to speak in other languages, according to the gifts the Spirit was giving them.

Right then, religious Jews from every nation in the world were staying in Jerusalem. When the sound came, a crowd gathered. They were surprised that each one heard them speaking in his own language. They asked themselves, "What does this mean?"

But some people joked and said, "They are full of new wine."

With the Eleven beside him, Peter shouted out, "Men of Judea and all of you who are staying in Jerusalem! This has to be explained to you, so pay attention to what I say. These men aren't drunk, as you think, because it's only nine in the morning. Instead, this is what the prophet Joel spoke about:

"'God says that this is what will happen in the last times: I will pour out my Spirit on all people, men and women. I will also show wonders in the sky above and signs on the earth below.'

"Listen to these words. As you know, Jesus of Nazareth was a man whom God supported with powerful miracles—wonders and signs that God did in your midst through him. By God's plan, this man was turned over to you, and you had pagans kill him by nailing him on the cross. But God raised him up. He could not be held by the power of death.

"God raised up this very man, Jesus, and all of us are witnesses to this. When he was lifted up to God's right hand and received from the Father the Holy Spirit that had been promised, he poured the Holy Spirit out, and this is what you are seeing and hearing. God has made Jesus both Lord and Messiah."

These words cut into their hearts. They said to Peter and the other apostles, "What should we do, brothers?"

Peter answered, "Have a change of heart. Let each one of you be baptized in the name of Jesus Christ, so your sins can be forgiven. Then you will receive the gift of the Holy Spirit, because this promise is for you and for your children, as well as for all those far away whom the Lord your God may call."

Everyone who accepted what he said was baptized. On that day about three thousand people joined them. They cen-

tered their lives around the teaching of the apostles, the sharing of their goods, the breaking of the bread and prayer.

## The Healing of a Lame Man

**Acts 3–5**

One day, Peter and John were going up to the Temple at three in the afternoon, which was the time for prayer. Every day a man who had been lame all his life was carried in and laid at the Beautiful Gate of the Temple, so he could beg from the people as they went in. When the man saw Peter and John, he asked them for money.

Instead, Peter, with John beside him, looked straight at the man and said, "Look at us!" So the beggar stared at them, hoping to get something.

Then Peter said, "I don't have silver or gold, but I'll give you what I do have. In the name of Jesus Christ, the man from Nazareth, walk." Then he took him by the right hand and helped him up.

Right away his feet and ankles became strong. He jumped up and began to walk. Then he went into the Temple with them, walking and jumping and praising God. All the people saw him walking and praising God, and they recognized him as the man who used to sit asking for money at the Beautiful Gate of the Temple. They were amazed at what had happened to him.

As he stood there, holding onto Peter and John, everyone ran to them.

Peter said to the people, "Men of Israel, why are you so surprised at this? Why are you staring as if we had made the man walk by our own power or holiness? The God of Abraham, Isaac and Jacob, the God of our ancestors, has given glory to his servant Jesus. Because of our faith in his name, he has given strength to this man whom you see and know. There is no other name under the sky by which we can be saved."

The priests and temple guards noticed the noise and excitement. They arrested Peter and John and put them in jail for the night. Meanwhile, many of the people who had listened to Peter believed in Jesus and joined his followers.

When Peter and John were taken for questioning the next day, Peter again said that the lame man had been healed by Jesus. So the religious leaders told Peter and John not to speak about Jesus anymore.

Peter and John answered, "You yourselves decide whether God thinks it right for us to listen to you rather than him. We can't help telling what we have seen and heard."

After warning them again, the leaders sent the apostles away. They couldn't find any way to punish them, because they were afraid of the people.

The community of believers was one in heart and soul. None of them called any of their possessions their own. They shared everything.

With great enthusiasm, the apostles kept speaking about the resurrection of the Lord Jesus. Through them, many miracles and signs were done among the people. They stayed together in Solomon's Porch and no one else dared to mix with them, but the people respected them very much.

Greater numbers of men and women began to believe in the Lord. Sick people were brought into the streets and laid there

on mats, so that at least Peter's shadow might fall on some of them as he walked by. People even came from nearby towns, bringing the sick, and they were cured.

## Stephen Is Killed

**Acts 6–7**

*There were two main groups in the Jerusalem community. Both groups were Jewish. But Luke calls only one of these groups "Hebrews." This was the group that used the Hebrew language when they prayed. He calls the other group "Hellenists." The Hellenists were Jewish, but they spoke and prayed in the Greek language and used a Greek translation of the Scriptures.*

Since the number of disciples kept growing, at a certain time the Hellenists began to complain against the Hebrews because their widows were overlooked when the daily portion of food was given out. So the Twelve called the community of the disciples and said, "Choose from among yourselves seven well-liked men who are filled with the Holy Spirit and wisdom, and we will put them in charge of this duty."

The whole community was pleased and elected Stephen, Philip, Prochorus, Nicanor, Timon, Parmenas and Nicolaus.

*These men were given the title "deacons," or "people who serve."*

Stephen was very outspoken, and his Hellenistic background got him into trouble with some Jewish leaders who were not followers of Jesus. For example, Stephen did not feel that the Temple was important, and he said so. He argued about it. So he was arrested and brought to trial.

At the trial, Stephen said that he could see Jesus standing next to God. This was a way of saying that Jesus himself was God.

The leaders shouted back, shutting their ears with their hands, and rushed at him together. Then they dragged him out of the city and began to stone him. They laid their cloaks at the feet of a young man named Saul.

*They had taken off their cloaks in order to throw better. Saul hadn't quite reached the legal age for taking part in the stoning, so he could only watch.*

As they were stoning him, Stephen prayed, saying, "Lord Jesus, receive my spirit!" Then, on his knees he cried out loudly, "Lord, don't hold this sin against them." After this he fell asleep [died].

## Philip Baptizes a Gentile

**Acts 8**

On that day a great persecution broke out in Jerusalem and the disciples scattered throughout the regions of Judea and Samaria—everyone except the apostles.

One of the other deacons, named Philip, began to travel around in Samaria and Judea. He told the Good News about Jesus and baptized people who wanted to follow "the Way"—as the religion of Jesus' followers was called.

An angel of the Lord spoke to Philip and told him, "Get ready and go toward the south, along the lonely road from Jerusalem to Gaza." So Philip got ready and left.

Suddenly he saw an official of the queen of Ethiopia, sitting in his carriage and reading. He had come to worship in Jerusalem and was on his way home. The Spirit said to Philip, "Go up to that carriage and stay near it."

So Philip ran up and heard him reading the prophet Isaiah. "Do you understand what you are reading?" Philip asked.

He answered, "How can I, if nobody will teach me about it?" He invited Philip to come up and sit beside him. Philip began to explain to him the Good News of Jesus.

As they went along the road, they came to some water, and the official asked, "Is there anything to prevent me from being baptized?"

So he ordered the carriage to stop, and both of them—Philip and the official—went down into the water, and Philip baptized him. After they had come up out of the water, the Spirit of the Lord took Philip away. The official didn't see him anymore but continued happily on his way.

## Saul Meets Jesus

**Acts 9**

Saul went to the high priest and asked for letters to the synagogues in Damascus, allowing him to arrest men and women who belonged to "the Way" and bring them back to Jerusalem.

But when Saul was coming near to Damascus, light from the sky suddenly surrounded him. He dropped to the ground and heard a voice say to him, "Saul! Saul! Why are you making me suffer?"

"Who are you, Sir?" Saul asked.

And the voice answered, "I am Jesus. You have been making me suffer. Get up now and go into Damascus. There you will be told what to do."

The men who were traveling with Saul stood there silently. They had heard the voice but hadn't seen anyone.

Saul got up from the ground. His eyes were open but he couldn't see. So they took him into Damascus, leading him by the hand. And he wasn't able to see for three days. He did not eat or drink.

In Damascus there was a disciple named Ananias. The Lord appeared to him in a vision and said, "Go to Straight Street. At the house of Judas ask for a man named Saul. He is praying and has seen in a vision a man named Ananias coming in and laying hands on him, so that he can see again."

But Ananias answered, "Lord, I've heard from many people about the harm this man has been doing to your holy people in Jerusalem. He's in town to arrest everyone who believes in you."

But the Lord said to him, "You must go. This man is someone special who will speak about me. I will let him know how much he will have to suffer for my sake."

So Ananias left and went to the house, and after he had laid his hands on Saul, he said, "Brother Saul, the Lord Jesus—who appeared to you while you were on the way here—has sent me so that you may recover your sight and be filled with the Holy Spirit."

Right away something like scales fell from Saul's eyes and he could see again.

He got up and was baptized. After he had eaten something, his strength came back to him.

Then the Church began to enjoy peace all through Judea, Galilee and Samaria. It grew and received much encouragement from the Holy Spirit.

Peter was traveling all around and visited the holy people living in Lydda. There he found a man named Aeneas. He was paralyzed and had been in bed for eight years.

Peter said to him, "Aeneas, Jesus Christ cures you. Get up and make your bed." He got up right away. The people in Lydda and Sharon knew this man, and they turned to the Lord.

## A Roman Begins to Follow the New Way

Acts 10

In Caesarea there was a man named Cornelius, a Roman officer who generously gave money to Jewish charities and prayed much to God. One afternoon in a vision he saw an angel, who came and said, "Cornelius, your prayers and donations have risen up to God. Send some men to Joppa to call a man named Simon Peter."

Cornelius sent two servants and a soldier to Joppa. They returned with Peter and some disciples. Peter had seen in a vision that it would be all right to enter a gentile's home to speak about Jesus.

Cornelius was waiting with his family and his servants.

Peter began to speak. "I believe that God has no favorites," he said. "He welcomes anybody who respects him and who does what is right, no matter what nation the person comes from. God sent Jesus of Nazareth, who went around doing good. Everyone who believes in him receives forgiveness of sins."

Peter was still speaking when the Holy Spirit came down on all the people listening to him. So Peter gave orders for them to be baptized.

## Peter Is Imprisoned

**Acts 11–12**

Even more gentiles came into the Church when Jesus' followers began to settle in Antioch in Syria, where they were given the name "Christians." A good man named Barnabas led the Church there and invited Saul to help teach the new Christians.

Meanwhile, trouble started in Jerusalem.

King Herod had James, the brother of John, killed by the sword. Then he had Peter put in prison and guarded by four squads of soldiers. The Church prayed hard for him.

On the night before his trial, Peter—bound with two chains—was sleeping between two soldiers. Guards were watching the gate of the prison. Suddenly an angel of the Lord appeared and a flash of light shone in the cell. The angel woke Peter and said, "Get up right away." The chains fell off Peter's hands. Then the angel said, "Put on your belt and sandals," which Peter did. "Wrap yourself in your cloak and follow me," said the angel.

Peter went out and followed him, but he couldn't believe that all this was real. He thought he was seeing a vision. They passed the first guard post and then the second. When they came to the gate leading to the city, it opened by itself. After they had walked a block, the angel suddenly disappeared.

Then Peter came to his senses and said, "It's true. The Lord has sent his angel and saved me from Herod's hands."

# Saul-Paul Begins His Journeys

**Acts 13**

One day, the leaders of the Church at Antioch were praying and fasting. That day the Holy Spirit made them see that it was time for someone to set out on a missionary journey. After praying, the community sent Saul and Barnabas off "to do the work for which God had chosen them."

They sailed to the island of Cyprus, then went on to Asia Minor, now called Turkey, speaking to the Jewish people first, and then to the gentiles. After several months, they returned to Syria. On this trip Saul began to use the Roman name "Paul"—which was more familiar to Greeks and Romans than the Jewish name "Saul."

On the next trip, Paul went with Silas and a boy named Timothy. After traveling through Asia Minor, they crossed a stretch of water into Macedonia, in what today is northern Greece. There they had some adventures in the city of Philippi.

*Luke was with the group now, so instead of saying "they" he says "we."*

On the Sabbath day we went outside the city gates to the river, where there was a place of prayer. We sat down and spoke the message to the women who had gathered there. The Lord opened the heart of a woman called Lydia to pay attention to what Paul was saying. She was baptized with her family.

One day, when we were on our way to the place of prayer, a slave girl came to-

ward us. She had a spirit by which she foretold the future and earned quite a bit of money for her owners. She followed close behind all of us, shouting out, "These men are servants of the most high God!"

After she had been doing this for several days, Paul had had enough. He turned and said, "In the name of Jesus Christ, I order you out of her." The spirit left her right away.

The girl's owners saw that their source of income was gone. They grabbed Paul and Silas, brought them to the city leaders and said, "These men are disturbing our city. They are encouraging a way of living that we Romans should not follow."

The city leaders had Paul and Silas beaten. Then they threw them into jail and gave the jailer orders to guard them very well. So he put them in the inner cell and fastened their feet.

Around midnight Paul and Silas were singing hymns to God and the other prisoners were listening. Suddenly, such a strong earthquake took place that the foundations of the prison were shaken. All the doors of the jail opened and everyone's chains fell off.

The jailer woke up and thought that all the prisoners had run away, so he took out his sword to kill himself. But Paul cried out in a loud voice, "Don't hurt yourself! All of us are here!"

So the jailer rushed in and threw himself down in front of Paul and Silas. He was shaking. Then he led them out and asked, "Brothers, what do I have to do to be saved?"

They answered, "Believe in the Lord Jesus and you will be saved—you and your family."

They spoke God's word to him and to

all his family and servants. He washed their wounds and was baptized, he and all who lived with him. Then he took them to his house, where he laid out a meal and celebrated his belief in God.

The next day the city leaders sent the police with the instructions, "Let those men go."

When the jailer told Paul to leave town quietly, Paul objected. Paul was a Roman citizen. It had been against the law for them to beat him and jail him with no trial.

Paul said, "They've beaten us in public without a trial, even though we're Roman citizens. They've thrown us into jail. And now do they think they'll push us out secretly? No way! They have to come and lead us out of here themselves."

The policemen told the leaders, who were afraid when they learned that these men were Roman citizens. So they went and apologized to them. They led them out and then begged them to leave the city.

## More Believers

**Acts 17–18**

In the land now called Greece, Paul went from one city to another, telling the Good News of Jesus. For a while, he traveled alone, while his friends stayed behind to continue teaching the new Christians.

At last Paul came to the famous city of Athens. There, he held discussions at the synagogue with Hebrews and other people who believed in God. He also spoke every day in the marketplace with anyone who came by.

Since the people of Athens liked to hear about anything different, some of them invited him to speak to a large, important group. Paul was happy to do this.

"People of Athens," he said, "I see how religious you are in every way. As I was walking around and carefully looking at the things you pray to, I saw an altar on which were written the words, 'To an unknown god.' So this is the one I want to tell you about—the one you pray to without knowing him. The God who made the world and everything in it is the Lord of heaven and earth. He gives everyone life and breath and everything else. He isn't far from any one of us We live and move in him, as one of your own poets has said."

Then Paul went on to speak about Jesus and his resurrection. Some of the people laughed, but others became Christians.

After that, Paul left Athens and went to Corinth, where he met a Jew named Aquila and his wife Priscilla. Since he did the same kind of work as they did, he stayed and worked with them. They were all tent-makers. Every Sabbath he held discussions in the synagogue and tried to win over both Jews and Greeks.

As usual, it wasn't easy, and Paul became discouraged.

One night the Lord said to him in a vision, "Don't be afraid. Keep speaking out. I am with you and nobody will attack and hurt you. I have many people in this city."

Paul settled down for a year and a half, teaching the Word of God.

On his second trip back to Antioch, Paul stopped in Ephesus, an important city in Asia Minor. He promised to return there.

## More Travels

Acts 19–26

On his next journey Paul returned to Ephesus, where he settled down for three years. Then Paul returned to the cities and towns he had visited on his second trip.

During this third journey, God worked a great miracle through Paul. A boy had fallen from a high window while Paul was teaching and had died, but Paul brought him back to life.

After his third journey, Paul set out for Jerusalem. On the way he stopped at Miletus, the seaport near Ephesus and sent a message to the Church leaders of Ephesus that he would like to see them.

When they arrived, he told them, "I'm on my way to Jerusalem, without knowing what will happen to me there. The Spirit keeps warning me in town after town that chains and sufferings are waiting for me. But I don't think of my life as valuable, as long as I carry out the ministry I've received from the Lord Jesus—to witness to the Good News of God's grace."

*Since Paul says he has been warned "in town after town," it seems that the Spirit was speaking to him through Christian prophets.*

When Paul reached Jerusalem, the warnings came true. A misunderstanding with some of the Jewish people led to a riot. Roman soldiers saved Paul from being killed, but they put him in prison because he had been accused of teaching against the Temple and of bringing Greeks into the part of the Temple that was only for Jews. Even though none of this was true, Paul suddenly found that many people wanted his death.

Was there a way out? Yes. Jesus appeared in a vision and encouraged him. "You will be my witness in Rome, too," he said. So Paul asked the governor to send him to Rome for trial.

## Shipwreck

**Acts 27**

Paul set off by ship for the capital of the empire. Luke and a disciple named Aristarchus went with him. Paul and other prisoners were guarded by Roman soldiers.

That ship took them as far as a port in Asia Minor. Then they boarded another ship, bound for Italy, which began to sail westward along the coast of the island of Crete. By now, winter was coming, and everyone began to worry about the weather.

Soon a northeaster began to blow. It rushed down the coast of the island. The ship was swept along by it. The sailors began to throw the cargo overboard. Neither the sun nor stars could be seen for many days, while the storm raged without letup. Almost everyone gave up hope of surviving.

One day Paul stood in the midst of everyone and said, "Take courage. Not a single one of you will be lost, only the ship. I'm saying this because last night an angel of the God whom I worship appeared to me and said, 'Don't be afraid. You will speak before the emperor. Everyone who is traveling with you is God's gift to you.' So take courage. We'll run aground on some island."

And that was what happened. Soon land was sighted. The sailors were steering for the beach when they struck a reef and the ship ran aground on it.

The soldiers wanted to kill the prisoners, since they were afraid some might escape. But the officer kept them from carrying out their plan. He ordered those who could swim to throw themselves overboard and reach shore first and the others to follow them, some on planks, some on other pieces of wreckage from the ship. In this way everyone was brought to land safely.

## The End of the Journey

**Acts 28**

We learned that the island was called Malta. The people there were very kind to us. They lit a bonfire, since it was rainy and cold, and made all of us feel at home.

Paul had gathered up a bundle of sticks that he put on the fire, and because of the heat a snake crawled out of the bundle and fastened itself onto Paul's hand. When the native people saw the snake, they said to one another, "For sure this man is a murderer. He escaped from the shipwreck but Justice didn't let him live."

Instead, Paul shook the snake off into the fire without being hurt. The island people expected that soon he would swell up or suddenly drop dead, but when nothing happened, they changed their minds and called him a god.

Nearby was some land owned by Publius, the ruler of the island. He welcomed us warmly and put us up as a real friend. His father was sick in bed. Paul cured him after praying and laying his hands on him. Because of this event, other islanders who were sick also came and were cured.

When spring came, the officer and his men took their prisoners aboard another ship and sailed for Italy.

And so we came to Rome. When the brothers there heard about us, they came out to meet us. When Paul saw them, he thanked God and took courage.

*Luke ends* Acts *with Paul's first weeks in Rome. Just as Luke's Gospel leads us from Nazareth by way of many places to Jerusalem, so* Acts *leads us from Jerusalem by way of many places to Rome. People around the Mediterranean Sea considered Rome the "center of the world," so Luke stops there.*

*Most experts think that Paul was set free after his trial but was martyred (killed for his beliefs) in Rome a few years later. His tomb and Peter's are both in Rome.*

# THE LETTER OF PAUL TO THE ROMANS

We are now in a section of the New Testament that contains letters written by apostles and other early followers of Jesus. Most of these letters were written to groups of Christians in different places. These letters are full of teachings about what Jesus asks us to believe and how he asks us to live. This kind of letter is sometimes called an *epistle*.

Several of the New Testament letters were written by Paul. Others, which have different styles, may have been written by people close to Paul, since they say things that Paul might have said. Paul's name is connected with thirteen letters in all.

The longest of St. Paul's letters is his letter to the Christians of Rome. It is a very important letter, but a bit hard to understand. We will quote some of the easier parts.

**Romans 1, 8**

Greetings from Paul, a servant of Christ Jesus, called to be an apostle and set apart to proclaim the Good News of God—to all in Rome, dear to God and called to holiness, grace and peace from God our Father and the Lord Jesus Christ.

*The New Testament letters help us understand what to believe and how to live. Here is an expression of trust in Jesus, who loves us so much and has done so much for us:*

If God is on our side—and he is—who can be against us? He did not spare even his own Son, but gave him up for all of us—so how can he not give us everything else, too?

Who can separate us from Christ's love? Can trouble or sufferings or persecution or hunger or danger? I am sure that neither death nor life nor any creature could ever separate us from the love of God, which we see in Christ Jesus our Lord.

## Living As Christians

**Romans 12**

*Later, Paul gives some practical points for our life:*

Your love must be real. You must hate evil and hold on to what is good. Love each other as brothers and sisters. See who can show the most respect for one another. Work hard; serve the Lord. Live in hope and joy. Put up with troubles patiently. Pray much and well. Help Christians who need help. Be happy with people who are happy and be sad with people who are sad. Get along well with each other. Be at peace with everyone.

300

# THE FIRST AND SECOND LETTERS OF PAUL TO THE CORINTHIANS

When Paul wrote to the Romans, he was writing to Christians whom he had not yet visited. Instead, when he wrote to the people of Corinth (who lived in what we today call Greece), he was writing to people with whom he had spent a year and a half. But no matter who the first readers were, there is always something in Paul's letters that can help us today, too. Scripture is for all times.

*The First Letter to the Corinthians is about many different topics. Maybe Paul was answering letters that the Corinthians had written to him.*

*At one point, Paul compares the Church with a human body. The whole body is Christ, and we are parts of Christ. This shows how much we need each other.*

**1 Corinthians 12–13**

The eye cannot say to the hand, "I do not need you," or again the head to the feet, "I do not need you." The parts should take care of one another. If one part suffers, all the other parts suffer with it. If a part is honored, all the other parts are happy, too.

*One of the most beautiful sections of this letter is Paul's famous "hymn to love." After talking about different gifts in the Church, Paul says that love is the best:*

If I can speak in all languages, but don't have love, I've become a noisy gong, a clanging cymbal. And if I know every mystery and have faith for moving mountains, but don't have love, I'm nothing.

Love is patient; love is kind. It isn't jealous; it doesn't brag. It isn't full of pride. It isn't rude. It's not self-seeking. It's hardly ever angry. It doesn't hold grudges. It's not happy when wrong is done. It's happy about the truth. Love never dies.

## Second Corinthians

**2 Corinthians 12**

*In this letter, Paul tells about his ministry as an apostle and states that God helps him when he is weak. Here is a famous section:*

The Lord told me, "My grace is enough for you." So I'm content with weakness, mistreatments, hardships and worries for the sake of Christ. For when I'm weak, then I'm strong.

# THE LETTERS OF PAUL TO THE GALATIANS AND EPHESIANS

The New Testament letters to groups that were written by St. Paul or contain his teachings are arranged in order of length, starting with the longest and ending with the shortest. Then come Paul's letters to individuals. Here are two more letters to groups.

The people of Galatia (in Asia Minor) seemed to be forgetting that the saving death and resurrection of Jesus are at the center of the Christian faith, so Paul stressed Jesus' death and resurrection. He told the Galatians not to be foolish by believing other teachings.

The letter to the people in or near the city of Ephesus is written in a different style and vocabulary. It may have been composed by one of Paul's disciples. It praises God for making us his children in the Church and invites us to "live in the light"—free from sin.

*The* Letter to the Galatians *and the* Letter to the Ephesians *say a lot about Jesus' death and resurrection and what they mean in our own lives.*

*Here (from* Galatians*) is one of Paul's most famous writings about sharing in Jesus' death and resurrection:*

---
**Galatians 2**

I have been crucified with Christ. I am still alive, but no longer myself—instead, Christ is living in me. I live by faith in the Son of God, who loved me and gave himself up for me.

*The closer Christians grow to Jesus, the better they understand this difficult passage of* Galatians. *Saints—holy people like Paul— always remain who they are, but they let Christ live and act through them for the good of the world and its people.*

## Praise for God's Plan of Love

**Ephesians 1**

*This is the opening of* Ephesians, *which praises God the Father for his wonderful plan to bring the world to him:*

Let us praise the Father of our Lord Jesus Christ, who in Christ has blessed us with spiritual gifts in the highest heavens. Out of love, he chose us in Christ before the creation of the world to be holy and without sin, and he planned to make us his children through Jesus Christ.

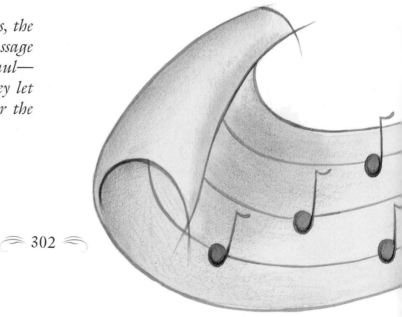

# THE LETTERS OF PAUL TO THE PHILIPPIANS AND COLOSSIANS

These letters to the Christians of Philippi (in modern Greece) and Colossae (in modern Turkey) contain pieces of early Christian hymns about Jesus. They also give us much good advice.

In its words and style, *Colossians* is much like *Ephesians,* and like *Ephesians* it may have been written by a disciple of Paul.

Philippians 2, 4

Make me completely happy by thinking the same way and having the same ideals. Be like Christ, who became like a servant.

*In the second part of his letter, Paul encourages the Philippians and us:*

Always be happy. Yes, always be happy. Let everyone see how kind you are. The Lord is near. Do not be anxious. Instead, tell God what you want. Ask and thank. Then the peace that comes from God will guard your hearts and minds in Christ Jesus.

Think about everything that is true, good, right and pure—everything that is beautiful and worth praising. Do whatever you have been told and have seen me do. Then God, who gives peace, will be with you.

## More on Christian Living

Colossians 3

*The Colossians seem to have been confused. They had some wrong ideas about religion and a wrong understanding about Jesus, who is the center of the Christian faith. So the author quotes a hymn that shows how important Jesus is.*

*In the second part of the letter, the author uses the image (word picture) of putting on special clothes. He means changing ourselves inside—in our spirit:*

As the chosen people of God that you are, put on kindheartedness, good will, humility, gentleness and patience. If anyone has a complaint against someone else, forgive each other, the way the Lord has forgiven you. On top of everything else, put on love, which holds everything together.

# THE FIRST AND SECOND LETTERS OF PAUL TO THE THESSALONIANS

The first of these letters was written about twenty years after Jesus Christ died and rose. At that time the teachings and miracles of Jesus were still being told aloud at the Eucharist and in other Christian gatherings. Within the next fifty years they would be written down to make up the four Gospels. All the rest of the New Testament, too, would be written during the next fifty years.

When Paul wrote his first letter to the Thessalonians, he was writing the first "book" of the Christian Scriptures that we have today.

*The people of the city of Thessalonica (in what is Greece today) were confused. They thought that the world was going to end very soon. Some of them were afraid. So from Corinth, Paul wrote a letter to help the Thessalonians better understand their Christian faith. First, he encouraged them:*

### 1 Thessalonians 1; 2 Thessalonians 2

From Paul, Silvanus and Timothy to the church of Thessalonica, which is in God the Father and in the Lord Jesus Christ. We wish you grace and peace.

We continually thank God for all of you and mention you in our prayers, for we always remember the way you show your faith, work in love and hold out in hope. News of your faith in God has spread everywhere.

*Toward the end of this letter, Paul spoke about the resurrection of the dead. But even after this, the Thessalonians were confused. Some of them stopped working. They may have thought, "Why work if the end of the world is coming?" Paul wrote a second letter, urging them not to worry about the end of the world. He said:*

While we were with you, we earned our bread, working day and night so as not to burden you. I say this because I hear that some of you are living in idleness. We direct such people to work for the food they eat.

# THE FIRST AND SECOND LETTERS OF PAUL TO TIMOTHY AND LETTER TO TITUS

These letters are addressed to individual people. They are very much alike in the way they are written and in the vocabulary used. They are different from the letters written or dictated by Paul himself: *Romans, Galatians, 1* and *2 Corinthians, Philippians, 1 Thessalonians* and *Philemon*. But from the time of the early Church, Paul's name has been connected with these three letters.

The *Acts of the Apostles* tells us that Timothy and Titus were disciples of Paul. These letters show us that Timothy and Titus became leaders of Christian communities. Since Church leaders are "pastors" ("shepherds"), all three letters are called "pastoral" letters.

*At some point, the leaders of the Christian communities or churches began to be called bishops.\* Timothy became the bishop of the Church in Ephesus, and Titus became the bishop of the Church on the island of Crete. (See the map on the next page.)*

## The First Letter to Timothy

**1 Timothy 2, 4**

*Here are some samples of good advice from 1 Timothy:*

I ask that prayers and thanks be offered for all people—for kings and all leaders, so our lives may be peaceful and religious. This is pleasing to God our savior. He wants all people to be saved and learn the truth.

Don't let anybody look down on you because you are younger. Be an example

to people in your conversation, in your lifestyle, in your love, faith and clean living. Be sure to read Scripture, to preach and to teach. Pay attention to yourself and what you are teaching. Keep doing these things, because in this way you will save yourself and those who listen to you.

## The Second Letter to Timothy

**2 Timothy 1–2**

*In 2 Timothy, the writer tells Timothy to be brave:*

God has not given us a spirit of fear. He has given us a spirit of courage, of love and of good judgment. Because of this, you must not be ashamed to be the Lord's witness. Join me in going through difficulties for the Good News. We are helped by the power of God, who saved us and called us to live a holy life, not because of anything we had done but because of his own plan and his grace, which he has given us in Christ.

---

*\*Bishops are the "shepherds" of the Church. They watch over the "flock."*

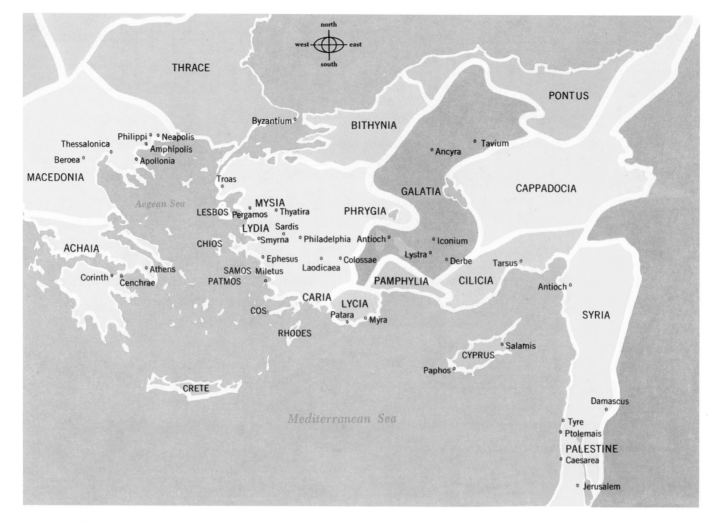

You must grow strong because of the grace that is ours in Christ Jesus.

Pass on to trustworthy persons the same teachings you learned from me. Then they will be able to teach others.

Stay on guard at all times. Take difficulties with patience. Tell the Good News and carry out your ministry completely.

## The Letter to Titus

**Titus 3**

*The* Letter to Titus *is much like the* First Letter to Timothy. *Titus had been sent to organize the Christian communities on the island of Crete.*

*The third chapter of this letter describes how Christians should live. The grace that comes to us from Jesus' death and resurrection makes us able to live a true Christian life. This grace comes through Baptism.*

Remind everybody to obey rulers and people in charge, and to be kind and gentle. God saved us in a way that matches his mercy. He saved us through the bath of rebirth by the Holy Spirit, whom he poured out on us in Jesus Christ our Savior, so that we could inherit everlasting life.

I want you to remind people about these things, so that those who believe in God will work at honest jobs that help them improve.

# THE LETTER OF PAUL TO PHILEMON

This short letter shows us how gentle and understanding Paul could be. He was kind and thoughtful toward the man he was writing to and also kind and thoughtful toward Onesimus, the runaway slave whom he was writing about. Here is the letter, almost complete.

*Philemon was a Christian who lived in Colossae. He owned slaves, as most rich people did in those days. One of his slaves, Onesimus, had stolen something and run away to Rome, a large city where it was easy to hide. While in prison, Paul somehow met Onesimus and persuaded him to go back to Philemon. In this letter Paul asks Philemon to take Onesimus back "as a brother."*

---

**Philemon**

Paul and our brother Timothy greet Philemon, our fellow-worker who is so dear to us. Grace and peace from God our Father and the Lord Jesus Christ.

I always mention you in my prayers and thank God for the reports I hear about your love and faithfulness toward the Lord Jesus and all his holy people. Your love has been a great joy and comfort to me.

Even though I am sure I could *tell* you to do the right thing, I would rather *ask* you to do it. I am writing about my "child," whose father I became while I was here in prison. I am talking about Onesimus, who has become very useful* to both of us—to you and to me.

I am sending him back to you. This means that I am sending you my heart. I would have liked to keep him with me, but I decided not to do anything without talking with you about it, so that the good you do will be what you freely choose.

Maybe the reason he left you for a while was so you could have him back forever, no longer as a slave but as a dear brother.

So, if you think of me as your friend, welcome him as if he were me. And if he has hurt you or owes you anything, I, Paul, will pay for it. I am writing this with my own hand.

*Paul often dictated his letters, but sometimes he wrote a few words to show that something was especially important to him.*

Please give joy to my heart in Christ. I am sure that you will do this.

May the grace of the Lord Jesus Christ be with you.

---

**"Onesimus" means "useful."*

# THE LETTER TO THE HEBREWS AND THE LETTER OF JAMES

The *Letter to the Hebrews* seems to have been written to Jewish people who had become Christians. This letter helps us understand the relationship of Jesus to the Hebrew Scriptures (our Old Testament). The writer explains why it is important to be loyal to Jesus.

The *Letter of James* is a very practical letter about Christian living. It seems to have been written for Christians in general, not for a particular person or community.

Experts don't know who wrote *Hebrews*, and they are not sure who wrote *James*, since at least three early Jewish Christians were called James. *James* may have been written by a cousin of Jesus, who was in charge of the Church at Jerusalem.

*The* Letter to the Hebrews *begins by explaining that Jesus is the greatest of all the prophets and that he is God himself:*

### Hebrews 1, 12

In the past, God spoke to our ancestors through the prophets, a little at a time and in different ways. Now in our times, he has spoken to us through his own Son. He is God's brilliant light and his very reflection. He keeps the universe together just by his word. He made up for our sins and then took his seat at the right hand of the great King.

*Toward the end of this book, the writer reminds us that Jesus died for us. We should love him in return.*

Let us run our race, throwing off the sins that weigh us down and keeping our eyes fixed on Jesus. He could see joy waiting for him while he suffered on the cross. Now he has taken his seat at the right side of God's throne. Think about this, so you will not grow tired or give up.

## James' Concerns

### James 2

*James saw that some Christians did not help others. So he wrote:*

What good is it to claim to have faith if you don't do anything? Suppose a brother or sister has nothing to wear or to eat, but you say, "Take care of yourself," without helping him or her, what good is that? Faith that does not result in good deeds is dead.

# THE FIRST AND SECOND LETTERS OF PETER

Like the *Letter of James*, these letters do not seem to have been written to a particular person or group.

*First Peter* was written to all the Christians in the area called "Asia Minor" (which today is the country of Turkey). In the early years of the Church, there were many Christians in that part of the world. This book may have been written by St. Peter, but more likely by one of his disciples.

*Second Peter* was written several years after St. Peter died, and the real author is unknown. (As we know, it used to be a custom to name books after famous people.)

*The* First Letter of Peter *talks about Baptism and what Jesus has done for us through this sacrament. Here is one of the sections of* 1 Peter *on Baptism.*

**1 Peter 1–2**

The Holy One who called you asks you to become holy yourselves in all your actions. This is why it is written, "You must be holy, because I am holy." You have been bought not with silver and gold, which do not last, but with the precious blood of Christ.

You have been given a new birth by God's living and lasting word—the Good News that has been told to you. You are chosen people, royal, holy, God's own people called by him out of darkness into his wonderful light.

## Christian Life

**2 Peter 1**

*The authors of 1 and 2 Peter encourage Christians to live as good followers of Jesus. Here is a section from 2 Peter:*

Our Lord Jesus called us through his own great deeds. Through them we have been given precious promises, so that we may be made sharers of God's own nature. Because of this you must work hard to add virtue to your faith, knowledge to your virtue, self-control to your knowledge, patience to your self-control, goodness to your patience and love to your goodness.

# THE FIRST LETTER OF JOHN

This letter speaks about light and life, darkness and death, love and hate. Light, life and love are also themes of John's Gospel. Experts think that the final editor of the fourth Gospel was also the author of the *First Letter of John*.

*The beginning of 1 John is very much like the beginning of John's Gospel:*

### 1 John 1

We are speaking of the Word of life, which has lived from the beginning, which we have heard, which we have seen with our eyes and touched with our hands. The eternal life that was with the Father became visible to us. We are telling you what we have seen and heard, so that you may share life with us, for we ourselves share life with the Father and with his Son, Jesus Christ.

## Christian Love

### 1 John 4–5

My dear ones, let us love each other, because love comes from God, and everyone who loves is born from God and knows God. Someone who doesn't love doesn't know God, because God is love.

God's love was shown in this way: he sent his only Son—his dear Son—into the world, so that we could have life through him. God loved us and sent his Son to make up for our sins.

If God has loved us like this, we have to love each other. Nobody has ever seen God. If we love each other, God stays with us and his love grows in us.

Anyone who says, "I love God," but hates a brother or sister, is lying. Someone who does not love a brother or sister who can be seen, can't love God, who can't be seen. Anyone who loves God must love others too.

We love God's children whenever we love God and keep his commandments. And for anyone who is a child of God his commandments are not hard.

God answers us no matter what we ask, as long as it agrees with his plan.

# THE SECOND AND THIRD LETTERS OF JOHN AND THE LETTER OF JUDE

All three of these letters are very short. *2 John* and *3 John* are very much alike. Because the words used are different from those in *1 John*, experts think that someone else wrote them.

The *Letter of Jude* might have been written by a cousin of Jesus.

*The* Second Letter of John *was written by "the elder" to "a chosen lady and her children." The "elder" was an important person in the Church. The "lady" seems to have been a group of people—maybe some leaders in a Christian community. The elder warned his readers not to follow anyone who taught anything different from what Jesus taught.*

**2 John**

My Lady, I am not writing down a new commandment for you, but the one we have had from the beginning—to love one another.

Anyone who does not hold onto the teaching of Christ, does not hold onto God. Anyone who does hold onto that teaching holds onto both the Father and the Son.

## Help for Missionaries

**3 John**

*The* Third Letter of John *is about a problem in a certain community. Their leader would not help a group of mission-aries who were passing through, so the writer asked one of his friends to help them.*

My dear friend, I pray that you are doing well in every way.

You are loyal in whatever you do for our brothers. You will do a good deed if you give them what they need for their journey. God deserves this. They are traveling for him.

## Keeping the Faith

**Jude**

*The* Letter of Jude *warns Christians to remember what they have been taught and not let anyone lead them into living a different way.*

My dear friends, remember what the apostles told you: "There will be people who will make fun of you and will live according to their own wrong desires." These people can get you to disagree with each other.

But you, instead, must encourage each other. Pray with the help of the Holy Spirit. Live in God's love, while you wait for the loving forgiveness of our Lord Jesus Christ to bring you to eternal life.

# THE BOOK OF REVELATION

*Revelation* (also called "the Apocalypse") is the only book of its kind in the New Testament. It seems to have been written in a community which regarded the Roman empire as a serious threat to Christianity. The writer used many symbols to describe a great struggle between good and evil. Through these symbols he taught that in the end God will win a great victory and everyone who loves God and is loyal to him will have happiness forever.

Just as there are relationships between certain New Testament letters that connect them in some way with Paul, so the *Book of Revelation* is related to John's Gospel and the *First Letter of John*. Some thoughts and words are alike. But there are also many differences. The author of the book calls himself "John," but his identity is unknown.

*The* Book of Revelation *is made up of different visions—unusual things that the writer saw and heard. The visions are full of symbols.*

*As the book opens, the writer tells us that he had been sent into exile for being a Christian. He was living on the island of Patmos, in the Aegean Sea near Asia Minor.*

**Revelation 1**

John, your brother who shares your sufferings and the kingdom of Jesus, ended up on the island of Patmos because of the word of God and Jesus' witness to it. One Sunday I heard a voice as strong as a trumpet blast, which said, "Write down in a book what you are going to see and send it to these seven churches."

The voice then named seven churches in Asia Minor.

I turned around to see who was speaking to me. When I turned, I saw seven gold lampstands. Among them stood someone like a Son of Man, wearing a long robe that ended at his ankles. There was a gold sash around his breast. His hair was as white as snow-white wool and his eyes were like a flame of fire. His feet were like brass and his voice was like the roaring of the ocean. He was holding seven stars in his right hand, and a sharp, two-edged sword came out of his mouth. His face was like the sun when it shines its brightest.

*If we were to use our imaginations, we would see a strange picture! But apocalyptic writing is about* meanings, *not* pictures. *Even the parts that are easier to imagine are full of symbols. For example, the long robe means that the man (Jesus Christ) is a priest, and the golden sash shows that he is a king. The snow-white hair (a sign of old age) means that he lives forever.*

*The fiery eyes tell us that Christ sees and knows everything. Feet "like brass" (a metal) show that he does not change. The voice like roaring waters and the shining face mean that he is more than a human being—he is God. The two-edged sword stands for God's word, which is very powerful.*

*The number seven is also a symbol. For the Hebrews it meant "all." So the "seven churches" meant all the communities of Christians.*

John was afraid, but the Son of Man—Jesus—encouraged him to tell what he saw. He was to write a message to each of the churches, to remind them how to live in a Christian way and avoid sin.

## More Visions

Revelation 4–5

Then John received a vision of God in heaven.

I saw a throne set up in heaven, and someone who sparkled like jewels was sitting on it. A rainbow circled the throne. Around the throne were twenty-four other thrones with twenty-four elders dressed in white robes and wearing crowns of gold on their heads. Flashes of lightning and thunder came out of the throne. In front of it seven lamps were burning, and there was what looked like a sea of glass or crystal.

Around the throne were four living things with eyes all over them. Each one of them had six wings. All the time, day and night, they repeated, "Holy, holy, holy is the Lord God, the all-powerful One. He was and is and will come."

In the right hand of the One sitting on the throne I saw a scroll, with writing on both sides. It was sealed with seven seals. Then I saw an angel who cried out in a loud voice, "Who is good enough to open the scroll and break its seals?"

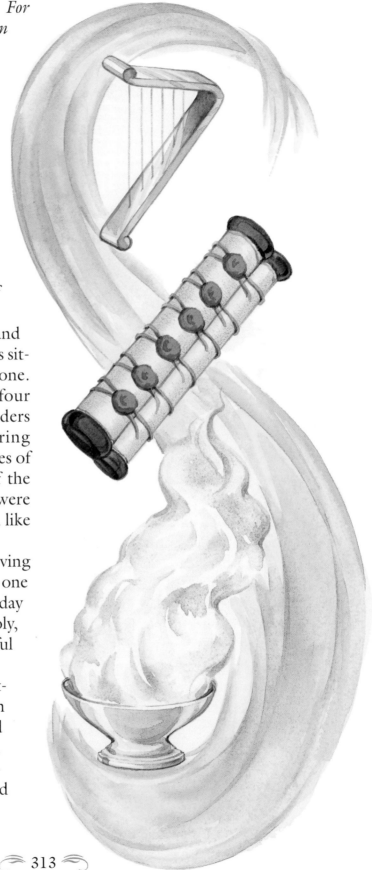

There was no one who could open the scroll and read it. I started to cry, because no one could open the scroll. Then one of the elders said, "Don't cry. Here comes the Lion of the tribe of Judah, the descendant of David. He has won the victory, so he will open the scroll with its seven seals."

Then between the throne and the elders I saw a Lamb standing. He looked as if he had been killed. The Lamb went and received the scroll from the right hand of the One seated on the throne.

The Lamb opened the seals one by one, revealing a great struggle between good and evil and the final victory of God in and through Jesus, the Lamb.

## The Woman and the Dragon

**Revelation 12**

*One of the most famous parts of the* Book of Revelation *tells about a woman, a dragon, and St. Michael:*

A great sign appeared in the sky—a woman with clothes like the sun, standing on the moon, wearing a crown of twelve stars on her head. She was about to have a baby. Another sign also appeared in the sky—a huge, red dragon that had seven heads and seven horns. There was a bright jewel on each head. Its tail dragged a third of the stars from the sky and threw them down to the earth.

The woman gave birth to a son, who was quickly taken up to the throne of God. Then the woman ran away for safety in the wastelands, where God had prepared a place for her.

War broke out in heaven. Michael and his angels fought against the dragon. The huge dragon is the serpent from years ago, who is called the devil or Satan. He leads the world away from God. He was thrown down to the earth and his angels were thrown down with him.

Then I heard a loud voice in heaven say, "Victory, power and kingship have now been given to our God and to Christ. Celebrate, you heavens and everyone who lives there! Too bad for you, land and sea, because the devil has gone down to you with great anger, since he knows he doesn't have much time left."

## Last Judgment, New World

**Revelation 18–22**

*An important part of this book for its first readers was the "fall of Babylon." In the* Book of Revelation, *"Babylon" is a code name for the Roman empire. (About two hundred years after the* Book of Revelation *was written, the empire would "fall" to God and the Church. People would be able to freely live their Christian faith.)*

At the end of the *Book of Revelation,*

God rewards or punishes everyone in the world according to how they have lived. Then the book describes a new world.

I saw a new sky and a new earth. The other sky and earth were gone.

I also saw the holy city, a new Jerusalem, coming down from heaven from God. I heard a voice say, "This is where God will live with his people. He will wipe away all tears from their eyes. There will be no more death or sorrow, crying or hard work."

*Revelation is the last book of the Bible. Its final vision ends with light, just as Genesis, the first book, opened with: "Let there be light."*

There will no longer be any night, and they will not need the light of a lamp or the light of the sun, for the Lord God will shine on them forever and ever.

*Jesus will come back at the end of the world, but he also comes to us in different ways in our daily lives. Let us pray the little prayer with which the Bible ends:*

Come, Lord Jesus.

# FINDING YOUR WAY IN THE BIBLE

When you use your family Bible, you will see that it contains many numbers. Each book of the Bible (unless it is already very short) is divided into smaller sections, called "chapters." These are numbered. The chapters are divided into even shorter sections, called "verses." These are numbered also. (In very short books, like *Obadiah* and *Jude*, there are no chapters—only verses.) This division can help people find anything they are looking for in the Bible. Suppose, for example, someone asked you to pick up your family Bible and read *John* 3:16. The table of contents in the Bible shows you what page *John* begins on. After turning to that page, you look for chapter 3. In chapter 3, you look for verse 16 and read the beautiful message it has for all of us.

When people quote something from the Bible, they often use letters and numbers to say where the quote came from. The numbers tell the chapter and verse or verses. The **letters** are abbreviations for the names of books of the Bible, such as *Gn* for *Genesis*. Different Bibles may use different abbreviations. Some abbreviations are given below.

In the *Bible for Young Catholics*, you will sometimes see two numbers with a hyphen between them, such as *Genesis* 29–31. This means that what you are reading comes from the *Book of Genesis*, chapters 29 and 31, with perhaps something from chapter 30 as well.

## ABBREVIATIONS OF THE NAMES OF THE BOOKS OF THE BIBLE
### (Alphabetical listing)

| | | | | | |
|---|---|---|---|---|---|
| Acts of the Apostles | Ac or Acts | Job | Jb | Obadiah | Ob |
| Amos | Am | Joel | Jl | 1 Peter | 1 Pt or 1 Pet |
| Baruch | Ba or Bar | John | Jn | 2 Peter | 2 Pt or 2 Pet |
| 1 Chronicles | 1 Ch or 1 Chr | 1 John | 1 Jn | Philemon | Phm or Phlm |
| 2 Chronicles | 2 Ch or 2 Chr | 2 John | 2 Jn | Philippians | Ph or Phil |
| Colossians | Col | 3 John | 3 Jn | Proverbs | Pv or Prv |
| 1 Corinthians | 1 Cor | Jonah | Jon | Psalms | Ps or Pss |
| 2 Corinthians | 2 Cor | Joshua | Js or Jos | Revelation | Rv or Rev |
| Daniel | Dn or Dan | Jude | Jude | Romans | Rm or Rom |
| Deuteronomy | Dt or Deut | Judges | Jg or Jgs | Ruth | Ru |
| Ecclesiastes | Ec or Eccl | Judith | Jt or Jdt | 1 Samuel | 1 Sm or 1 Sam |
| Ephesians | Ep or Eph | 1 Kings | 1 Kg or 1 Kgs | 2 Samuel | 2 Sm or 2 Sam |
| Esther | Es or Est | 2 Kings | 2 Kg or 2 Kgs | Sirach | Si or Sir |
| Exodus | Ex or Exod | Lamentations | La or Lam | Song of Songs | Sg |
| Ezekiel | Ez or Ezk | Leviticus | Lv or Lev | 1 Thessalonians | 1 Th or 1 Thes |
| Ezra | Ezr | Luke | Lk | 2 Thessalonians | 2 Th or 2 Thes |
| Galatians | Ga or Gal | 1 Maccabees | 1 Mc | 1 Timothy | 1 Tm or 1 Tim |
| Genesis | Gn or Gen | 2 Maccabees | 2 Mc | 2 Timothy | 2 Tm or 2 Tim |
| Habakkuk | Hb or Hab | Malachi | Ml or Mal | Titus | Ti |
| Haggai | Hg | Mark | Mk | Tobit | Tb |
| Hebrews | Heb | Matthew | Mt or Matt | Wisdom | Ws or Wis |
| Hosea | Ho or Hos | Micah | Mi | Zechariah | Zc or Zec |
| Isaiah | Is or Isa | Nahum | Na | Zephaniah | Zp or Zep |
| James | Jm or Jas | Nehemiah | Ne or Neh | | |
| Jeremiah | Jr or Jer | Numbers | Nm or Num | | |

# GLOSSARY WITH COMMON PRONUNCIATIONS OF LESS FAMILIAR NAMES

## Pronunciation Key for Vowels, Some Consonants

| | | | | | | | |
|---|---|---|---|---|---|---|---|
| a | as in pat | e | as in met | o | as in hot | sh | as in shine |
| ah | father | ee | meet | oh | so | th | think |
| ahr | mark | eer | ear | oi | boy | th | they |
| air | dare | eye, ye | eye | oo | pool | u | put |
| aw | saw | g | get | oor | poor | uh | but |
| ay | say | i | is | or | for | uhr | blur |
| yoo | mew | zh | vision | | | | |

**Aaron** (air´uhn)—Moses' brother and the first Israelite priest of the tribe of Levi (*Exodus-Numbers*)

**Abel** (ay´buhl)—the Bible's name for the second son of Adam and Eve (*Genesis*)

**Abinadab** (uh-bi´nuh-dab´)—one of Saul's sons (*1 Samuel*)

**Abishai** (uh-bye´shye)—one of David's nephews and warriors (*1 and 2 Samuel*)

**Abraham** (ay´bruh-ham)—the ancestor of the Jewish people; he traveled from Haran to Canaan around 1900 B.C. (*Genesis*)

**Abram** (ay´bruhm)—Abraham's name before God changed it (*Genesis*)

**Absalom** (ab´suh-luhm)—one of David's sons; he wanted to be king and led a revolt against his father (*2 Samuel*)

**Achish** (ay´kish)—the Philistine king of Gath who helped David (*1 Samuel*)

**Acts**—the *Acts of the Apostles*, a book of the Bible (see p. 280)

**Adam**—"man"—the Bible's name for the first man (*Genesis*)

**Ahab** (ay´hab)—a king of Israel in the 9th century B.C.; he married Jezebel, a worshipper of Baal (*1 and 2 Kings*)

**Ahaz** (ay´haz)—a king of Judah in the 8th century B.C.; he rejected God's help (*2 Kings, 2 Chronicles, Isaiah*)

**Alexander the Great**—the leader of the Greeks who conquered the Holy Land in the 4th century B.C.

**Almighty** (awl-mye´tee)—a name for God; it means "the One who is all-powerful"

**Amalekites** (uh-mal´uh-kytes)—warlike people who lived on the Sinai Peninsula in Old Testament times (*Exodus, 1 Samuel*)

**Ammon** (am´uhn)—an area east of the Jordan River in Old Testament times

**Amorites** (am´uh-rytes)—people who lived east of the Jordan River at the time of Moses (*Numbers*)

**Amos** (ay´muhs)—a prophet of the 8th century B.C.; a prophetical book bears his name (see p. 195)

**Ananias** (an´uh-nye´uhs)—the Christian whom God called to baptize Saul of Tarsus (*Acts*)

**Andrew**—the brother of Simon Peter and one of Jesus' first followers (*Gospels*)

**Aner** (ay´ner)—one of Abraham's friends (*Genesis*)

**Anna**—Tobit's wife; another Anna lived in Jerusalem at the time Jesus was born (*Luke*)

**Antioch** (an´tee-ok)—a city in Syria that served as a base for Paul's missionary journeys; also, a city in Asia Minor that Paul visited (*Acts*)

**Antiochus IV** (an-tye´uh-kus the fourth)—the ruler of Syria who started a religious persecution of the Jewish people in the 2nd century B.C. (*1* and *2 Maccabees*)

**Apostles**—the group of disciples whom Jesus chose to be the first leaders of his Church (*Gospels*)

**Aram** (air´uhm)—an old name for Syria, a nation north and east of the Holy Land

**Arioch** (air´ee-ok)—an official of the Chaldean king in the *Book of Daniel*

**ark**—a box-like boat (see *Genesis*); a box in which the Israelites kept and carried the ten commandments (*Exodus, Joshua, 1* and *2 Samuel*)

**Artaxerxes** (ahr´tuh-zuhrk´seez)—the name of three Persian emperors, one or two of whom are mentioned in *Ezra* and *Nehemiah*

**Asher** (ash´uhr)—a son of Jacob (*Genesis*) and ancestor of a tribe of Israel

**Asonath** (az´uh-nath)—the wife of Joseph, son of Israel (*Genesis*)

**Assyria** (uh-seer´ee-uh)—a powerful and cruel nation at the time of the two kingdoms (*2 Kings, 2 Chronicles*)

**Atonement** (uh-tohn´muhnt)—a Jewish holy day in early autumn, known to us as Yom Kippur

**Azariah** (az-uh-rye´uh)—the name used by the angel Raphael when in disguise (*Tobit*); also, one of the three young men thrown into the fiery furnace (*Daniel*)

**Baal** (bay´uhl)—one of the gods of the Canaanites

**Babel** (bay´buhl)—a place where God confused people's language so they could no longer understand one another (*Genesis*)

**Babylonians** (bab´uh-loh´nee-uhnz)—or Chaldeans—people who ruled Mesopotamia and nearby lands after the Assyrian empire weakened and fell

**Balaam** (bay´luhm)—a professional "seer" employed to curse the Israelites when they invaded Canaan (*Numbers*)

**Balak** (bay´lak)—the king of Moab at the time the Israelites invaded Canaan (*Numbers*)

**Barak** (bair´ak)—the judge who with Deborah led the Israelites to victory against Sisera of the Canaanites (*Judges*)

**Barnabas** (bahr´nuh-buhs)—a follower of Jesus' teachings who led the Church in Antioch and traveled with Paul on his first missionary journey (*Acts*)

**Bartholomew** (bahr-thol´uh-myoo)—an apostle—probably the one also called Nathanael (*Gospels*)

**Baruch** (bair´uhk)—a book of the Bible that bears the name of Jeremiah's secretary (see p. 182)

**Bashan** (bay´shuhn)—a land east of the Jordan River at the time the Israelites invaded Canaan (*Numbers*)

**Beatitudes** (bee-at´uh-toodz´ or bee-at´uh-tyoodz´)—promises of God's special favor for persons who have the attitudes of mind and heart that Jesus asks of his followers (*Matthew, Luke*)

**Belshazzar** (bel-shaz´uhr)—a Chaldean king in one of the stories told in the *Book of Daniel*

**Benjamin** (ben´juh-muhn)—the younger son of Jacob and Rachel (*Genesis*) and ancestor of a tribe of Israel

**Bethel** (beth´uhl)—"house of God," also spelled Beth-el: a holy place in Canaan, mentioned often in the Bible

**Bethlehem** (beth´li-hem)—"house of bread" —a village in the hills south of Jerusalem where both David and Jesus were born (*1 Samuel, Matthew, Luke*)

**Bethulia** (bi-thoo´lee-uh)—the beseiged city in the *Book of Judith*

**Bible**—a collection of writings that are holy to Jews and Christians; the Bible is also called Scripture or the Scriptures

**Boaz** (boh´az)—the man who became Ruth's husband (*Ruth*)

**Booths**—the final harvest feast of the year— around the beginning of October (*Leviticus*)

**Caesarea** (sez´uh-ree´uh)—a city on the coast of the Holy Land (*Acts*)

**Caesarea Philippi** (fi-lip´eye)—a city in the pagan territory north of Galilee (Gospels)

**Cain** (kayn)—the name the Bible gives to the first son of Adam and Eve (*Genesis*)

**Caleb** (kay´luhb)—one of the explorers of Canaan during the Exodus; with Joshua, he was loyal to Moses (*Numbers*)

**Calvary** (kal´vuh-ree)—the small hill on which Jesus was crucified—also called Golgotha (Gospels)

**Canaan** (kay´nuhn)—a land that was promised by God to Abraham and his descendants—later conquered by the Israelites (*Genesis, Deuteronomy, Joshua, Judges*)

**Canaanites** (kay´nuh-nytes)—some of the people who lived in the land of Canaan

**Capernaum** (kuh-puhr´nay-uhm)—a city by the Sea of Galilee where Jesus worked many miracles (Gospels)

**Carmel** (kahr´muhl)—the only mountain on the coast of the Holy Land; it is located north of the Plain of Sharon

**Catholics**—Christians who belong to the Catholic Church; the word dates back to the early 2nd century

**Chaldeans** (kal-dee´uhnz)—the rulers of Mesopotamia and nearby lands after the decline and fall of Assyria

**cherubim** (chair´uh-bim)—the plural of cherub—a kind of winged being common in the art and artifacts of the ancient Middle East; this word can also mean angels

**Chinnereth** (kin´uhr-eth)—the name of the Sea of Galilee in Old Testament times

**Christ**—the Greek translation of the Hebrew term "Messiah"

**Christians**—followers of Jesus

**Chronicles** (kron´i-kuhlz)—two historical books of the Bible (see p. 132)

**City of David**—a section of Jerusalem; also, a name for Bethlehem

**Colossians** (kuh-losh´uhnz)—the Christians of Colossae in Asia Minor, to whom a letter was written in Paul's name (see p. 303)

**commandments**—laws given by God (*Exodus*)

**Corinthians** (kuh-rin´thee-uhnz)—the Christians of Corinth in Achaia (Greece), to whom Paul wrote two letters (see p. 301)

**Cornelius** (kor-neel´yuhs)—one of the first Romans to become Christian (*Acts*)

**covenant** (kuhv´uh-nuhnt)—an agreement to be loyal (for more explanation, see p. 338) (*Genesis, Exodus*)

**creation** (kree-ay´shuhn)—making something from nothing; also, a thing made from nothing (see p. 12)

**crucifixion** (kroo´si-fik´shuhn)—a Roman form of execution: death on a cross, hanging from one's arms (Gospels)

**Cyrene** (sye-ree´nee)—a city and region in northern Africa

**Cyrus** (sye´ruhs)—the Persian ruler in the 6th century B.C. who let the Jews return to their homeland (*2 Chronicles; Ezra*)

**Damascus** (duh-mas´kuhs)—an ancient city in Syria, mentioned several times in the Bible

**Dan**—a son of Jacob *(Genesis)* and ancestor of a tribe of Israel

**Daniel**—a hero—perhaps legendary—of the book of the Bible that bears his name; Daniel is listed as a major prophet (see p. 187)

**Darius** (duh-rye´uhs)—a Persian emperor *(Ezra);* also, a Median king *(Daniel)*

**David**—the second and most famous king of Israel; he lived in the 11th and 10th centuries B.C. *(1 and 2 Samuel, 1 Kings, 1 Chronicles)*

**Dead Sea**—the Holy Land's largest lake and the lowest spot on the earth's surface; its water is very salty

**Deborah**—the woman judge of Israel *(Judges)*

**Decapolis** (di-kap´uh-lis)—"ten cities"—a Greek-speaking district near Galilee at the time of Jesus

**Delilah** (di-lye´luh)—the woman who helped the Philistines capture Samson *(Judges)*

**Deuteronomy** (doo´tuh-ron´uh-mee)—the last book of the Pentateuch (see p. 68)

**devils**—the angels who rebelled against God *(Revelation);* their leader, Satan, tempted Adam and Eve *(Genesis)* and even Jesus (Gospels)

**Dinah** (dye´nuh)—Jacob's daughter *(Genesis)*

**disciple** (di-sye´puhl)—a person who follows a master (teacher), believing the master's teachings and living the way the master lives

**Ebed-melech** (ee´bid-mee´lik)—a servant at the palace of Zedekiah; he saved Jeremiah from starvation *(Jeremiah)*

**Ecclesiastes** (i-klee´zee-as´teez)—one of the wisdom books (see p. 172)

**Eden**—the garden Adam and Eve lived in before they sinned *(Genesis)*

**Edom** (ee´duhm)—a land south and somewhat east of the Holy Land in Old Testament times

**Egypt** (ee´jipt)—a powerful nation during the early history of Israel

**Eleazar** (el´ee-ay´zuhr)—a son of Aaron and priest of the Israelites *(Leviticus, Numbers);* also, a martyr at the time of the Maccabees *(2 Maccabees)*

**Eleven, the**—the group of the apostles after Judas left and before Matthias was added (Gospels, *Acts)*

**Eli** (ee´lye)—a priest who took care of the ark of the covenant at Shiloh in the 11th century B.C. *(1 Samuel)*

**Elijah** (i-lye´juh)—a prophet in the northern kingdom at the time of Ahab and Jezebel in the 9th century B.C. *(1 and 2 Kings)*

**Elisha** (i-lye´shuh)—Elijah's assistant and successor as a prophet *(1 and 2 Kings)*

**Elizabeth**—Mary's cousin, the wife of Zechariah; she became the mother of John the Baptizer *(Luke)*

**Emmanuel** (i-man´yoo-uhl)—also spelled Immanuel—"God with us"—a name in the prophecy of Isaiah that is referred to in *Matthew*

**Emmaus** (i-may´uhs)—a town near Jerusalem where the risen Jesus appeared to two disciples *(Luke)*

**Ephesians** (i-fee´zhuhnz)—people living in the city of Ephesus, to whom a letter was written in Paul's name (see p. 302)

**epistle** (i-pis´uhl)—a letter written in order to teach something; the 21 New Testament letters are epistles

**Esau** (ee´saw)—a son of Isaac and Rebekah, born shortly before his twin, Jacob *(Genesis)*

**Esdraelon** (ez´druh-ee´luhn)—a valley that crosses the Holy Land from east to west

**Eshcol** (esh´kol)—one of Abraham's friends *(Genesis)*

**Esther** (es´tuhr)—a Jewish woman who as queen of Persia used her position to save her people; also, the book of the Bible that tells her story (see p. 148)

**Eucharist** (yoo´kuh-rist)—the Body and Blood of Jesus, under the appearances of bread and wine (Gospels, *1 Corinthians*)

**Euphrates** (yoo-fray´teez)—an important river in Mesopotamia

**Eve**—"mother of everyone living"—the name the Bible gives to the first woman *(Genesis)*

**Exile** (eg´zyle or ek´syle)—the 50-60-year period that the people of Judah spent in Babylonia away (exiled) from their homeland *(Isaiah, Jeremiah, Ezekiel, Daniel)*

**Exodus** (ek´suh-duhs)—the journey (13th century B.C.) of the Israelites from slavery in Egypt to freedom as God's people in Canaan *(Exodus, Leviticus, Numbers, Deuteronomy);* also, the book of the Bible that is named after this event (see p. 44)

**Ezekiel** (i-zee´kee-uhl)—a priest living in Babylon during the Exile (6th century B.C.) who was called to be a prophet; also, the Prophetical Book that bears his name (see p. 183)

**Ezra** (ez´ruh)—a priest-scibe who is called the father of Judaism; he journeyed from Mesopotamia to Jerusalem to bring about religious reform; one of the Historical Books bears his name (see p. 133)

**Gabael** (gab´ay-uhl)—one of Tobit's relatives *(Tobit)*

**Gabriel** (gay´bree-uhl)—an angel who brought messages from God to Daniel, Zechariah and Mary

**Gad**—a son of Jacob *(Genesis)* and ancestor of a tribe of Israel

**Galatians** (guh-lay´shuhnz)—people of a region of Asia Minor; also, a letter that Paul wrote to these people (see p. 302)

**Galilee** (gal´uh-lee)—the section of the Holy Land west of the Sea of Galilee

**Genesis** (jen´uh-sis)—"the Beginnings"—the first book of the Bible (see p. 12)

**Gennesaret** (gi-nes´uh-ret)—a town near the Sea of Galilee; also, another name for the Sea of Galilee

**Gethsemane** (geth-sem´uh-nee)—a garden on the slopes of the Mount of Olives, near Jerusalem (Gospels)

**Gibeon** (gib´ee-uhn)—a town in south central Canaan whose people tricked Joshua into protecting them *(Joshua)*

**Gideon** (gid´ee-uhn)—one of the judges of Israel *(Judges)*

**Gilboa** (gil-boh´uh)—a mountain near the valley of Esdraelon, which gave its name to the battle in which Saul was killed *(1 and 2 Samuel)*

**Gilead** (gil´ee-uhd)—part of the Israelite territory east of the Jordan river

**Gilgal** (gil´gal)—the place in Canaan that Joshua made his base at the beginning of the Israelites' conquest *(Joshua)*

**God**—the creator of the universe; he watches over human beings with the concern of a father and is often called "Father"

**gods**—world rulers imagined and worshipped by people who don't know that there is only one God

**Golgotha** (gol´guh-thuh)—a small hill, also called Calvary, which in Roman times was just outside the walls of Jerusalem (Gospels)

**Goliath** (guh-lye´uhth)—the Philistine giant whom David killed *(1 Samuel)*

**Gomorrah** (guh-mor´uh)—one of the cities on the "Jordan plain" that was destroyed at the time of Abraham and Lot *(Genesis)*

**Gorgias** (gor´juhs)—governor of Idumea and a leader of Syrian troops at the time of Judas Maccabeus *(1 and 2 Maccabees)*

**Goshen** (goh´shuhn)—the part of the Nile delta in Egypt where the Israelites settled

**Gospels** (gos´puhls)—the four books of the New Testament that tell what Jesus did and taught; "gospel" means "good news" (see p. 206)

**great commandment(s)**—two principles for right-living found in the Hebrew and Christian Scriptures: to love God above all things (to put God first in our lives) and to love others (wish them well; do good to them) the way we love ourselves

**Habakkuk** (huh-bak´uhk or hab´uh-kuhk)—a prophet in Judah around 600 B.C.; also, the Prophetical Book that bears his name (see p. 200)

**Hagar** (hay´gahr)—an Egyptian woman who was Sarah's slave; she became the mother of Ishmael *(Genesis)*

**Haggai** (hag´eye)—a prophet in Judah after the Exile (6th century B.C.); also, the Prophetical Book that bears his name (see p. 201)

**Ham** (ham)—one of the sons of Noah *(Genesis)*

**Haman** (hay´muhn)—the enemy of the Jewish people in the *Book of Esther*

**Hananiah** (han´hu-nye´uh)—one of the young men thrown into the fiery furnace *(Daniel)*

**Hannah** (han´uh)—Samuel's mother *(1 Samuel)*

**Hanukkah** (hah´nuh-kuh)—a Jewish religious celebration held every year in December; it recalls the rededication of the Temple by Judas Maccabeus *(1* and *2 Maccabees)*

**Haran** (hair´uhn)—the city on the plain of Syria from which Abraham migrated to the land of Canaan *(Genesis)*

**Hathach** (hay´thak)—one of Esther's servants *(Esther)*

**Hebrews** (hee´brooz)—the descendants of Abraham, Isaac and Jacob (at different periods also called Israelites and Jews); also, a book of the New Testament, that may have been written for Jewish Christians (see p. 308)

**Hebrew Scriptures**—the Scriptures (the Law, the Prophets and the Writings) that Jewish people accept as the Word of God; the Hebrew Scriptures make up the greater part of the Catholic Old Testament (see p. 11)

**Hebron** (hee´bruhn)—a city west of the Dead Sea where Abraham and Sarah were buried and much later David was crowned king of Judah *(Genesis, 2 Samuel)*

**herald** (hair´uhld)—a messenger who announces good news, such as the news that someone important is coming

**Herod** (hair´uhd)—"the Great"—a king of the Jewish people at the time Jesus was born; also, Herod Antipas, a son of the first Herod, who was king during Jesus' ministry *(Gospels)*

**Hezekiah** (hez´uh-kye´uh)—a king of Judah at the time of the Assyrian threat *(2 Kings, 2 Chronicles)*

**Historical Books**—books of the Bible that relate history or tell stories (see p. 71)

**Holy Land**—the region where most of the Old and New Testament events took place; in early times it was called Canaan; later, Israel and Judah; under the Romans, Palestine; today, Israel and the territory of the Palestinian Arabs

**Holy Spirit**—the Third Person of the Blessed Trinity; he is God like the Father and the Son

**Horeb** (hor´eb)—another name for Sinai, the mountain near the tip of the Sinai peninsula where God spoke to Moses *(Exodus)*

**Hosea** (hoh-zay´uh)—a prophet in the northern kingdom in the 8th century B.C.; also, the Prophetical Book that bears his name (see p. 194)

**Hoshea** (hoh-shee´uh)—the king of Israel when it was conquered by Assyria *(2 Kings)*

**Hushai** (hoosh´eye)—a friend of David's who helped him escape from Absalom *(2 Samuel)*

**idol** (eye´duhl)—anything worshipped as if it were a god

**Isaac** (eye´zik)—the son of Abraham and Sarah *(Genesis)*

**Isaiah** (eye-zay´uh)—a prophet of Judah, who lived in the 8th century B.C.; the book of the Bible called "Isaiah" contains his prophecies as well as those of an unknown prophet from the time of the Exile (see p. 174)

**Ishmael** (ish´may-uhl)—the son of Abraham and an Egyptian slave, Hagar *(Genesis)*

**Ishmaelites** (ish´may-uh-lytes)—descendants of Abraham's son, Ishmael *(Genesis)*

**Israel** (iz´ray-uhl)—the name God gave to Jacob *(Genesis)*; later, the name of the Hebrew nation *(Exodus–1 Kings)*; afterwards, the name of the northern kingdom *(1* and *2 Kings)*

**Israelites** (iz´ray-uh-lytes)—the descendants of Abraham, Isaac and Jacob (Israel) at the time of the Exodus and settlement of Canaan; later, the people of the northern kingdom

**Issachar** (is´uh-kahr)—a son of Jacob *(Genesis)* and ancestor of a tribe of Israel

**Jacob** (jay´kuhb)—a son of Isaac and Rebekah, born after his twin, Esau *(Genesis)*

**Jael** (jay´uhl)—the woman who killed the Canaanite general Sisera *(Judges)*

**James**—Zebedee's son, an apostle, sometimes called James the greater; also, another apostle, sometimes called James the less; also, one of Jesus' cousins, who may have been the author of the *Letter of James* (see p. 308)

**Japheth** (ja´feth)—one of the sons of Noah *(Genesis)*

**Jason** (jay´suhn) of Cyrene—the author of five scrolls about the persecution by Antiochus and the Maccabean revolt (2nd century B.C.); his work is summarized in *2 Maccabees* (see p. 160)

**Jebusites** (jeb´yoo-sytes)—the inhabitants of Jerusalem before David captured it *(2 Samuel, 1 Chronicles)*

**Jehoiachin** (ji-hoh´yah-kin)—a son of Jehoiakim; he was taken into exile by the Chaldeans *(2 Kings, 2 Chronicles)*

**Jehoiakim** (ji-hoh´yah-kim)—a son of king Josiah; he ruled Judah in the late 7th century B.C. *(2 Kings, 2 Chronicles)*

**Jeremiah** (jair´uh-mye´uh)—a prophet who spoke God's message in Judah in the late 7th and early 6th centuries B.C.; also, the Prophetical Book that bears his name (see p. 178)

**Jericho** (jair´uh-koh)—an ancient city that the Bible connects with the Israelite invasion of Canaan *(Joshua)*

**Jeroboam I** (jair´uh-boh´uhm the first)—the first king of Israel after it broke away from Judah in the 10th century B.C. *(1 Kings)*

**Jerusalem** (ji-roo´suh-luhm)—the capital of David's kingdom and of the kingdom of Judah; the site of the Temple; the site of Jesus' death and resurrection

**Jesse** (jes´ee)—David's father *(1 Samuel)*

**Jesus ben Sira** (sye´ruh)—the author of the wisdom book called *Sirach*; he lived in the 2nd century B.C.

**Jesus Christ**—the name by which Jesus is often called in the New Testament letters; it means "Jesus, the Messiah"

**Jethro** (jeth´roh)—Moses' father-in-law *(Exodus, Numbers)*

**Jezebel** (jez´uh-bel)—a princess from Sidon who became the wife of Ahab, king of Israel *(1 and 2 Kings)*

**Jezreel** (jez´ree-uhl)—another name for the valley of Esdraelon

**Joab** (joh´ab)—one of David's nephews and commander of David's troops *(1 and 2 Samuel)*

**Job** (johb)—the main character in the book of the same name, which is a dramatic poem about innocent people's sufferings (see p. 166)

**Joel** (joh´uhl)—a prophet who lived around the 5th or 4th century B.C.; also, the Prophetical Book that bears his name (see p. 194)

**John**—an apostle, brother of James and son of Zebedee; a Gospel and three letters bear his name (see pp. 260, 310, 311)

**John Hyrcanus** (heer-kay´nuhs)—a nephew of Judas Maccabeus; he succeeded his father, Simon, as ruler of the Jewish nation *(1 Maccabees)*

**John the Baptizer**—Jesus' cousin; God called him to urge people to change their lives because the Messiah was coming (Gospels)

**Jonah** (joh´nuh)—the main character of the biblical book of the same name (see p. 196)

**Jonathan** (jon´uh-thuhn)—one of Saul's sons—David's friend *(1 and 2 Samuel)*

**Jordan**—the main river in the Holy Land

**Joseph**—the elder son of Jacob and Rachel and ancestor of the "Joseph tribes," Ephraim and Manasseh *(Genesis);* also, the husband of Mary and stepfather of Jesus *(Matthew, Luke)*

**Joseph of Arimathea** (air´uh-muh-thee´uh)—a follower of Jesus who had the Lord's body placed in his own tomb, near Calvary (Gospels)

**Joshua** (josh´yoo-uh)—Moses' successor, who led the Israelites into Canaan in the late 13th or early 12th century B.C.; also, the book of the Bible that bears Joshua's name (see p. 71)

**Josiah** (joh-sye´uh)—a reforming king of Judah who lived in the 7th century B.C. *(2 Kings, 2 Chronicles)*

**jubilee** (joo´buh-lee) year—every fiftieth year—a time for debts to be canceled and slaves set free *(Leviticus)*

**Judah** (joo´duh)—a son of Jacob *(Genesis)* and ancestor of a tribe of Israel

**Judaism** (joo´duh-iz´uhm)—the religion of the Hebrew (Jewish) people, on which Christianity is based

**Judas Iscariot** (joo´duhs is-kair´ee-uht)—the apostle who offered to show Jesus' enemies where to capture him (Gospels)

**Judas Maccabeus** (joo´duhs mak´uh-bee´uhs) —the military leader of a family who led the Jewish revolt against the persecutor Antiochus IV in the 2nd century B.C. *(1 and 2 Maccabees)*

**Judea** (joo-dee´uh)—in Roman times, the area of the Holy Land around Jerusalem; more or less, Judea was the old land of Judah

**Judges** (juhj´iz)—a book of the Bible that tells about the Israelite leaders of the 12th and early 11th centuries B.C (see p. 80)

**Judith**—the heroine of the book of the Bible of the same name (see p. 142)

**Kadesh** (kay´dish)—an oasis on the Sinai Peninsula from which the Israelites explored the land of Canaan *(Numbers)*

**Kenites** (ken´ytes)—a group of nomads (wanderers) in the region of the Sinai peninsula *(Numbers, Judges)*

**Kings**—two books of the Bible, covering the period from David's death to the Exile (see pp. 118, 124)

**Laban** (lay´buhn)—Rebekah's brother, the father of Leah and Rachel *(Genesis)*

**Lamentations** (lam´en-tay´shuhnz)—a book of the Bible that reflects the sorrow of the Jewish people over the destruction of Jerusalem by the Chaldeans (see p. 182)

**last supper**—the Passover meal that Jesus ate with his disciples the night he was betrayed *(Gospels)*

**Lazarus** (laz´uh-ruhs)—one of Jesus' friends, who lived in Bethany, a town near Jerusalem *(Luke, John);* also, a character in a story that Jesus told *(Luke)*

**Leah** (lee´uh)—Laban's elder daughter and Jacob's wife, mother of several of his children *(Genesis)*

**leprosy** (lep´roh-see)—a severe skin disease, which was incurable in biblical times

**Levi** (lee´vye)—a son of Jacob *(Genesis)*, ancestor of the priestly tribe of Israel

**Levites** (lee´vytes)—men of the tribe of Levi who helped the priests

**Leviticus** (li-vit´i-kuhs)—the 3rd book of the Bible, named after the priestly tribe, Levi, and dealing with religious rules (see p. 59)

**Lord**—a title of respect used both for men and for God; out of reverence, the Jews call God "Lord" rather than "Yahweh," which was the holy name that God revealed to Moses

**Lot**—Abraham's nephew, who migrated to Canaan with him *(Genesis)*

**Luke**—an evangelist (Gospel-writer) who traveled with Paul and wrote *Luke* and *Acts* (see pp. 238 and 280)

**Maccabees** (mak′uh-beez)—two books of the Bible, named after Judas Maccabeus (see pp. 154, 160); this name is also used for the brothers of Judas Maccabeus

**Maccabeus** (mak′uh-bee′uhs)—a nickname given to Judas, a Jewish military leader of the 2nd century B.C. who led a revolt against foreign oppression (*1* and *2 Maccabees*)

**major prophets**—Isaiah, Jeremiah, Ezekiel and Daniel—called "major" because the books by or about them are lengthy and well known

**Malachi** (mal′uh-kye)—a prophet of the 5th century B.C.; also, the Prophetical Book that bears his name (see p. 202)

**Malchishua** (mal′ki-shoo′-uh)—one of Saul's sons (*1 Samuel*)

**Mamre** (mam′ree)—one of Abraham's friends (*Genesis*)

**Manasseh** (muh-nas′uh)—a son of Joseph; also, the tribe of Israel that was descended from him (*Genesis*); also, one of the kings of Judah (*2 Kings, 2 Chronicles*)

**manna** (man′uh)—a food tasting somewhat like bread, but shaped like flakes, which God gave to his people in the desert (*Exodus, Numbers, Deuteronomy*)

**Mark**—one of the evangelists; also, the Gospel that bears his name (see p. 228)

**Martha**—one of Jesus' friends; she lived in Bethany, a town near Jerusalem (*Luke, John*)

**Mary**—the mother of Jesus (Gospels, *Acts*); also, the name of one or two other women who stood near Jesus on Calvary (Gospels)

**Mary Magdalen** (mag′duh-luhn)—one of Jesus' most loyal disciples (Gospels)

**Mary of Bethany** (beth′uh-nee)—the sister of Martha and Lazarus (*Luke, John*)

**Mattathias** (mat′uh-thye′uhs)—a Jewish priest who, with his five sons, started the Maccabean revolt (*1 Maccabees*)

**Matthew**—one of the apostles, whose name is connected with one of the Gospels (see p. 206)

**Matthias** (muh-thye′uhs)—the disciple of Jesus who was chosen to replace Judas as an apostle (*Acts*)

**Media** (mee′dee-uh)—a country northeast of Mesopotamia at the time of the Assyrians and Chaldeans

**Melchizedek** (mel-kiz′uh-dek)—a priest "of God most high" who sacrificed bread and wine; he blessed Abraham (*Genesis*)

**Meribaal** (mair′i-bay′uhl)—Jonathan's son (*2 Samuel*)

**mercy** (muhr′see)—undeserved forgiveness or help

**Mesopotamia** (mes′uh-puh-tay′mee-uh)—the "land between the two rivers"—the region that Abraham came from (*Genesis*)

**Messiah** (muh-sye′uh)—God's agent in history—a leader expected by the Jewish people; Christians regard Jesus as the Messiah

**Micah** (mye′kuh)—a prophet of the 8th century B.C.; also, the Prophetical Book that bears his name (see p. 200)

**Michal** (mye′kuhl)—Saul's daughter, whom David married (*1* and *2 Samuel*)

**Midian** (mid′ee-uhn)—the land east of the Sinai Peninsula; in Moses' time even part of Sinai was called Midian (*Exodus*)

**minor prophets**—Hosea, Joel, Amos, Obadiah, Jonah, Micah, Nahum, Habakkuk, Zephaniah, Haggai, Zechariah and Malachi; most of their writings are shorter than those of the major prophets

**Miriam** (meer′ee-uhm)—the sister of Moses and Aaron (*Exodus, Numbers*)

**Mishael** (mish′ay-uhl)—one of the young men thrown into the fiery furnace in a story found in the *Book of Daniel*

**Moab** (moh´ab)—a country east of the Dead Sea in Old Testament times

**Modein** (moh´deen)—a town in the foothills west of Jerusalem—where the Maccabean revolt began *(1 Maccabees)*

**Mordecai** (mor´duh-kye)—Esther's cousin, who had raised her *(Esther)*

**Moriah** (mor-eye´uh)—the mountain where Abraham prepared to sacrifice Isaac *(Genesis)*

**Moses** (moh´ziz)—a great Old Testament leader who lived in the 13th century B.C.; he led the Israelites from Egypt to the land of Canaan *(Exodus, Leviticus, Numbers, Deuteronomy)*

**Naaman** (nay´uh-muhn)—an Aramean (Syrian) general who was cured of leprosy by Elisha *(2 Kings)*

**Nahum** (nay´huhm)—a prophet of the 7th century B.C.; a Prophetical Book bears his name (see p. 200)

**Naomi** (nay-oh´mee)—Ruth's mother-in-law *(Ruth)*

**Naphtali** (naf´tuh-lye)—a son of Jacob *(Genesis)* and ancestor of a tribe of Israel

**Nathan** (nay´thuhn)—a prophet who lived at the time of David *(2 Samuel)*

**Nathanael** (nuh-than´ay-uhl)—one of the twelve apostles—also called Bartholomew (Gospels)

**Nazareth** (naz´uh-rith)—the town in Galilee where Mary lived when she was invited to become the mother of the Messiah *(Luke);* Jesus grew up in Nazareth *(Matthew, Luke)*

**Nebo** (nee´boh)—a mountain east of the Jordan river and Dead Sea, from which Moses was able to see the land of Canaan before he died *(Deuteronomy)*

**Nebuchadnezzar** (neb´uh-kuhd-nez´uhr)—the Chaldean (Babylonian) emperor at the time of the destruction of Jerusalem in 587 B.C. *(2 Kings, 2 Chronicles);* he also appears in the *Book of Judith*

**Necho** (nee´koh)—a pharaoh (king) of Egypt, who became an ally of Chaldea against Assyria *(2 Kings)*

**Negeb** (neg´eb)—a dry region between the Sinai Peninsula and the hill country of Judah (Judea)

**Nehemiah** (nee´huh-mye´uh)—a governor of Jerusalem in the 5th century B.C.; also, the book of the Bible that bears his name (see p. 133)

**New Testament**—the Christian Scriptures—the section of the Bible made up of the four Gospels, the *Acts of the Apostles,* letters written by early Christians and the *Book of Revelation* (see p. 203)

**Nile**—Egypt's great river

**Nineveh** (nin´uh-vuh)—the capital city of the Assyrian empire

**Noah** (noh´uh)—the hero of an Old Testament story about a good-living family that was saved from a great flood *(Genesis)*

**Numbers**—a book of the Pentateuch, named after the censuses of the Israelites that it mentions (see p. 60)

**Obadiah** (oh´buh-dye´uh)—a prophet who lived around the 5th century B.C.; also, the Prophetical Book that bears his name (see p. 195)

**Old Testament**—the section of the Bible that contains the Hebrew Scriptures; for Catholics and some other Christians, the Old Testament also contains other Scriptures written before Jesus' time (see p. 11)

**Omri** (om´ree)—one of the kings of Israel; he built the city of Samaria *(1 Kings)*

**Onesimus** (oh-nes´uh-muhs)—an escaped slave whom Paul reconciled with his master *(Philemon)*

**Onias** (oh-nye´uhs)—a Jewish priest of the early 2nd century B.C. *(2 Maccabees)*

**pagan** (pay´guhn)—a worshipper of many gods or someone with little or no religion

**Palestine** (pal´uh-styne)—the name that the Romans gave to the Holy Land

**parable** (pair´uh-buhl)—a story that hides a message; Jesus often taught with parables (Gospels)

**Paran** (pay´ruhn)—a region in the northern part of the Sinai Peninsula (*Numbers*)

**Passover**—a Jewish religious celebration held in the early spring; it recalls God's deliverance of the Israelites from slavery in Egypt (*Exodus, Leviticus*)

**patriarchs** (pay´tree-ahrks)—the "great fathers" of the Jewish people: Abraham, Isaac and Jacob

**Paul**—the name by which Saul of Tarsus was known after he became a Christian and apostle (*Acts*)

**Pentateuch** (pen´tuh-took or pen´tuh-tyook)—"five books"—the first five books of the Bible, which Jews call the Torah (see p. 12)

**Pentecost** (pen´ti-kost)—a late spring harvest feast; the "birthday of the Church"

**Persia** (puhr´zhuh)—a country east of Mesopotamia that conquered the Chaldeans and formed an empire

**Peter**—the leader of the apostles; Jesus gave him this name, which means "rock" (*John*)

**pharaoh** (fair´oh)—the title of the king of Egypt in Old Testament times

**Pharisees** (fair´uh-seez)—a group of religious leaders at the time of Jesus

**Philemon** (fi-lee´muhn)—a friend of Paul's; also, Paul's letter to his friend (see p. 307)

**Philip**—one of the twelve apostles (Gospels); also, one of the deacons in the early Church (*Acts*)

**Philippians** (fi-lip´ee-uhnz)—people of a certain city in Macedonia; also, the letter Paul wrote to the Christians there (see p. 303)

**Philistines** (fi-lis´tinz or fil´is-teenz´)—people who invaded Canaan from the Mediterranean Sea and settled along the coast

**pilgrim**—a person who travels to a holy place to pray there

**Pilate** (pye´luht)—the Roman governor of Judea who ordered Jesus' death (Gospels); he was called "Pontius" after his homeland, Pontus, in Asia Minor

**plagues of Egypt**—disasters that happened to the Egyptians just before the Exodus (*Exodus*)

**prehistoric** (pree´his-tor´ik)—before history (before written records)

**priest**—a person who offers sacrifices to God or to gods

**Promised Land**—Canaan at the time of the Exodus; this land had been promised by God to Abraham and his descendants

**prophet** (prof´it)—a person who speaks for God or writes God's message

**Prophetical** (proh-fet´i-kuhl) **Books**—books of the Bible that contain the writings of prophets or their disciples and/or tell about the prophets' lives (see p. 174)

**Proverbs** (prov´uhrbz)—a book of the Bible that is chiefly composed of short, wise sayings (see p. 170)

**Psalms** (sahmz)—a book of the Bible composed of 150 prayer-songs (see p. 168)

**Purim** (pyoo´rim)—a Jewish celebration whose origin is explained in the *Book of Esther*

**Qoheleth** (koh-hel´ith)—another name for the book of the Bible called *Ecclesiastes*

**Rachel** (ray´chuhl)—Jacob's favorite wife, mother of Joseph and Benjamin (*Genesis*)

**Raguel** (ruh-gyoo´uhl)—one of Tobit's relatives (*Tobit*)

**Rahab** (ray´hab)—a woman of Jericho who helped two Israelite spies (*Joshua*)

**Ramah** (ray´muh)—Samuel's hometown

**Rameses** (ram´uh-seez)—a pharaoh who ruled Egypt around the time of the Exodus (13th century B.C.)

**Raphael** (raf´ay-uhl or ray´fee-uhl)—the angel in the *Book of Tobit*

**Rebekah** (ri-bek´uh)—the wife of Isaac, mother of Jacob and Esau *(Genesis)*

**Rehoboam** (ree´huh-boh´uhm)—Solomon's son, who became King of Judah *(1 Kings)*

**resurrection** (rez´uh-rek´shuhn)—rising or being raised from the dead; Jesus' resurrection showed that he is God

**Reuben** (roo´bin)—a son of Jacob *(Genesis)*, ancestor of a tribe of Israel

**revelation** (rev´uh-lay´shuhn)—God's message for human beings, part of which we find in the Bible

**Revelation** (rev´uh-lay´shuhn)—the last book of the Bible (see p. 312)

**Romans** (roh´muhnz)—the people of Rome; also, the letter that Paul wrote to the Roman Christians (see p. 300)

**Ruth**—a woman from Moab who became an ancestor of King David; also, the book of the Bible that tells her story (see p. 94)

**Sabbath** (sab´uhth)—a day to rest and worship God *(Exodus, Leviticus);* Jews observe it on Saturday; Christians, on Sunday

**sabbatical** (suh-bat´i-kuhl) year—every seventh year, when farmlands were to be left unplowed, so minerals could be restored to the soil *(Leviticus)*

**Salome** (suh-loh´mee)—one of the women who followed Jesus *(Mark);* also, the daughter of Queen Herodias

**Salt Sea**—another name for the Dead Sea

**Samaria** (suh-mair´ee-uh)—the capital of the northern kingdom, which eventually gave its name to the whole region

**Samaritans** (suh-mair´uh-tuhnz)—people of mixed background who worshipped the Lord somewhat differently than the people of Judah did

**Samson** (sam´suhn)—one of the judges of Israel *(Judges)*

**Samuel** (sam´yoo-uhl)—the last of the judges, who was also a priest and prophet; also, the two books of the Bible that were named after him (see pp. 98 and 112)

**Sanballat** (san-bal´at)—a governor of Samaria, 5th century B.C. *(Ezra, Nehemiah)*

**Sarah** (sair´-uh)—Abraham's wife, the mother of Isaac *(Genesis);* also, the young woman in the *Book of Tobit*

**Sarai** (sair´eye)—Sarah's name before God changed it *(Genesis)*

**Satan** (say´tuhn)—the leader of the angels who rebelled against God *(Revelation);* Satan is also called Lucifer, Enemy, the devil, the evil one (see also p. 166)

**Saul** (sawl)—the first king of Israel *(1 and 2 Samuel)*, who lived in the 11th century B.C.; also, a former persecutor of the Christians who became Paul the apostle *(Acts)*

**scepter** (sep´tuhr)—a special staff which is a symbol of a king's power *(Numbers, Esther)*

**Second Isaiah**—a name given to an unknown prophet or group of prophets of the 6th century B.C.; also, the second part of the *Book of Isaiah*

**Sennacherib** (suh-nak´uh-rib)—an Assyrian emperor of the 8th century B.C. *(2 Kings)*

**seraphs** (sair´ufs) or **seraphim** (sair´uh-fim)—angels that always worship God

**Seth**—the name the Bible gives to the third son of Adam and Eve *(Genesis)*

**Shalmaneser** (shal´muh-nee´zuhr)—one of the Assyrian emperors; he is mentioned in the *Book of Tobit*

**Sheba** (shee´buh)—a country in Arabia at the time of King Solomon; also a rebel leader at the time of David *(2 Samuel, 1 Kings)*

**Shechem** (shek´uhm)—an ancient city in central Canaan

**Shem**—one of Noah's sons; he was called the ancestor of the Semites, the ethnic group to which the Hebrews belonged *(Genesis)*

**Shiloh** (shye´loh)—the location of the ark of the covenant at the time of the judges

**Shimei** (shim´ee-eye)—a relative of Saul's who cursed King David when the king was fleeing from Absalom *(2 Samuel)*

**signs**—in John's Gospel, the miracles of Jesus (see p. 260)

**Silas** (sye´luhs)—one of Paul's companions on his second missionary journey *(Acts)*

**Simeon** (sim´ee-uhn)—a son of Jacob *(Genesis)* and ancestor of a tribe of Israel; also, an old man who recognized Jesus as the Messiah *(Luke)*

**Simon** (sye´muhn)—a brother of Judas Maccabeus *(1 Maccabees);* also, the name of Peter and another apostle (Gospels)

**sin**—disobeying God's law; doing what is wrong (bad, evil)

**Sinai** (sye´nye)—a peninsula between two arms of the Red Sea; also, a range of mountains on the peninsula and the particular mountain (also called Horeb) where God spoke to Moses *(Exodus)*

**Sirach** (sye´ruhk)—one of the Wisdom Books (see p. 173)

**Sisera** (sis´uh-ruh)—the leader of the army of the Canaanite king, Jabin *(Judges)*

**Sodom** (sod´uhm)—one of the cities destroyed in Abraham's time *(Genesis)*

**Solomon** (sol´uh-muhn)—one of David's sons and the third king of Israel *(1 Kings)*

**Solomon's Porch**—one of the outer areas of the Temple at the time of Jesus

**Son of God**—a term that could simply mean a person very close to God, but it means much more when it refers to Jesus, who truly is the Son of God the Father

**Son of Man**—an expression that has different meanings in Scripture; in *Ezekiel* it means simply "man"; in *Daniel* it means someone who sits in the place of honor at God's right hand; Jesus uses it of himself, perhaps to stress his humanity while hinting at his divinity

**Song of Songs**—one of the Wisdom Books (see p. 172)

**Stephen**—one of the deacons of the early Church and the first follower of Jesus to die for his beliefs *(Acts)*

**Susa** (soo´suh)—an important city in the Persian empire

**synagogue** (sin´uh-gog)—a place for worship, Scripture-reading and instruction in the Jewish religion

**synoptics** (sin-op´tiks)—the three Gospels that are most alike: *Matthew, Mark* and *Luke*

**Syria** (seer´ee-uh)—a nation northeast of the Holy Land

**Temple**—the great building in Jerusalem where priests offered sacrifices to the Lord in the name of the people; the Temple was also a place of prayer

**Thaddeus** (thad´ee-uhs)—one of the twelve apostles, also called Jude or Judas (Gospels)

**Theophilus** (thee-of´uh-luhs)—"someone who loves God," to whom the *Gospel As Told by Luke* and the *Acts of the Apostles* are addressed

**Thessalonians** (thes´uh-loh´nee-uhnz)—the people of a city in Macedonia; also, two New Testament letters addressed to them in Paul's name (see p. 304)

**Thomas**—one of the twelve apostles (Gospels)

**Tiberias** (tye-beer´ee-uhs)—another name for the Sea of Galilee

**Tigris** (tye´gris)—one of the two main rivers in Mesopotamia

**Timothy**—one of Paul's disciples; two letters addressed to Timothy in Paul's name (see p. 305)

**Titus** (tye´tuhs)—another of Paul's disciples; also, a letter addressed to him in Paul's name (see p. 305)

**Tobiah** (toh-bye´uh)—one of the main persons in the *Book of Tobit;* also, a governor of Ammon in the 5th century B.C.

**Tobit** (toh´bit)—one of the main persons in a story about an Israelite family living in Nineveh; the book of the Bible named after him (see p. 136)

**Torah** (tor´uh)—the Hebrew name for the first five books of the Bible; it means "the teaching" or "the law"

**Trinity** (trin´i-tee)—a word that means the three divine Persons: the Father, the Son and the Holy Spirit

**transfiguration** (trans-fig´yoo-ray´shuhn)—the event on the mountaintop when Jesus' appearance became radiant with light and the Father's voice spoke from heaven (Gospels)

**Twelve (the)**—the group of twelve men chosen by Jesus to symbolize his mission to Israel and be the foundation of his Church—the apostles

**Unleavened Bread**—a religious celebration of the first grain harvest in the spring; it occurred right after Passover

**Uz**—Job's homeland (Job)

**Uzziah** (uh-zye´uh)—a king of Judah in the 8th century B.C.; also, the ruler of Bethulia in the Book of Judith

**wasteland**—land with little or no plant-life, often rocky or sandy

**wisdom** (wiz´duhm)—knowledge about the right way to live

**Wisdom** (wiz´duhm)—the name of one of the Old Testament Wisdom Books (see p. 173)

**Wisdom Books**—some Old Testament literary works, plus various books that teach how to please God and/or get along with other people (see p. 166)

**Xerxes** (zuhrk´seez)—the Persian king (emperor) of the Book of Esther

**Yahweh** (yah´way)—the Hebrew name for God, which Jewish people do not even say, because of their respect for it; God revealed this name to Moses (Exodus)

**Zacchaeus** (za-kee´uhs)—a tax collector whom Jesus visited in Jericho (Luke)

**Zealots** (zel´uhts)—Jews of the 1st century who wanted to revolt against Rome and free their homeland

**Zebedee** (zeb´uh-dee)—the father of the apostles James and John (Gospels)

**Zebulun** (zeb´yuh-luhn)—a son of Jacob (Genesis) and ancestor of a tribe of Israel

**Zechariah** (zek´uh-rye´uh)—a prophet of the 6th century B.C.; also, the Prophetical Book that bears his name (see p. 202); also, the father of John the Baptizer (Luke)

**Zedekiah** (zed´uh-kye´uh)—the last king of Judah, captured by the Chaldeans after he escaped from Jerusalem (2 Kings, Ezekiel)

**Zephaniah** (zef´uh-nye´uh)—a prophet of the 7th century B.C.; also, the Prophetical Book that bears his name (see p. 201)

**Zion** (zye´uhn)—one of the mountains on which Jerusalem was built; also, a name for the whole city of Jerusalem

# IMPORTANT EVENTS AND PERSONS IN BIBLICAL HISTORY

| Period | Persons | Events | Dates | Books of the Bible |
|---|---|---|---|---|
| (Pre-history) | (Adam and Eve) (Cain and Abel) (Noah) | (Great Flood) (Tower of Babel) | | Genesis |
| The time of the Patriarchs (the "great fathers") | Abraham, Isaac Jacob-Israel Joseph and his brothers | Journey of Abraham to Canaan<br><br>Migration of Israel's family to Egypt | about 2000–1700 B.C. | Genesis Job |
| The Exodus | Moses Aaron | Passage through the sea<br><br>Covenant at Mt. Sinai<br><br>Years spent in the desert | around the 13th century B.C. | Exodus Leviticus Numbers Deuteronomy |
| The conquest of Canaan | Joshua Deborah Barak Gideon Samson Ruth | Settlement of the Israelites in Canaan | about 1200–1050 B.C. | Joshua Judges Ruth 1 Chronicles (part) |
| From separate tribes to a united kingdom | Samuel Saul David Solomon | Saul—Israel's first king<br><br>David—builder of a strong kingdom | about 1050–922 B.C. | 1 and 2 Samuel 1 Kings (part) 1 and 2 Chronicles (parts) |
| The two kingdoms | Ahab Elijah Elisha Ahaz Isaiah | Separation of the northern tribes (Israel) from Judah<br><br>Conquest of Israel by Assyria | 922–721 B.C. | 1 Kings (part) 2 Kings Amos Hosea Isaiah (part) Micah 2 Chronicles (part) Jonah, Tobit |
| The last days of the kingdom of Judah | Hezekiah Manasseh Josiah Jeremiah | Reform by King Josiah<br><br>Seige and fall of Jerusalem | 721–587 B.C. | 2 Kings Jeremiah (part) Zephaniah Nahum Habakkuk Judith |

# AND THE BOOKS OF THE BIBLE RELATED TO THEM

| Period | Persons | Events | Dates | Books of the Bible |
|---|---|---|---|---|
| Chaldean rule | Ezekiel | The Exile | 587–539 B.C. | Jeremiah *(part)* Lamentations, Baruch Ezekiel, Isaiah ("2 Isaiah") Daniel *(part)* |
| Persian rule | Ezra Nehemiah | Rebuilding of the Temple | 539–333 B.C. | Daniel *(part)* Haggai Zechariah Esther Ezra, Nehemiah Obadiah Malachi Joel Song of Songs Psalms *(final version?)* Proverbs *(final version?)* |
| Greek rule (from Egypt) | | | 333–200 B.C. | Sirach Ecclesiastes? |
| Greek rule (from Syria) | Mattathias Judas Maccabeus Jonathan Simon | Persecution by Antiochus IV Maccabean revolt | 200–135 B.C. | 1 and 2 Maccabees |
| Jewish independence | | | 135–63 B.C. | |
| Roman rule | Jesus Mary Peter, the Twelve Mary Magdalene Stephen Philip Paul | Birth, ministry, death and resurrection of Jesus Beginning of the Church Destruction of the Temple Destruction of Jerusalem | 63 B.C.– A.D. 135 | Wisdom? Gospels Acts Letters Revelation |

N.B. Often books of the Bible were *about* one period but written in another. This chart stresses the period that each book of the Bible is *about*.

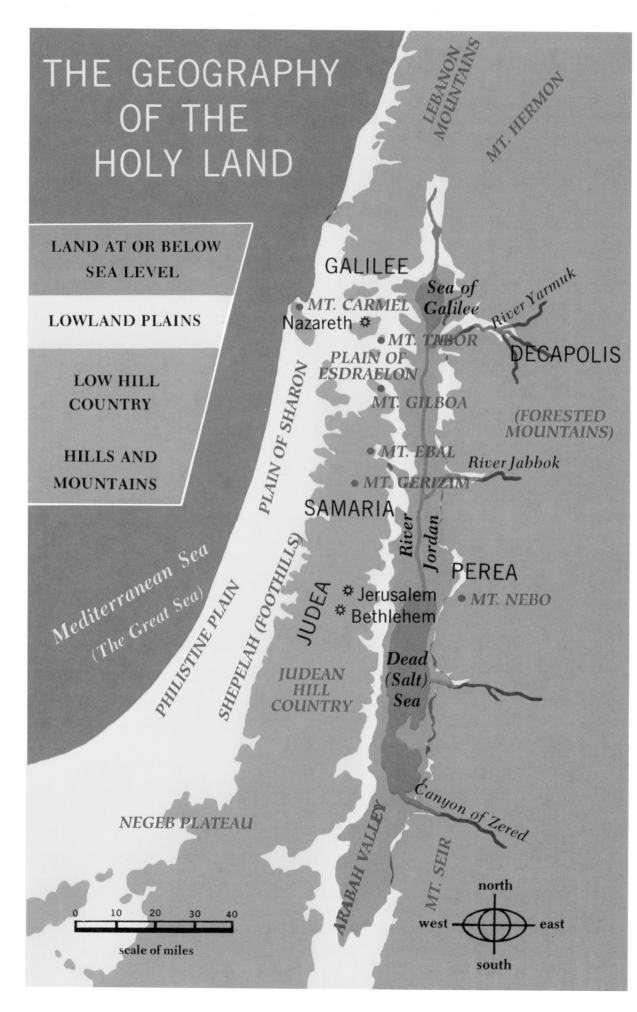

# THE WORLD OF THE BIBLE

The Bible tells us about God's involvement in the history of the Hebrew, or Jewish, people and continues with the history of the early Church, whose members were both Jewish and non-Jewish Christians.

Sometimes it's hard to understand an event or teaching that we find in the Bible, since we don't know the place, customs or history related to it. For that reason, people study the **geography, archaeology** and **history** of the Holy Land in order to better understand the Bible. Many books contain information about biblical times and places.

# HISTORY—SHAPED BY GEOGRAPHY

Here are some facts to start you thinking: The Holy Land was located between two places where important civilizations grew up. Southwest was Egypt, a land green with crops in the midst of desert. It was watered by a mighty river, the Nile. To the east (on the other side of another great desert) was the green "land between the two rivers"—sometimes called Mesopotamia. One people after another settled there between the Tigris and Euphrates Rivers. They grew crops and built civilizations—and later those civilizations were replaced by others.

Find Africa on a globe—and Egypt in the northeastern section of it. Run your finger along the Nile River from south to north, then along the eastern edge of the Mediterranean Sea (the Holy Land and Syria), eastward to the northwestern part of the land between the two rivers (modern Iraq) and southeast to the Persian Gulf. You have traced a half-circle or crescent. Because this area was good farmland in the midst of deserts, it has been called "the fertile crescent." In the fertile crescent, crops and civilizations grew. Up and down the fertile crescent armies marched, because the peoples of Egypt and Mesopotamia were often at war with each other.

The Holy Land lay on the fertile crescent between the powerful nations at both ends. This is one of the reasons why the history of God's people was filled with wars and battles.

Geography within the Holy Land also influenced its history. For example, along the Mediterranean coast there were almost no natural harbors, so the Hebrews did not become great sea traders, like their northern neighbors, the Phoenicians.

During the Israelites' early years in Canaan, they found it difficult to capture cities from the Canaanites and Philistines, because those cities were on the plains, where the Hebrews' enemies could fight with horse-drawn chariots. At first, the Israelites didn't have this advantage, so they settled in the rugged hill country (a ridge of low mountains running down the land from north to south). Only in David's time did they gain control of the cities on the plains.

An important trade route passed up the coastal plain from Egypt, across the land by way of the Valley of Esdraelon (Jezreel), and along the Sea of Galilee. For this reason, the region where Jesus did much of his teaching and healing (Galilee) was a place where people from different nations and backgrounds met one another. (At one point the Gospels mention people from Tyre and Sidon in Phoenicia who came to see Jesus.)

The Sea of Galilee was shaped something like an ancient harp and was called Lake Chinneret, which means "harp." In the Gospels, the lake is sometimes called Lake Gennesaret or the Sea of Tiberias (because of the city of Tiberias which the Romans had built on its shores). Fishing was an important occupation in Galilee,

so it is not surprising that some of Jesus' disciples were fishermen.

The Sea of Galilee drains into the Jordan River, which winds southward through a deep gorge and ends in the Dead Sea—the lowest spot on the earth's surface. Another gorge—the Arabah—extends from the southern end of the Dead Sea to an arm of the Red Sea. All these are part of a geological fault—an "earthquake zone." Earthquakes may have had something to do with the destruction of Sodom and Gomorrah (now under the Dead Sea) and with the stopping of the Jordan's waters when Joshua entered the land of Canaan at the time of the spring floods.

The Jordan River formed a natural barrier against invaders from the desert to the east.

# HISTORY—UNDERSTOOD THROUGH ARCHAEOLOGY

Biblical archaeology began in the 1800s, when people discovered that the low, round hills called *tells* that are common in the Holy Land and Mesopotamia were the sites of ancient cities. In fact, usually a tell contains not just one buried city, but several cities, one on top of the other. Centuries after a city had been destroyed by enemies and filled with windblown sand, people would see the mound of earth and decide that it was a good place to build, since there was visibility on all sides to help them prepare against enemy invasions.

Styles of pottery and radio-carbon dating have enabled archaeologists to identify and date different cities. Objects that have been found show much about the life of the people—what their musical instruments were like, whether they used coins, what sort of decorations they had in their homes. (Some rich people in the northern kingdom had beds of carved ivory!)

Of the 5,000 tells in the Holy Land, approximately fifty have been investigated. Biblical archaeology takes money, time and patience, but it is interesting and exciting.

# HELP YOUR CHILDREN LEARN ABOUT...THE PENTATEUCH

## Background for yourself

**1** The opening chapters of *Genesis* are a work of literature and theology, rather than science and history.

In chapter 1, the order of the events of creation isn't to be taken literally. This creation account is a poem in which the events form a pattern: creation of light; creation of sea and sky; creation of land and plants; coalescence of light into sun, moon and stars; population of sea and sky with fish and birds; population of land with animals and human beings.

The theological truths taught in chapter 1 include the following:

- There is only one God, and he existed before the universe.

- Everything else that exists was created by God.

- God is good and so are the things he created.

- Human beings are more like God than plants and animals are.

Chapter 2 of *Genesis* presents a second creation account, different in many respects from the first but again showing that human beings are more like God than other animals are. The theory of evolution is not ruled out by this account:

the biblical message is simply that the human race began as part of God's plan of creation.

Here are some of the truths taught through the symbolism of chapters 2 and 3:

- Men and women are equal in dignity. (Eve was "taken from Adam's side," not from his head or his feet.)

- Marriage is meant to last. (In the complete text, Adam exclaims that a man will leave his parents and cling to his wife and the two will become one flesh. Jesus explains that this text indicates that human beings should not separate those whom God has joined together—cf. *Mark* 10).

- The first human beings were created free from sin but rebelled against God in pride and disobedience. (The serpent tricked them into believing that by disobeying God they could place themselves at God's level.)

- As a result of their disobedience, their descendants became more inclined toward committing sin. (This is shown in the stories of Cain and Abel, Noah and the tower of Babel in *Genesis* 4–11.)

**2** The Sinai covenant *(Exodus, Deuteronomy)* became the great bond between God and Israel. It was modeled on a type of secular agreement between a king and petty rulers, who thus became his vassals. In such agreements the king would pledge himself to protect and defend his vassals if they fulfilled certain conditions. God likewise promised to protect the Israelites, who were to become his special people. Their part of the covenant centered around the ten commandments—a written expression of the natural law that God has implanted within every human heart.

## Particular points

- Each "day" of creation starts in the evening, because that was the way the Hebrews counted days—from the moment the first stars began to appear.

- Some of the peoples of the ancient Middle East believed that the sky was a dome containing floodgates that released water in the form of rain. *Genesis* 1:6–8; 14–18 reflects this concept.

- The books of the Pentateuch were composed from oral traditions. After these traditions had been set down in writing, editors tried to merge them—not always successfully, as can be seen by reading the complete account of Noah and the ark (*Genesis* 6:5–8:19).

- God's command to Abraham to sacrifice Isaac was only a test, as the Bible itself make clear (*Genesis* 22:1); *Hebrews* 11:17–19; *James* 2:21–22). The *New Jerome Biblical Commentary* calls it the greatest of Abraham's trials and states that through his obedience, "Abraham entrusts his life and his future unconditionally to the God who calls him" (p. 25). Isaac was the aging Abraham's whole life; he was the future of the promise.

- The plagues and the manna *(Exodus, Numbers)* may all have been natural phenomena. This includes even the "water turned into blood," since reddish, evil-smelling water occurred in the Nile at certain times. However, the timing of the plagues and the abundance of the manna gave both a miraculous character: God was at work through natural phenomena. The same is true of the crossing of the Israelites at a shallow fording place and the return of the waters to impede the passage of the Egyptian army.

- In the *Book of Numbers,* we find the Lord telling Moses and Aaron that because of some fault of theirs they wouldn't live to see the Promised Land.

What had displeased the Lord? Here are some possibilities:

1. Moses and Aaron didn't believe that the miracle would happen if they only *spoke* to the rock instead of striking it;

2. God was very willing to give the people water, since they really needed it, but Moses and Aaron were angry, because of the people's complaints and didn't want to give them a drink;

3. Moses and Aaron didn't believe that the Lord was so good that he would continue to give the people water.

- The jubilee year of *Leviticus* has become a Catholic tradition. Jubilees are celebrated at the beginning of every century (in honor of Jesus' incarnation) and at other times for various reasons. Pilgrimages to the main churches of Rome or to local churches and shrines are part of Catholic jubilee celebration.

## References in this book

—The introductions to the Bible and to the Old Testament (pp. 9–11).

—The introductions to *Genesis–Deuteronomy* and the explanations throughout the text (pp. 12–70).

—The first flyleaf map, which offers information about the Exodus.

## To read together from the family Bible

*Genesis* 50:14–21 (what happened after Jacob's death).

*Exodus* 15:1–20 (the song of Moses, Miriam and the Israelites after passing through the sea). This may have been composed somewhat later and embellished as it was resung. Hence, the addition of the name "Red Sea." Enjoy the poetry of this early Hebrew epic, which is sung during the Easter Vigil.

*Hebrews* 11:1–31 (Old Testament men and women of faith).

## Activities

1. Call your child's attention to the first three paragraphs under "History, Shaped by Geography" in "The World of the Bible," p. 335. On a globe, trace the fertile crescent from modern Egypt through Israel and Syria to Iraq. Then, invite your child to trace Abraham's journey from Mesopotamia to Canaan. Abraham may have been born at Ur, near where the Tigris and Euphrates rivers join. If so, he later journeyed to Haran in the plain of Syria. From Haran he journeyed to Canaan (modern Israel) and on into Egypt, returning later to Canaan, where he died.

2. The Israelites spent many years in the desert, longing for their new homeland. The only home they had known was Egypt, where they had been slaves.

   Share experiences of being lost. Imagine how people from other countries must feel in our country until they become adjusted.

   Is there some way your family can help an immigrant?

3. Teach the children how to look up citations in the family Bible.

## Prayers

*Psalm 104* (103 in another numbering system) is about all God's creatures; *Psalm 8* places more stress on human beings.

If only one Bible is available, pray these in the way that psalms are prayed at

Mass—one person reading and the others responding with an antiphon.

Suggested antiphon for each section of *Psalm 104:* **How great you are, O Lord, our God!**

Suggested antiphon for each verse or two of *Psalm 8:* **Lord, our Lord, we see your greatness everywhere.**

*Psalm 114 (113)* is a brief psalm about the Exodus and the crossing of the Jordan into Canaan. Pass the family Bible from one person to another, each one reading two verses. Discuss the imagery in the psalm.

## Other sources

(Parents) *Catechism of the Catholic Church*, Boston: Pauline Books & Media, 1994, nn. 50–141, 198–421.

*Jesus Is the Promise,* by Celia Sirois (sixth grade text in the Alive in Jesus religious education series), Boston: Pauline Books & Media, 1990, pp. 10–39, 73–74; 178–189.

*A Crowd of Witnesses, vol. 1,* by Enzo Crocetti and Mario Giordano, Boston: Pauline Books & Media, 1994, pp. 9–17, 21–50.

# ...THE HISTORICAL BOOKS

## Background for yourself

**1** The Exile was the great watershed in the history of the Chosen People. The exiles found themselves in a strange land, with no Temple and no sacrifices. Their king was a prisoner. Yet, God had not abandoned them. Through the prophets whom he sent, they began to discover that their God was the God of the whole earth.

They began to give more importance to what they still had: their weekly holy day (the Sabbath) and the Scriptures, especially the Torah (Pentateuch). Men called scribes edited the Scriptures and copied them. This was also when synagogues began. These were places where people went to listen to the Scriptures and to pray.

The Hebrew religion as it emerged from the Exile is called Judaism.

**2** The concept of life after death appears very late in Old Testament literature. The Historical Book that brings it out clearly is *2 Maccabees,* which contains references to the resurrection of the dead, purification after death and intercessory prayers (prayer by the living for the dead and by the dead for the living).

## Particular points

- The Catholic Old Testament contains more books than do the Hebrew Scriptures and many Protestant Bibles. These books are called deuterocanonical (which means that their authenticity was established later), but the Church places them on an equal footing with the rest of the Old Testament. They are: *Tobit, Judith, Wisdom, Sirach, Baruch, 1* and *2 Maccabees.* Parts of *Esther* and *Daniel* are also deuterocanonical.

  In the Hebrew Scriptures, the following constitute single books: *Samuel, Kings,* the *Minor Prophets, Chronicles, Ezra-Nehemiah.*

- Not all the descriptions in *Joshua* and *Judges* are to be taken literally. The message of these books is that the Israelites could not have settled the land of Canaan without the help of God.

- The selection from *Ruth* omits a scene that could be problematic. (On Naomi's advice, Ruth approaches Boaz when he is sleeping among his harvesters on the threshing floor and lies at his feet.) If the children read this story, some comment may be needed. You could tell them that Ruth's action was not as imprudent as it seems, since Naomi trusted in the virtue of both Boaz and Ruth. On the other hand, the Bible is not offering this episode for our imitation.

## References in this book

—The introductions to *Joshua–2 Maccabees* and the explanations throughout the text (pp. 71–165).
—The map and text on pp. 334–336.
—"Important Events and Persons" (pp. 332–333).

## To read together from the family Bible

*2 Samuel* chapter 7 (the Lord's promise to David and David's grateful response).

*Psalm 89 (88)*—recollection of God's promise and a plea for restoration of the monarchy.

*Hebrews* 11:32–40 (more Old Testament men and women of faith)

## Activities

Invite the children to compare the maps on pp. 78 and 164 and notice how the boundaries of the Chosen People's territory changed between the time of Joshua and the formation of the two kingdoms. The division at the time of Joshua was idealistic, and the Israelites never possessed the whole territory until around the time of David's death. By the time of Israel's secession from Judah, territory was already being lost. Boundary changes continued throughout Old Testament times.

## Prayers

*Psalm 15 (14)* presents the attitude of the *anawim*—the poor ones of the Lord, who trust only in him. Pray it with the family Bible, using as an antiphon: **Lord, who shall live on your mountain?**

Try praying *1 Samuel* 3:10 whenever you pause for prayer or wait for Mass to begin: **Speak Lord. Your servant is listening.** Encourage your children to do the same.

## Other sources

*Handbook of Life in Bible Times*, by J. A. Thompson, Leicester, England: Inter-Varsity Press, 1986.

*Jesus Is the Promise*, op. cit., pp. 46–57; 65–69; 75.

*A Crowd of Witnesses, vol. 1*, op. cit., pp. 51–77, 93–104.

# ...THE WISDOM AND PROPHETICAL BOOKS

## Background for yourself

**1** *Job,* first of the Wisdom Books, presents the problem of the suffering of the innocent. *Job* does not solve that problem, although the main character's trust in God grows stronger as a result of his testing. The New Testament sheds light on suffering, showing us that Jesus accepted his sufferings (Gospels) and used them to redeem the human race (*Romans* 5:18). St. Paul teaches that if we suffer with Jesus, we will live with him in glory (*Romans* 8:17). St. Augustine says that God permits bad things to happen and is able to bring about good results from them.

**2** One of the concepts presented in the *Psalms* is that of *hesed* and *emet*—God's loving-kindness and faithfulness. There are many translations for these terms, including "grace and truth" and "faithful love." They will be seen again in chapter 1 of *John*. *Hesed* has to do with God's relationship with his people—the kinship that he has established with them—which "obliges" him to look out for their well-being. *Emet* (related to *Amen*—"So shall it be") has to do with rocklike fidelity.

**3** Related to *emet* is the concept of redeeming. A *goel* or redeemer in ancient Israel was someone who rescued a member of his family (as Boaz married Ruth to provide an heir for Ruth's deceased husband, Mahlon, thus keeping Mahlon's property in the family). Speaking through Isaiah, God proclaims himself Israel's redeemer (*Isaiah* 41:41 and elsewhere).

In becoming our brother and giving his life for us, Jesus would be our redeemer *par excellence*.

**4** In his "Temple sermon" Jeremiah warned the people of Judah not to think that God would save them from their enemies no matter how they themselves lived. Many of them had turned away from the Lord and were worshipping other gods, yet they felt that God would protect them. This kind of mistaken belief is called presumption. There is also a reverse form of presumption: belief that a person doesn't need God's help. The right outlook for Christians is to cooperate with God: to ask God's help, to trust him and meanwhile to do our best ourselves.

## Particular points

- Some of the prophets had *disciples*. This term will also appear in the New Testament. Disciples are followers who learn not only what a master (teacher and exemplar) tells them but also the way the master lives.

- The prophets often used poetic imagery in relaying God's messages. For example, to indicate that the Messiah would be a man of peace, Isaiah spoke of a wolf being a guest of a lamb (11:6). To say that the Exile was about to end, the prophet told Zion (Jerusalem) to stand on a mountain-top as a herald and cry out that the Lord was coming (40:9–10). To describe the rebirth of the nation, *Ezekiel* spoke of a vast field of bones coming back to life (37:1–14)

- Some people think that when "Second Isaiah" wrote about the suffering servant, he was writing about the people of Israel itself. There are also other ideas about "Second Isaiah's" meaning, and one interpretation does not exclude others.

  From the time of the early Church, Christians have taught that the servant songs in *Isaiah* may be seen as foretelling the sufferings and death of Jesus. Jesus himself helped his disciples and apostles to see his role as a suffering servant (see *Mark* 10:45 and *Luke* 24:13 ff.).

- Daniel's vision of a statue made of different substances refers to the various kingdoms that would rule the people of Judah until the time of the Maccabees. (The *Book of Daniel* is believed to have been written at the time of the Maccabees.)

- The expression "O King, live forever!" (*Daniel*) might sound strange to us, but it was a normal form of address at that time. An echo is found in our own times in nations that have a monarchy: "Long live the king!" or "God save the queen!"

## References in this book

— The introductions to *Job-Malachi* and the explanations throughout the text (pp. 166–202).

## To read together from the family Bible

*Psalm 29* (God's majesty in a storm) and *Psalm 51* (a famous prayer of repentance).

*Isaiah* 43:1–21 (God's love for his people, whom he will free from captivity in Babylon).

## Activities

1. Ask the children to compare God's call of Isaiah with that of Jeremiah. The complete texts are: *Isaiah* 6:1–8 and *Jeremiah* 1:4–10;17–19. In both cases,

the prophet needs to be encouraged, but for different reasons. God works with people as they are.

2. Invite the children to identify the psalm verses and proverbs in the text that they like the best.

## Prayers

The second half of *Psalm 19 (18)* may be prayed with this antiphon: **Your laws, Lord, are more precious than gold.**

*Psalm 23* may be prayed with the antiphon: **The Lord is my shepherd; there is nothing I shall want,** or *Psalm 138* may be prayed with: **I thank you, Lord, with all my heart.**

## Other sources

(Parents) *Catechism of the Catholic Church*, op. cit., nn. 2568–2597.

*Jesus Is the Promise*, op. cit., pp. 59–63, 70–73.

*A Crowd of Witnesses, vol. 1*, op. cit., pp. 18–20, 78–92.

For Parents and Teachers—

# ...THE FOUR GOSPELS

## Background for yourself

Just as the material in the Old Testament historical books was first transmitted orally, so was the content of the Gospels. The Vatican II constitution on divine revelation *(Dei Verbum)* and the Biblical Commission's document on the historical character of the Gospels *(Sacra Mater Ecclesia)* explain:

"The Church has firmly held and continues to hold that the four Gospels... faithfully hand on what Jesus Christ, while living among men, really did and taught for their eternal salvation until the day he was taken up into heaven. After the ascension of the Lord, the apostles handed on to their hearers what he had said and done. This they did with that clearer understanding which they enjoyed after they had been instructed by the glorious events of Christ's life and taught by the light of the Spirit of truth" *(DV 19)*.

"This primitive instruction was passed on orally at first and later written down. Indeed it was not long before many attempted 'to draw up a narrative' of the events connected with the Lord Jesus. The sacred authors, each using an approach suited to his specific purpose, recorded this primitive teaching in the four Gospels, for the benefit of the churches. Of the many elements at hand they reported some, summarized others, and developed still others in accordance with the needs of the various churches. They used every possible means to ensure that their readers would come to know the validity of the things they had been taught" *(SME)*.

The Gospels were probably written over a period of thirty-five years (from the mid-60's to the end of the century), with *Mark* first and *John* last.

Each Gospel has its own particular characteristics, as is pointed out in the introductions and explanations. Together they give us a portrait of Jesus (not a chronological biography) and tell us what he did and taught.

## Particular points

- The Gospel writers are called *evangelists*. This means "tellers of the good news." The word comes from the Greek word for Good News or Gospel: *evangelion*.

- Important words associated with Matthew's Gospel include "beatitudes," "mercy" and "transfiguration" (see glossary).

- Mark's Gospel speaks of the "brothers and sisters" of Jesus. This has led some people to think that Mary and Joseph had other children. But the Catholic Church has always taught that Mary did not have other children. The culture of the Middle East and the Gospels themselves suport the Church's teaching. At that time, people didn't have a separate word for "cousin," so cousins were simply called brothers and sisters. This is still true in many places today. *Mark* 6 speaks of Jesus' "brothers" James and Joses; *Mark* 15 says that "the mother of James and Joses" watched Jesus' death from a distance with some other women. This indicates that the mother of James and Joses was not the same person as Jesus' mother.

- Related to the above is the question of Mary's continuing virginity. Again, the Church teaches that Mary remained a virgin after the birth of Jesus. One of the biblical supports for this teaching is *Luke* 1: Mary asked how her son would be conceived, since she was a virgin. Such a question could only mean that Mary intended to remain a virgin.

- Matthew's story of the wise men shows that Jesus came for everyone. The wise men represented the gentile (non-Jewish) peoples of the world.

- The parable of the good Samaritan (*Luke* 10) will have more meaning if one keeps in mind that the Jews and Samaritans had been unfriendly for centuries. Jesus was saying that *everybody* is our neighbor.

## References in this book

—The introduction to the New Testament (p. 203).
—The map and text on pp. 204 and 205.
—The introductions to *Matthew–John* and the explanations throughout the text (pp. 206–279).
—The second flyleaf map with its explanations.

## To read together from the family Bible

*Psalm 22* (the psalm that Jesus began to pray aloud on the cross) could be recited using the antiphon: ***My God, my God, why have you abandoned me?***

## Activities

1. Invite the children to read the passage of *Exodus* where God reveals himself to Moses as I AM (*Exodus* 3:14) and *John* 8:58, in which Jesus says, "Before Abraham was, I AM." This was one of the times that Jesus revealed his divine identity.

2. Invite them to compare *Zechariah* 9:9 with *Matthew* 21:1–9, which narrates the fulfillment of the prophecy about the Messiah's entrance into Jerusalem, riding on a donkey. This is one of the many Old Testament prophecies that was fulfilled (attained a deeper meaning) in Jesus.

## Prayers

Pray *Luke* 1:46–55 (Mary's *Magnificat* or hymn of praise to God) and 1:68–79 (Zechariah's hymn, the *Benedictus*). Both of these hymns have become part of the official prayer of the Church, the Liturgy of the Hours. The *Benedictus* is prayed at morning prayer, and the *Magnificat* at evening prayer.

## Other sources

(Parents) *Catechism of the Catholic Church*, op. cit., nn. 422–682, 2598–2622.

(Parents) *The Historicity of the Gospels (Sacra Mater Ecclesia)*, instruction of the Pontifical Biblical Commission, April 21, 1964, Boston: Pauline Books & Media.

*Jesus Is the Promise*, op. cit., pp. 82–111; 118–123.

*A Crowd of Witnesses, vol. 2, Interviews with Famous New Testament Men and Women*, by Enzo Crocetti and Mario Giordano, Boston: Pauline Books & Media, 1994, pp. 9–74; 88–117.

# …ACTS, THE LETTERS, REVELATION

## Background for yourself

**1** The rapid spread of Christianity was the result of the great activity of the Holy Spirit together with what may have been a set of circumstances ordained by divine providence.

Stories like the one of Philip on the road toward the desert and the conversion of Cornelius and his household show the Spirit's impulse to broaden the Church and extend it outward. Another name for the *Acts of the Apostles* is "the Gospel of the Holy Spirit."

The spread of Christianity was also favored by the earlier scattering of Hebrews throughout the Roman empire. Wherever they were, they had their synagogues. The Scriptures had been translated into Greek. Through these Jewish colonies, gentiles had come to know about the one God. Some of them attended the synagogue services as "God-fearers," people sympathetic to the religion of Israel. Meanwhile, the situation of relative peace, coupled with an excellent network of Roman roads, enabled the apostles and other missionaries to carry the Good News far and wide.

## Particular points

- In *Acts*, when Peter says that God has made Jesus "both Lord and Messiah," he is referring to Jesus' divinity. The key word is "Lord," since the Messiah was not expected to be divine. The Greek word used for "Lord" is *Kyrios*, the same word used in the Greek translation of the Old Testament to identify God.

- Who is the woman in *Revelation* chapter 12? Most Bible experts say that the woman is a symbol for the people of God. But some Catholics like to think that this section might also be about Mary. That is why pictures or statues of Mary sometimes show twelve stars around her head.

## References in this book

—The introductions to *Acts–Revelation* and the explanations throughout the text (pp. 280–315).

—"Important Events and Persons" (p. 333).

## To read together from the family Bible

*Acts* 20:7–12 (Paul brings a dead boy back to life).

*Philippians* 2:1–11 (Paul urges the Christians of Philippi to be good to one another and points to the example of Jesus by quoting an early Christian hymn).

## Activities

Invite the children to look at the map on p. 306. This shows some of the first lands to which Christianity spread.

## Prayers

*Ephesians* 1:3–10 (a hymn of praise for God's goodness in making us his people). The antiphon could be: **Praised be the name of our Lord Jesus Christ. "Come, Lord Jesus."**

## Other sources

(Parents) *Catechism of the Catholic Church*, op. cit., nn. 683–747.

*Jesus Is the Promise*, op. cit., pp. 124–147.

*A Crowd of Witnesses, vol. 2*, op. cit., pp. 75–92; 118–138.

**Pauline**
**BOOKS & MEDIA**

The Daughters of St. Paul operate book and media centers at the following addresses. Visit, call or write the one nearest you today, or find us on the World Wide Web, www.pauline.org

**CALIFORNIA**
3908 Sepulveda Blvd, Culver City,
 CA 90230   310-397-8676
5945 Balboa Avenue, San Diego,
 CA 92111   858-565-9181
46 Geary Street, San Francisco,
 CA 94108   415-781-5180

**FLORIDA**
145 S.W. 107th Avenue, Miami,
 FL 33174   305-559-6715

**HAWAII**
1143 Bishop Street, Honolulu,
 HI 96813   808-521-2731
 Neighbor Islands call: 800-259-8463

**ILLINOIS**
172 North Michigan Avenue,
 Chicago, IL 60601
 312-346-4228

**LOUISIANA**
4403 Veterans Memorial Blvd,
 Metairie, LA 70006
 504-887-7631

**MASSACHUSETTS**
885 Providence Hwy, Dedham,
 MA 02026   781-326-5385

**MISSOURI**
9804 Watson Road, St. Louis,
 MO 63126   314-965-3512

**NEW JERSEY**
561 U.S. Route 1, Wick Plaza, Edison,
 NJ 08817   732-572-1200

**NEW YORK**
150 East 52nd Street, New York,
 NY 10022   212-754-1110
78 Fort Place, Staten Island,
 NY 10301   718-447-5071

**PENNSYLVANIA**
9171-A Roosevelt Blvd, Philadelphia,
 PA 19114   215-676-9494

**SOUTH CAROLINA**
243 King Street, Charleston,
 SC 29401   843-577-0175

**TENNESSEE**
4811 Poplar Avenue, Memphis,
 TN 38117   901-761-2987

**TEXAS**
114 Main Plaza, San Antonio,
 TX 78205   210-224-8101

**VIRGINIA**
1025 King Street, Alexandria,
 VA 22314   703-549-3806

**CANADA**
3022 Dufferin Street, Toronto, Ontario,
 Canada  M6B 3T5   416-781-9131
1155 Yonge Street, Toronto, Ontario,
 Canada  M4T 1W2   416-934-3440

¡También somos su fuente para libros, videos y música en español!